AF411551

World Society and the Middle East

Rethinking Peace and Conflict Studies

Series Editor: **Oliver P. Richmond**, Professor, School of International Relations, University of St Andrews

Editorial Board: **Roland Bleiker**, University of Queensland, Australia; **Henry F. Carey**, Georgia State University, USA; **Costas Constantinou**, University of Keele, UK; **A.J.R. Groom**, University of Kent, UK; **Vivienne Jabri**, King's College London, UK; **Edward Newman**, University of Birmingham, UK; **Sorpong Peou**, Sophia University, Japan; **Caroline Kennedy-Pipe**, University of Sheffield, UK; **Professor Michael Pugh**, University of Bradford, UK; **Chandra Sriram**, University of East London, UK; **Ian Taylor**, University of St. Andrews, UK; **Alison Watson**, University of St Andrews, UK; **R.B.J. Walker**, University of Victoria, Canada; **Andrew Williams**, University of St Andrews, UK.

Titles include:

Jason Franks
RETHINKING THE ROOTS OF TERRORISM

Vivienne Jabri
WAR AND THE TRANSFORMATION OF GLOBAL POLITICS

James Ker-Lindsay
EU ACCESSION AND UN PEACEKEEPING IN CYPRUS

Roger MacGinty
NO WAR, NO PEACE
The Rejuvenation of Stalled Peace Processes and Peace Accords

Carol McQueen
HUMANITARIAN INTERVENTION AND SAFETY ZONES
Iraq, Bosnia and Rwanda

Sorpong Peou
INTERNATIONAL DEMOCRACY ASSISTANCE FOR PEACEBUILDING
The Cambodian Experience

Sergei Prozorov
UNDERSTANDING CONFLICT BETWEEN RUSSIA AND THE EU
The Limits of Integration

Oliver P. Richmond
THE TRANSFORMATION OF PEACE

Bahar Rumelili
CONSTRUCTING REGIONAL AND GLOBAL ORDER
Europe and Southeast Asia

Chandra Lekha Sriram
PEACE AS GOVERNANCE

Stephan Stetter
WORLD SOCIETY AND THE MIDDLE EAST
Reconstructions in Regional Politics

Rethinking Peace and Conflict Studies

Series Standing Order ISBN 1-4039-9575-3 (hardback) & 1-4039-9576-1 (paperback)

You can receive future titles in this series as they are published by placing a standing order. Please contact your bookseller or, in case of difficulty, write to us at the address below with your name and address, the title of the series and one of the ISBNs quoted above.

Customer Services Department, Macmillan Distribution Ltd, Houndmills, Basingstoke, Hampshire RG21 6XS, England

---

World Society and the Middle East

Reconstructions in Regional Politics

Stephan Stetter
Professor of International Politics
Universität der Bundeswehr München, Germany

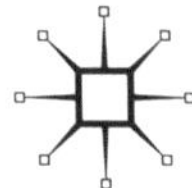

First published 2008 by
PALGRAVE MACMILLAN
Houndmills, Basingstoke, Hampshire RG21 6XS and
175 Fifth Avenue, New York, N.Y. 10010
Companies and representatives throughout the world

PALGRAVE MACMILLAN is the global academic imprint of the Palgrave Macmillan division of St. Martin's Press, LLC and of Palgrave Macmillan Ltd. Macmillan® is a registered trademark in the United States, United Kingdom and other countries. Palgrave is a registered trademark in the European Union and other countries.

ISBN-13: 978–1–4039–9577–3   hardback
ISBN-10: 1–4039–9577–X   hardback

This book is printed on paper suitable for recycling and made from fully managed and sustained forest sources. Logging, pulping and manufacturing processes are expected to conform to the environmental regulations of the country of origin.

A catalogue record for this book is available from the British Library.

Library of Congress Cataloging-in-Publication Data
Stetter, Stephan, 1972–
World Society and the Middle East : reconstructions in regional politics / Stephan Stetter.
p.cm — (Rethinking peace and conflict studies)
Includes bibliographical references and index.
ISBN 1–4039–9577–X (alk. paper)
1. Middle East—Politics and government. 2. Interregionalism—Middle East. 3. Group identity—Middle East. 4. Politics and war—Middle East. 5. Globalization—Middle East. I. Title.
JQ1758.A58S74 2008
320.956—dc22   2008015914

10 9 8 7 6 5 4 3 2 1
17 16 15 14 13 12 11 10 09 08

Printed and bound in Great Britain by
CPI Antony Rowe, Chippenham and Eastbourne

Contents

Preface

> Music is the only thing that's in tune with what's happening
> Bob Dylan[1]

We need something to connect us with what is happening. And even more so if that which is happening is important to us. My connection with the Middle East began more than a decade ago and since then my attachment with this colourful and interesting region and its people has become ever stronger. This book, which is the result of many fascinating encounters with the rhythms and tunes of the Middle East vibrant throughout world society, would not have been possible without the friendship, support and help I am proud to have received from many colleagues and friends in academia and beyond. I would like to thank Oliver P. Richmond, the editor of this book series, Amy Lankaster-Owen, Alison Howson, Alexandra Webster and Gemma d'Arcy-Hughes from Palgrave Macmillan as well as Barbara Slater. They have offered great support for this project at all stages. Many thanks also to the anonymous referee.

Very special thanks to Mona Hatoum – as well as Sophie Greig from White Cube London – for sharing the passion of constructing and deconstructing. I am grateful indeed to Mona for granting permission to reproduce parts of her artwork on the cover of this book.

Various parts of this book have been presented at conferences, workshops and lectures and I would like to express my sincere gratitude for the many productive and insightful discussions I had on various drafts and chapters at the ECPR (European Consortium for Political Research) conference in Bologna in 2004, the pan-European conferences of the SGIR (Standing Group on International Relations) in The Hague (2004) and in Turin (2007), the World International Studies Conference (WISC) in Istanbul 2005, the ISA (International Studies Association) annual meeting in San Diego in 2006, the DAVO (Deutsche Arbeitsgemeinschaft Vorderer Orient) conferences in Hamburg in 2005 and 2006, the meeting of the *Nahostnetzwerk* at the Helmut-Schmidt-University in Hamburg in 2006, the meeting of the *Netzwerk Konstruktivistische Konfliktforschung* in Marburg in 2007, the *Sektionstagung* of the *Sektion Internationale Politik* of the DVPW (Deutsche Vereinigung für Politische Wissenschaft) in Mannheim 2005, and the *Forschungskolloquium* at Bielefeld University as well as at Departmental Seminars in Aarhus (2006), Istanbul and

Birmingham (2007). I also presented parts of this book at the University of the Bundeswehr in Munich and I am grateful for the stimulating inputs I have received there.

I am particularly indebted to Mathias Albert, not only for reading and commenting on many parts of this book which I submitted in November 2007 as my *Habilitationsschrift* at the Faculty of Sociology at the University of Bielefeld. Working with Mathias in Bielefeld has always been an invaluable and unique experience, both personally and intellectually. In that context also many thanks to Mathias as well as to Mario, Stephan, Giovanni and Christian for the stunningly entertaining time we had together in our band project *Die Musik der Gesellschaft*.

I would like to thank in particular Klaus P. Japp for his insightful and thought-provoking comments on this book. Many thanks also to Thomas Diez for his support and critical reading of this book. With my friend Tobias Werron I also had many stimulating discussions on world society and all that it entails and I would like to thank Tobias for reading and commenting on the entire final draft of this book.

Many thanks to Raffaella A. Del Sarto and René 'Moshe' Wildangel for countless superb discussions on Middle East politics. *Shukran* to my excellent Arab language teachers at the *Landesspracheninstitut Nordrhein-Westfalen* – as well as to the Faculty of Sociology at the University of Bielefeld and the *Deutsche Forschungsgemeinschaft* for providing research funding. Moreover, I am grateful to Jan Busse, who was an excellent student assistant at an early stage of this project. I also want to thank André Bank, Martin Beck, Hermann Bünz, Micky Drill, Majed Elhewaihi, Cilja Harders, Knud Erik Jørgensen, Annette Jünemann, Philipp Misselwitz, Rami Nasrallah, Naseef Naem, Roby Nathanson, David Newman, Michelle Pace, Sharon Pardo, Bahar Rumelili, Klaus Schlichte, Shlomo Shpiro, Alfred Tovias, Mike Turner, Morten Valbjørn, Haim Yacobi and all other friends and colleagues who have commented on parts of this book at various occasions. Many thanks also to Barbara Lüders, Rike Geisler and Alexandra Nocke. My greatest thanks go to my family, in particular to my wife Anna and our daughter Sophia, to Annegret, Franz, Judith and Barbara Stetter, to my grandma Philippine Läufer as well as to Agnes and Erwin Sigl. Many thanks also to Andreas Läufer for offering accommodation (and great DVDs) in Hanover where parts of this book were written.

I dedicate this book to Anna for making it happen.

Stephan Stetter

Foreword

Mathias Albert

Having worked closely with its author for the last five years, I can witness that *World Society and the Middle East* has failed completely regarding one goal which the author had set for his project. Under the '007-goal', the self-confessed James Bond fan Stephan Stetter wanted to integrate the title of every Bond movie into the text in a meaningful way. However, it turned out that while in a book on the Middle East some titles could be integrated quite easily -- 'The World is Not Enough' and, arguably, quite sadly, 'Live and Let Die' could also have been fitted in with little problem – most presented bigger (but not insurmountable) problems (for example, 'From Russia with Love'). However, in the end it proved all but impossible to integrate 'Goldfinger' (save in an analysis on unequal income distribution in some of the oil states) or 'Moonraker' (save in attempts to describe the lack of simple-mindedness of those systems theorists used extensively in the argument). Of course, the book's failure to achieve its '007-goal' can easily be forgiven by somebody with less enthusiasm for Commander Bond than for Captain Kirk and colleagues: even without using the titles of Bond movies in its argument, *World Society and the Middle East* still manages 'to boldly go where no one has gone before'.

Since such assertions of course are a standard feature of most forewords, I would like to elaborate at least a little bit on why I think this indeed is the case here in particular. What makes *World Society and the Middle East* so remarkable is that it not only brings together literatures which so far had little (or in fact nothing) to do with each other. It also succeeds in making important contributions to each of these literatures themselves. Thus, as it argues itself, the book stands out in the literature on the Middle East in a narrower sense as it could arguably be seen as one of the very few books which venture into the subject at a rather high level of theoretical sophistication. That it does so using what can probably be seen as one of the most complex social theories around today, namely the modern systems theory of world society pioneered particularly by the sociologist Niklas Luhmann, and that it does so without losing touch with an extremely deep empirical knowledge about the region makes it stand out in the Middle East literature in the social sciences. That said, however, it also succeeds in making a significant contribution to systems theory in at least two important respects: first, it connects systems theory to concrete themes (conflict) and regions (the Middle East) which it has mostly ignored so far; second, it challenges some inconsistencies within the theory, particularly when it comes to insisting on its own postulate of a primacy of a functional differentiation of world society against some notable tendencies within contemporary systems-theoretical thought to 're-naturalize' space. Finally, and perhaps least explicitly, *World Society and the Middle East* makes an important contribution to the field of international relations, particularly because it does what could be seen as an almost ideal form of IR scholarship – that is, not to float at entirely remote theoretical heights or crawl on the theory-averse grounds of pure empirical research, but to be able to combine thorough theoretical reflection with rich empirical analysis.

Speaking to very different literatures is a risky business for any author as much as it is risky to try and sit between the chairs occupied by disciplinary orthodoxy. All the more the present book is to be lauded for taking such risks and pursuing what is in many respects a truly transdisciplinary exercise. It demands from its readers, particularly those not already versed in, most notably, world society theory, a significant amount of intellectual openness and effort. Yet the intellectual investment in the reading of this book certainly pays off. Not necessarily in terms of showing new and surprising, previously unexplored pathways to conflict resolution in the Middle East – rather it offers more a perspective on the real size of the problems standing in the way of many conflict resolution strategies (not least the main form of differentiation of world society itself). However, what *World Society and the Middle East* forcefully demonstrates is that climbing the heights of social theory helps to get a fresh perspective on the entire region. Under this perspective, conflicts and problems do not wither away, but they look markedly different and allow more sophisticated assessments of the prospects as well the limits of attempts to 'unfreeze' the Middle East.

Part I

World Society and the Middle East

1
Introduction: Globalization, World Society and the Study of the Middle East in International Relations

Fields of diamonds in the sky, worlds are whirling right on by
Johnny Cash, 'Fields of Diamonds'[1]

World society and the Middle East: introductory remarks

This book proposes a framework for analysis of Middle East politics. It is, thereby, guided by theoretical and empirical curiosity. From an empirical perspective two main research questions can be highlighted as its starting point. First, why have the manifold liberalization and peace processes in the region, which emerged in the 1990s and at the beginning of the 2000s and which were accompanied with great expectations, lost momentum? Leadership changes in Jordan, from King Hussein to his son Abdallah, and in Syria from Hafiz Al-Assad to his son Bashir Al-Assad, might have paved the way for some cautious economic (Syria, Jordan) and political (Jordan) openness, yet they left the overall authoritarian structures (more so in Syria, yet in milder forms in Jordan, too) intact. Democratization and constitutionalization processes in Lebanon and Palestine became stalled. The assassination of former Prime Minister Rafiq Hariri, ongoing heavy interference by neighbouring states Syria and Israel – but also by Iran, Saudi-Arabia and Western governments – as well as the stalemates in overcoming the deep divides between the different confessional sects impeded an overall transformation of conflict constellations in Lebanon. In Palestine, the nascent democratic structures, symbolized by Palestine's self-confident parliament, the Palestinian National Assembly, as well as a vibrant private sector, always stood in tension with the charismatic and autocratic governing style of former president Yassir Arafat. Moreover, the overall pervasiveness of democratization efforts is constrained by both

Israeli occupation and severe internal confrontations between the Hamas movement and the Fatah movement, which still claims a post-revolutionary, quasi-natural monopoly of power in Palestine. Finally, while Israel is a well-functioning democracy, the liberal features of polyarchic governance often encounter their limits in governing practices vis-à-vis the Palestinian national minority (20 per cent of Israel's overall population) as well as when the practices of occupation in the West Bank and Gaza Strip are taken into perspective.

In addition, interregional political, cultural and economic cooperation is rare and Middle Eastern states and people have so far failed to develop a comprehensive regional security community. Finally, relations between the 'West' and the Middle East are strained. This not only relates to the military confrontations between Western (and Middle Eastern) governments, on the one hand, and Islamist fundamentalists, on the other. It also relates to the massive (mutual) stereotypes between Westerners and Muslims, Jews, Arabs and Israelis. In this environment, the much hoped for peace dividends did not materialize. While Israel has concluded peace agreements with Egypt (1979) and Jordan (1994) and has developed formal (Mauritania) and semi-formal (for example, Morocco, Tunisia, Oman and Qatar) diplomatic contacts with several Arab states, relations have soured in the context of the Second Intifada (2000–04) and are a (very) cold peace at best, hardly extending beyond narrower government and business circles. This only underpins the mutual suspicions and strained relations between many Arab countries in the 'new Arab cold war',[2] for example, ongoing tensions between Lebanon and Syria as well as Syria and Jordan. Central to all these dynamics is the gradual erosion of the Oslo peace process between Israel and Palestine and the severe domestic (for example, the assassination of Israeli Prime Minister Yizhak Rabin by a Jewish fundamentalist; violent confrontations between Hamas and Fatah in Palestine) and bilateral (suicide bombings against Israeli civilians by Islamist and secular Palestinians groups; targeted killings, the erection of a fence/wall and ongoing settlement-building activities and army intrusions of Israel in the West Bank and the Gaza Strip) ramifications of entrenched forms of hostility. These developments direct attention to the second key research question of this study. Thus – and notwithstanding the many patterns of cooperation and coexistence which do exist in regional politics – why are adversarial identities and conflicts still so central to Middle East politics?

These questions are more difficult to answer than might initially be assumed – and serve to direct attention towards the theoretical premises of this study. Thus, long after the age of colonialism has formally ended, Orientalism still casts a long shadow on many writings (and concrete politics) on the Middle East. Hence, the projection of negative stereotypes onto Middle Eastern cultures and peoples which, in turn, form the basis of various reifications of a quasi-natural inclination of Middle Eastern states and populations to deceit, violence and conflict is still a powerful mode of explanation for the Middle East's 'regional exceptionalism'.[3] This unfortunate tendency has had a strong renaissance in the past decade with the Middle East in general, and Islam/Arabism in particular, becoming subject to all kinds of crude assumptions about an alleged (naturally or socially-generated) conflict obsession of these 'cultures' and 'civilizations' – and similar things can be said about the massive stereotypes which exist in the West and Arab countries vis-à-vis Jews and Israelis. The way out from such empirically and theoretically unconvincing 'compartmentalizations' of an entire region and its people is, however, not as straightforward as might initially appear. Thus, critics of Orientalist practices have been stunningly 'uncritical towards their own references [and] insofar there is no reflexive hierarchy'[4] between the undisputable prejudices against Middle Easterners in the Orientalist tradition, on the one hand, and the often uncritical and apologetic celebration of local practices, which more often than not simply replicate structures of violence, discrimination (for example, against women and national minorities) and racism (for example, against an allegedly decadent West), on the other.

Thus, Middle Eastern studies are still haunted by the spectre of Orientalism, and both the Orientalist as well as the anti-Orientalist traditions – which in their various 'realist' or 'critical' facets still constitute a key segment of Middle East studies – are deeply implicated within an overall 'Orient/Occident divide'[5] which pitches them against one another as if they were ontologically given, positivist objects. Consequently, the reasons for the pervasiveness of antagonistic identities and conflicts in the region are seen either in specificities of the 'Hobbesian' regional political system (including its cultural dimension)[6] or the subtle patterns of domination by a politically, economically and culturally hegemonic West.[7] This has larger conceptual, empirical and theoretical ramifications than might initially be suspected. More precisely, both traditions nurture an explicit or implicit reification of the Middle East as a distinct territorial/cultural container characterized by regional identities (which are either problematized or celebrated), on the one hand, and conflict patterns (as either a structurally given feature of the regional system or the result of a hegemonic export of Western patterns of domination), on the other.

The major problem with both traditions is that they re-inscribe notions of antagonistic identities and conflicts into their respective research programmes on identities and conflicts in the Middle East. In a nutshell, and referring to a major argument unfolded throughout this book, political, scientific and many other societal discourses are subject to a creeping antagonization of Middle East politics, that is, a subtle logic of thematizing opposing identities and conflicts when writing and acting on Middle East politics on a local, regional and global scale. The task ahead is, thus, quickly described: to write about the obvious centrality of antagonistic identities and conflicts in the Middle East without implicitly reproducing assumptions about their objective status. Yet, due to the subtle ways through which antagonistic notions about the region encroach into even seemingly 'critical', benevolent or benign practices, its implementation is much less straightforward. What is at least required, on a theoretical level, is a truly self-referential theory 'which cannot presuppose that its own form is given and prescribed. [Such a theory] only clarifies its status when encountering itself within its own research subjects',[8] rather than mystically regarding itself as immune from its societal environs, as this shapes both the 'realist' and 'critical' tradition in Middle East studies. Empirically, this argument for autological research – well known to many deconstructivist, radical constructivist and post-structuralist theories – has strong repercussions insofar as any theory must then be measured against the yardstick of its ability to constantly formulate its theoretical concepts and models against the background of a (necessarily constructed) social reality – and in that sense it always already is 'empirical theory'.[9] However, 'a general licence for autological research admittedly contains only few instructions; it does not yet clarify what has to be done'.[10]

It is for that reason that any theory must mark its starting points, its unavoidable *petitio principii* which results from the very fact that any theory is already intractably interlinked with and embedded into what it seeks to explain.[11] By building on the theory of world society in modern systems theory, this book starts from the assumption that rather than being constituted by ontologically given objects (such as actions or actors) society constitutes itself and constantly evolves on the basis of communications as its basic unit. It is then the 'boundless potential for surprise'[12] which the inaccessible horizon of all actualized and potential communications, which occur at any given (and, indeed, un-given) moment in time, entails, which renders any linear, causal theory of society, in general, and politics, in particular, over-simplistic.[13] Hence, such a focus on communications necessarily requires a *globalized* perspective on all empirical topics (including Middle East politics) since, by definition, both the reach of actualized communications and the inaccessible pool of potential communications cannot be limited by territorial, identity-related (symbolic) or functional borders. However, and notwithstanding this general remark, society always is a *historical* society which constantly produces and re-produces its internal (world) societal boundaries on these very territorial, symbolic and functional levels. This requires making explicit which boundaries are particularly decisive in structuring and confining world societal communications. In that context various theories of globalization (both in international relations and the social sciences more generally) have underlined the permeability of territorial and symbolic borders. This does not mean that these borders are unimportant – quite the contrary, as the above discussion on the underlying reification of cultures and territories in Middle East politics and the dramatic consequences such bordering practices have on the life of people in the region and beyond shows. Yet, what the debate on global governance, global 'cobwebs', world society and patterns of global hegemony as well as the global diffusion of cultural models shows is that it is *primarily* the level of functional divisions which is the motor of globalization and societal differentiation – and these approaches then only disagree with regard to the (crucial) questions whether, first, one (and then: which) or several functional spheres are central to societal differentiation and, second, to what degree other forms of differentiation matter, too. However, the general relevance of functional differentiation – that is, the pervasive logic of political, economic, religious, academic, legal, art-related and other functionally separated yet highly interdependent societal spheres – can hardly be disputed. Notwithstanding this argument, to which this and subsequent chapters will return, functional differentiation is of course also a form which is not ontologically given but rather results from ever-evolving and highly contingent changes in (world) society – which through history has encountered many other forms of primary and secondary differentiation. Without embarking at this stage further on these arguments,[14] it suffices to say that this short discussion of key theoretical points of departure not only has the purpose of highlighting (in the sense of the aforementioned autological tradition) the theoretical and intellectual traditions to which this study strongly relates. In addition, and from an empirical perspective, it also strongly suggests that whatever else is needed in a study on Middle East politics the focus on 'globalization', 'functions' and 'societal differentiation' is essential. What is required, in other words, is an adequately complex *and* empirically-oriented theoretical framework – and it is on this basis that this book opts for the theory of world society in modern systems theory as a promising candidate.

Briefly then, and with a view to the key research questions which have been highlighted above, the task ahead is to take the centrality of (antagonistic) identities and conflicts in Middle East politics seriously – rather than writing them off as an Orientalist conspiracy – while at the same time avoiding any reification of these antagonistic features in the form of culturalist or civilizational paradigms. World society theory offers a useful way out of this dilemma, since it disposes of conceptual lenses which allow us to 'regard this normality as unlikely',[15] thereby taking both the historical reality and the contingent and dynamic character of these societal discourses and structures sufficiently into perspective. Seen from that angle, it clearly comes to the fore that the communicative dynamics which shape the patterns of identity and interest politics, conflict, cooperation and peace in the Middle East are always part of structurally global forms of differentiation and distinction. In other words, conflicts and identities in the Middle East are not following a separate regional logic of societal differentiation and neither are they the result of a misfit between (Western) modernity and (regional) tradition. The Middle East is in its entirety already part of a structurally debordered and global (political) order. And, functional differentiation is, consequently, not a specific form of differentiation in the West but rather a universal – and often highly conflictive – mode of operation. This and subsequent chapters will look in great detail at these important empirical and theoretical issues.

Addressing globalization and the Middle East

'Globalization' has become an indispensable buzz-word in the study of the Middle East in International Relations (IR) and other social science disciplines. There is hardly an analysis which does not stress in one way or another the intractable linkages on the political, economic and cultural levels which entangle this region with other parts of the world. While scholars differ with regard to their assessment of whether the Middle East forms a region which adheres to its own (cultural) laws and principles[16] or whether Middle East politics and society are in fact subject to 'global' and 'universal' dynamics,[17] widespread references to the (deep) linkages and dependencies connecting this region with the rest of the world can be found in most contemporary analyses.[18] This centrality of 'globalization' certainly corresponds with a wider trend in the social sciences, in which not only various empirical studies on global interconnectedness but also theories of globalization, world-systems and world society prosper.[19] This trend is not confined to the disciplinary borders of globalization studies and sociology, but also affects the discipline of IR which is deeply 'perturbated' by the advent of globalization.[20]

The popularity of 'globalization' is particularly related to developments since the end of the Cold War and the demise of the bipolar, allegedly state-centred order. These developments render analyses of world politics based on the assumption of the primacy of nation-states ever more difficult. Disparate literatures such as those on 'new wars', regional integration processes, securitization dynamics, the global human rights regime and the political economy of globalization all bear witness to the growing relevance of adopting both a 'globalized' *and* a wider societal perspective when addressing issues of crucial importance to IR. Thus, more than 30 years after his seminal critique on 'the unfortunate title'[21] of IR, with its emphasis on inter-state (*vulgo* inter-national) relations, John W. Burton's plea for a world society approach to global politics has made some headway – moving from the margins to the centre of the discipline. Burton argued that addressing the 'many transactions in addition to those regulated by governments within states that cut across state boundaries'[22] in the analysis of world politics in IR leads to conceptual consequences which necessitate a more systematic and theoretically coherent approach to global interconnectedness and societal interactions. Ultimately, such a 'methodological cosmopolitanism'[23] proves to be both theoretically and empirically more compelling for an analysis of major developments in world politics than the traditional tools of culture-oriented 'methodological regionalism' in area studies and the state-centred 'methodological (inter-)nationalism' in classical IR.[24]

When addressing the way in which the literature on Middle East politics in IR and neighbouring disciplines has responded to this development, a somewhat shadowy image emerges. On the one hand, the literature on the Middle East in IR is heavily under-theorized and if the literature is theory-guided it still tends to follow classical state-centred and interest-focused positivist theories, such as various strands of realism, liberalism, institutionalism and, at least partly, middle-ground social constructivism.[25] On the other hand, however, the analysis of global structural interrelations, dependencies and (in-)equalities as well as the embedding of Middle East politics within a wider societal setting is central to a vast literature on the Middle East, at least in an implicit manner.[26] Yet, the underlying theoretical assumptions on concepts such as 'globalization' and 'society' employed in Middle East studies often remain ambiguous and amorphous. They are ambiguous insofar as many debates centre around the main concern of the 'area study controversy',[27] namely the question of whether global or local/regional dynamics have primacy in accounting for major developments in Middle East politics, as if the one could be thought without the other. Similarly, a vast amount of ink is spilled on assessing the status of 'society' vis-à-vis politics, as if politics was detached from its societal environs.[28] Debates are then amorphous to the extent that 'globalization' and 'society' are often treated as self-explanatory variables, which do not require further specification and theoretical clarification. However, this diagnosis contrasts markedly with the aforementioned increasing theoretical relevance of 'globalization' and 'society' in many studies within IR and beyond. Consequently, the main venture of this book is to let theoretically rich approaches on 'globalization' and 'society', on the one hand, and the impressive literature on Middle East politics, on the other, speak to each other. This dialogue between Middle East and globalization studies not only promises new insights into the underlying dynamics of politics and society in this fascinating region in relation to an encompassing global interconnectedness, but will also allow us to address – and to critically question – the reach of globalization theories when seen through the prism of obvious local/regional and cultural peculiarities.

Given this objective, it is the main aim of this introductory chapter to outline in greater detail the way in which 'globalization' and 'society' as central theoretical concepts are addressed in this book. This is based on the observation that neither of these terms is self-explanatory, let alone uncontested. While the analysis in this book is based on world society theory in modern systems theory, as initially developed by Niklas Luhmann, it also takes regard of crucial insights from other comprehensive theories of globalization as well as from other radical (de-)constructivist theories. As will be outlined in this chapter and in the introductory sections of each subsequent chapter, world society theory offers a rich, theoretically compelling toolbox with which developments in Middle East politics can be tackled within the context of a systematic *and* critical theoretical framework.[29] At the same time, however, this framework does not sacrifice the obvious complexities and factual richness of empirical phenomena in the region to the goddess of sterile theoretical abstraction. Rather, world society theory combines a firm commitment to universal and constructivist theorizing on structures, patterns, systems and societal regularities with a critical and deconstructivist epistemology which directs attention to paradoxes, contradictions and polycontextuality. The choice for world society theory derives, thus, in particular from the fact that this theory allows us to address universal global features and regional peculiarities at the same time, thereby avoiding a generally unproductive separation between these two modes of observation.

The following sections of this chapter will discuss in greater detail the main reasons why embarking on world society theory in a book on Middle East politics is indeed a worthwhile endeavour. This necessitates, first, a short discussion on how world society theory relates to other comprehensive theories of globalization, such as theories of complex interconnectedness and cobwebs, world-systems analysis, world polity theory and theories of multiple modernities. It will also include a discussion on how crucial insights from these theories can be incorporated into a world society framework. As a next step, this chapter will then delineate the main contours of the theory of world society in modern systems theory as far as this is relevant for the specific empirical focus on Middle East politics. It will focus in particular on (global) communications, societal differentiation and homogeneity/heterogeneity as central themes stemming from the adoption of this theoretical framework. The final section outlines the structure of this book, thereby briefly summarizing the theoretical rationale and empirical content of the five subsequent chapters on key developments in Middle East politics.

From an empirical perspective, this book focuses on politics in the region of *bilad as-sham*, that is, historical Syria, which today comprises mainly the states of Israel, Jordan, Lebanon and Syria as well as the Occupied Territories in the West Bank and the Gaza Strip, governed by the Palestinian Authority (PA) – with special emphasis being given to the Israel-Palestine arena.[30] This region, also referred to as the Middle East, the Levant, *al-mashreq* or *as-sharq al-awwsat* in Arabic and *ha-mizrach ha-tichon* in Hebrew, provides an interesting case for 'grounding' the theory of world society within a concrete regional setting.[31] Thus, the theory of world society explicitly claims to be a universal theory of the evolution of human society. However, empirically, most of its proponents draw from Western and European empirical examples, while the application – and possible refinement – of the theory when confronted with non-Western settings – although occasionally referred to[32] – has so far a rather rudimentary status in world society theory. However, it seems obvious from the outset that the Middle East as a region of ancient human civilizations and cultures, as the origin of three major *world* religions as well as our alphabet, and as a region whose political and economic structures, whose conflicts as well as peace processes not only affect worldwide media reporting but also have a tremendous impact on society well beyond its regional borders[33] must have a powerful role to play in any comprehensive theory of globalization.

What drives this study is not the hardly tantalising goal of aseptically mapping the theory of world society onto Middle East politics. It rather attempts to let the theory of world society be irritated by an analysis of key developments in the region. Such an irritation might prove helpful for at least two reasons. First, it is a contribution to the theoretically promising yet still early reflections in world society theory on an adequate theoretical concept of 'region' within a comprehensive theory of globalization.[34] Second, by addressing the role of 'power' and 'politics' from a systems theoretical perspective, this study attempts to clarify the 'location of power' in modern systems theory, thereby challenging the widespread suspicion that modern systems theory fails to have a comprehensive and critical understanding of 'power'.[35] In a nutshell, rather than mechanically applying world society theory to the Middle East, this study is guided by empirical curiosity and theoretical ambition. Similar arguments can, on a theoretical level, be brought up with regard to the linkages of world society theory and other comprehensive theories of globalization and society. Thus, in the same way as concrete developments in Middle Eastern politics 'perturbate' the theoretical framework, so do alternative theories of globalization, on the one hand, and alternative comprehensive theories of society, on the other. As this study will argue again and again, it is fruitful to incorporate notions from other comprehensive globalization theories and theories of society into this study's analysis of Middle East politics. However, rather than engaging at this stage in an abstract and detailed reasoning on this relationship between different theories of globalization/society, subsequent chapters will introduce selected concepts from world society theory and other theories of globalization/society in relation to the more specific issues discussed therein. The aim of this chapter is rather to offer a more systematic and general overview on the usefulness of world society theory for a study on Middle East politics, and the ways in which alternative theories of globalization and society can be usefully related to such an endeavour.

Notwithstanding this strong plea for a 'global' perspective on Middle East politics, this study also has something to offer for readers from a strong Middle Eastern studies' background. By drawing extensively from the Middle East literatures in IR, political science, sociology, religious studies, geography and anthropology and by re-reading this literature through the lenses of world society theory, this book also aims to contribute directly to area studies. If successful in this enterprise, it is probably the key objective of this book to make a small contribution to overcoming the spectre of Orientalism[36] which has haunted Middle East studies for more than thirty years. As Fred Halliday has rightly observed, Orientalism tends to throw the (theoretical) baby out with the bath-water.[37] Thus, the (laudable) critical purpose of Orientalism in unmasking all subtle and direct practices of re-inscribing (negative) ontological assumptions about Middle Easterners into scientific and political discourses has over time transformed into a powerful counter-hegemony which provides the basis for dismissing the application of universal theories to the Middle East on the basis of the argument that such endeavours ultimately are (Western) distorted images of the 'real' Middle East. By showing that there can and indeed must be a globalized approach to the study of politics and society in the Middle East and that this approach can *at the same time* be sufficiently sensitive in incorporating local/cultural perspectives, the analysis in this book asserts that critical purpose and systematic, universalist theorizing are but two sides of the same coin.

Theories of globalization and world society

Notwithstanding these arguments on an implicit allegation of Orientalism, which underpins many theoretical generalizations on the Middle East, it has nevertheless become commonplace to analyse societal developments in the Middle East against the backdrop of the deep impact that globalization has had on local politics, economics and culture.[38] This interest in globalization and global dynamics relates to several analytical levels. Thus, a central theoretical concept of globalization in the context of Middle East studies relates to those works which emphasize various forms of global interaction and interrelations, such as for example the linkages between 'diaspora' communities and their respective homelands.[39] Hardly surprising, given the tendency in popular discourses to equate globalization with global *economic* interrelations, the focus on the impact of globalization on the Middle East has also been a common theme in countless studies in economics and international political economy, which have analysed the global linkages and networks which permeate economic structures in the region, be it on the level of capital flows, migration, remittances, trade or – arguably the key issue – rent-seeking dynamics related to petroleum resources in many Middle East countries.[40] More recently, with the rise of Islamist fundamentalism, global (in-)security structures – in particular the globalized networks in which fundamentalist terrorism operates – have entered the scene.[41] One could, of course, argue that this 'new' threat which pitches an allegedly 'modern' West against an allegedly 'traditional' Middle East[42] has only replaced the traditional, pre-1990 focus in IR on how the Cold War has affected the region and how, in turn, it relates to global politics in the current period.[43] Notwithstanding this observation, the focus on the global dimension of Islamism and Islamist violence – which however has been and still is primarily a political phenomenon within the Middle East – has also given rise to a renewed interest in the relationship between (world) religions and global politics. Scholars of Middle East politics have discovered the Muslim *'umma* and the legal framework set in place by the *shari'a* as relevant for understanding political developments in the region and have even embarked on exegesis of the *qur'an* for the rather profane purpose of IR.[44] This closely relates to a further 'globalized' perspective which characterizes the Middle East literature. Thus, given the Middle East's image as a 'perennial conflict region',[45] such an overview on globalized approaches would not be complete without mentioning those studies which focus on the impact of global – and mostly Western – political dynamics on the region. This relates primarily to the analyses of how Middle East conflicts, and in particular the Palestinian-Israeli conflict, affect political developments on a global scale. These analyses also deal with global military interrelations – such as US policies in the region, or strategic global linkages as they are, for example, embodied in democracy-promotion policies and other multilateral policies of the US and the EU.[46] In this context, a quantity of research has focused on the strong global involvement in aid policies vis-à-vis the Palestinians, be it in the context of UNRWA (United Nations Relief and Works Agency) or individual states' developmental policies.[47] However, despite this 'conflict image' of the Middle East, there has always been an interest in (and hope for) cooperation and integration in the region, as for example with regard to the long-term impact of the Oslo process.[48] This closely links to a research tradition which – nurtured by the cyclical peace processes (for example, in Israel-Palestine and Lebanon) as well as changes in leadership in Arab countries – focuses on the dynamics of democratization or – at least – liberalization and elite-change in the region and its impact on improving national and regional security.[49]

A second trail of globalized perspectives in Middle East studies are those studies which apply universal theories developed in political science, IR and other social sciences disciplines to the analysis of politics in the region. Most prominent in that regard, still heavily borrowing from the classical IR focus on the state and the allegedly anarchical structure of the world political system, is the focus on state emergence and state behaviour in the realm of foreign politics of Middle Eastern states.[50] Consequently, as Martin Beck has observed, most studies are guided by an underlying rationality assumption typical for positivist theories.[51] These studies hence emphasize that states and their leaders behave (more or less) rationally and are primarily concerned with state survival in a rather unfriendly regional environment – although there is disagreement on whether the state really is central to an 'anarchical Middle East' or whether its role is rather overstated.[52] In this context, one can also identify a number of studies which look at domestic political structures in the Middle East, thereby addressing the more or less subtle mechanisms through which leaders uphold their power in the light of outspoken or suppressed opposition and contestation.[53] Yet, reflecting on the close linkage between traditional IR theories and studies on the Middle East, it is telling that most of these studies closely follow a state-centred orthodoxy, either from 'above' by referring to an anarchical Middle Eastern (sub-)system or (fragile) regional (in)security regimes in the tradition of (neo-)realist and institutional approaches or from 'below' by referring to the way in which domestic coalitions and structures shape the foreign policy behaviour of national governments and autocratic rulers. Moreover, since the 1990s (middle-ground) social constructivist approaches have been increasingly applied to the study of Middle East politics, in particular addressing the way in which specific identities such as Arab nationalism, Zionism or Islamism affect domestic, regional and international politics in the Middle East and, thereby, guide state behaviour.[54]

The extent to which such an application of IR theory to the Middle East can really be equated with 'globalized' perspectives on the region must, of course, be qualified. None of these approaches takes its point of departure from a specific theory of globalization, but rather from an often implicit acknowledgement that global structures and dynamics have a role to play in regional politics. In other words, what is adopted is a more or less systematic *perspective on globalization*, rather than an explicit *theory of globalization*. This correlates with a critical re-reading of the area-controversy in Middle East studies, in which area-specialists had to tackle the problem that 'with emphasis increasingly placed on scholarship that is global in perspective and informed by social science theory', regional/local accounts of Middle East politics were coming under stress.[55] However, the battle between 'global' and 'local' perspectives is not as one-sided as suggested here. Safeguarded by the counter-hegemony of the Orientalism debate, the plea for local peculiarities and distinctions often has normatively flavoured undertones which justify a strong focus on regional distinctiveness in contrast to allegedly 'Western' simplifications.[56] Often drawing from anthropological or ethnographic methods, various studies focus on societal patterns allegedly specific to the Middle East, such as tribal structures or wider family relations and power relations therein. There is also an emphasis on distinct historical trajectories which are, in their specific dynamics, unique to the region, such as the experiences of colonialism and de-colonialization in the Arab context, the history of anti-Semitism and the Holocaust for the Israeli case or other societal features unique to Arabness, Jewishness or Muslimness.[57] This emphasis on specific features of Middle East society and politics finally resounds in what could be referred to as the 'territorial claim' of Middle East studies, namely the assertion that, after all, there is an inside and outside perspective on the region, understood not in terms of expertise but rather in terms of primordial linkages which allow insiders better to 'sense' how the Middle East operates.[58]

This is not the place to repeat the area-studies controversy and neither is it the place to point to the inherent problems of Orientalism which have been discussed at length elsewhere.[59] Yet, in the light of this book's emphasis on the world societal embedding of the Middle East, it might be useful to point to the paradoxical way in which Orientalism itself becomes subject to its own diagnosis. It ultimately rests on an ontological inside/outside distinction, thereby implying that it has a better and deeper understanding of the 'real' Middle East. However, as necessary as local expertise is, one needs to avoid treating the region as being composed of idiosyncratic and ultimately autonomous units that can only be grasped from a dialogical encounter with the 'pure' self. Thus, while this study questions the ontological basis from which arguments of regional distinctiveness originate, such approaches nevertheless pose a twofold challenge which any globalized theoretical perspective on society and politics in the Middle East must seriously consider. The first challenge is to reconcile a globalized theoretical approach with the richness, complexity and diversity of concrete empirical facts related to the Middle East. The second challenge then is to acknowledge the existence of undisputable regional societal dynamics without adopting a problematic understanding of regions as territorially confined containers. As this book shows, a world society perspective can indeed make an important contribution to the debate on society and politics in the Middle East in an ever-globalizing world while at the same time systematically considering the complexities of regional politics, culture and history.[60]

However, before outlining in greater detail the theoretical credentials of world society theory, this section aims to identify key elements of other central theories of globalization which are useful in complementing a world society perspective and which are therefore on various occasions referred to throughout this book. It is not the aim of this book fully to integrate these alternative theories of globalization into a world societal framework and reference to these theories throughout the book will consequently be made in a non-systematic manner. Thus, rather than discussing the linkages between world society theory and other complex theories of globalization in greater detail, which would indeed be a topic for another book, the purpose of this *tour d'horizon* in relation to other globalization theories is the observation that various contributions in Middle East studies have, often implicitly, picked on key themes addressed in these globalization literatures. This observation provides further evidence for one of the major claims of this book, namely that any comprehensive theory of Middle East politics needs systematically to address the embedding of this region into a globalized setting. By drawing from four key theories of globalization, namely theories of communicative interconnectedness and cobwebs, world-systems theory, world polity theory and the theory of multiple modernities, this section outlines the extent to which the 'global' has indeed figured prominently in the Middle East literature in IR and beyond – at least in an implicit manner (and, as a useful side effect, the subsequent chapters will occasionally refer to overlaps between world society theory and these alternative theories of globalization). There is no intention of providing a comprehensive overview on these four key theories of globalization – this book primarily draws from the theory of world society in modern systems theory – the aim is rather to try to show in a cursory fashion that Middle East studies, often unconsciously, relate to some of the theoretical core assumptions therein, thereby indeed providing further evidence for the need to integrate Middle East studies into a comprehensive theory of globalization.

According to widespread basic definitions, globalization refers to processes of worldwide interconnectedness and interrelations. This has been well summarized by Keohane and Nye who have argued that globalization can be understood as a 'network of interdependence at multi-continental distances'.[61] In more general terms, Robertson has referred to globalization as 'the compression of the world and the intensification of consciousness of the world as a whole'.[62] In other words, there is no identity or form of action that could be conceived of independently of its linkages to the world as a whole – world being understood both figuratively (the world as the horizon of what can be thought) and literally (the world as the globe) – referred to throughout this book as the *double* world horizon of all societal processes. More generally speaking, globalization is understood as the compression of worldwide space and time distances. As Innis and others have pointed out, this is accelerated by communications media such as the internet, telephone, television and others – but should nevertheless not be confined to nineteenth or twentieth-century communications media, as the tremendous impact of the invention of the alphabet or book printing illustrate.[63] In his theory of world society – which must not be confused with world society theory in modern systems theory – John W. Burton specified such notions of global interconnectedness and interrelations by adopting an explicitly communication theoretical framework. By addressing 'communications or links between units that create systems',[64] Burton developed the theoretical framework for a multi-layered map of global 'cobwebs' which transcends notions of world society based on territorial configurations.[65] This focus on communicative cobwebs – and the way in which the zillions of different cobwebs which exist at a specific point in time overlap, intersect and change – is of particular relevance for the study of regions in world society, such as the Middle East. Following Burton, regions can be understood as globalized cobwebs, which cannot be adequately understood in mere geographical terms. In other words, regions are globalized cobwebs which constitute de-territorialized spaces on the basis of 'cultural, religious, ethnic and ideological ties'.[66]

In contrast to the intellectual trend of 'temporalo-centrism',[67] which views globalization as a comparatively recent phenomenon, studies of global interconnectedness are well suited to showing that the dynamics of globalization are in fact a long, historical, non-linear process.[68] Interconnections between the Americas, Eurasia and Africa – as well as Australia – can be traced back to the fifteenth and sixteenth centuries, with interconnectedness between Eurasia and (northern and north-eastern) Africa being much older. There are few places where this would be more visible than in the Middle East, which virtually for millennia has been at the intersection of cross-continental movements, be they of migratory, spiritual, economic or cultural nature. Consequently, there are manifold studies which have identified the various linkages which historically bind the Middle East with neighbouring regions in Europe, Asia and Africa.[69] Seen from that perspective, it is somewhat unfortunate that elements of the Middle East literature fall victim to 'temporalo-centrism' by equating globalization with post-Cold War economic liberalization and/or Western political domination.[70] However, at least in an implicit manner, the Burtonian notion of cobwebs shimmers through in the literature on global diaspora communities and their political impact on Middle East politics and society, such as the manifold studies on Jewish and Arab communities in the Americas and Europe. Similar arguments can be made with regard to the impact of global media reporting on the Middle East, such as, in particular, reporting on the Israeli-Palestinian conflict, the emergence of Al-Jazeera and Al-Arabiyya as globalized Arab information providers within the modern media system and, more generally, the spread of the internet in the Middle East and the repercussions that this has on societal and political developments.[71] It is an interesting aside here that a focus on the trans-border impact of communication media has already played a central role in studies on the spread of Nasserist ideology to Jordan and Syria through the radio station *sawt al-arab* in the 1950s.[72] Taken together, the focus on global interconnectedness and global cobwebs gives a hint on the way in which the constitution of regions through globalized communication patterns materializes with regard to the Middle East as a region only partly defined by geographical categories.[73]

Of course, such global (or at least interregional) interconnectedness has neither from a contemporary nor a historical perspective been detached from power distributions. In fact, interconnectedness has regularly given rise to short-term or structural dependencies, hegemony, domination and conflict. This is well reflected in current critical globalization literature with its emphasis on global resistance, processes of 'McDonaldization', and Westernization more generally.[74] An often heard claim in these literatures – mirroring some of the key arguments of the Orientalism debate – is that local cultures are structurally dominated by hegemonic (Western) institutions and cultural frames. However, the literature is ambivalent with regard to the status of the agency of the non-Western periphery. While some stress the powerlessness of the periphery vis-à-vis the Western core, others argue that the periphery – and in particular the Middle East – becomes a space of resistance against Western economic, cultural and political hegemony.[75] From a systematic globalization perspective this focus on structural dependencies has arguably been most coherently addressed in world-systems analysis in the tradition of Immanuel Wallerstein.[76] By adopting a long historical perspective, Wallerstein argues that 'over 400 years... successive expansions have transformed the capitalist world economy from a system located primarily in Europe to one that covers the entire globe'.[77] As a result of this process, 'the peoples of the globe became linked into one integrated unit: the modern world-system', in which Western economic, cultural and political powers prevail.[78] What is, however, important is to note that hegemony in world-systems theory cannot be attributed to single actors, such as the US, but rather is a structural feature of the world-system.[79]

In an implicit manner, this focus on global interconnectedness plus structural domination by the West – often in the context of a globalized world economy – has been an underlying theme in a wide array of research on the Middle East. In particular in the aftermath of the Cold War, there have been plenty of studies which focused on the unleashing dynamics of capitalist modes of production in a globalized world economy and the responses of Middle Eastern states to this.[80] While this is particularly true for the rent-seeking literature on oil- and gas-producing countries in the Gulf and other Middle Eastern regions,[81] it has not been confined to this set of countries. With regard to the Mashreq, such broad trends of economic globalization are a key theme in the international political economy literatures of the 1990s, such as in manifold studies on the (economic) liberalization processes in Syria and Jordan[82] or as documented in studies on the benefits of economic integration between Israel and her Arab neighbouring countries.[83] However, the analysis of global interconnectedness and global dependencies has not been limited to the narrow realm of economic interrelations. The consideration of how global geopolitical constellations relate to the Middle East (and how the Middle East shapes these constellations) has always played a prominent role in Middle East studies, both during and after the Cold War. While several studies have emphasized the agency of Middle East states vis-à-vis the Cold War superpowers or, nowadays, the West, the more widespread assumption – in particular from Middle East scholars – is the observation of political-cultural dominance by the West. This debate is usually framed in geostrategic terms, thus reflecting the neorealist dominance in security studies on the Middle East.[84] In that context there has always been a tradition of interpreting the Middle East as a place of resistance to processes of Western domination. This focus on resistance – which becomes, for example, evident in assertions of Arabness and Islamism in a geopolitical context – fits well with the observation by Wallerstein that the contemporary world-system is based on two principal ideologies, these being universalism, on the one hand, and racism-sexism, on the other. According to Wallerstein, these ideologies 'are not opposites but a symbiotic pair'.[85] One does not need to stretch analogies too far to argue that it has been a particular strength of area studies to identify how these two ideologies simultaneously work as a subtext of political and cultural constructions of the Middle East, in particular in Western academic and political circles. Thus, stereotypical attributions of Middle Easternness, which date back to historical images of the Levant[86] and are associated with violence, backwardness and filth, serve from that perspective as a stabilizing mechanism for a Western-dominated world-system. Thus, the pure, rational universal modes of production and progress embodied by capitalism and modern science, can be contrasted with the irrational, untrustworthy and violent particularistic culture of Islam and/or the Middle East.[87] It is on this basis that 'the universal work ethic justifies all existing inequalities' and becomes the 'cultural' explanation for underdevelopment and the need for ongoing Western interventions.[88]

While sharing world-systems theory's analytical focus on global interrelations and structural dependencies, yet without its emphasis on economic production and cultural hegemony, world polity approaches in the tradition of the Stanford School have focused in particular on the identification of patterns of global isomorphic reproduction. Thus, John W. Meyer and collaborators have looked at the dynamics of global institutional diffusion (in particular the spread of the state system, educational organizations and others)[89] as well as the spread of the cultural modes on which these global institutions rely. The latter are, in particular, notions of rationality, sovereignty and progress, all of which are particularly well developed in the Middle East. World polity approaches are helpful in showing that globalization does not weaken the (nation)-state but has rather been the prime reason for its emergence and consolidation.[90] Yet, by doing so, the Stanford School almost automatically shifts the observational lenses away from the obvious differences between states and regions and is, rightly, chilled by the remarkable structural similarities on the basis of which all states and other organizations operate. World culture refers in that context to the specific cognitive frames to which organizations relate, while the concept of world polity addresses the structural institutions which operate within these frames.[91] Particular attention is then devoted to the analysis of the role of the state within the world polity. Thus, 'contemporary constructed "actors", including the nation state, routinely organize and legitimate themselves in terms of universalistic (world) models like citizenship, socioeconomic development, and rationalized justice',[92] underpinned by the emergence of shared formal structures of the state apparatus and other organizations – such as universities, schools, hospitals and so on – throughout the world. As a result, in the course of the twentieth century 'world society has been consolidated'.[93] Of course, world polity approaches acknowledge that these diffusion processes are indeed 'eclectic' and, therefore, regional differences – and even conflict between these different models – endure.[94] Thus, it would be unfair to repeat the often voiced criticism that the Stanford School underestimates heterogeneity and difference, although it might nevertheless be argued that world polity approaches are on a conceptual level not well equipped to account for both isomorphization *and* heteromorphization in world society in a way that would be coherent with the overall texture of this theory.[95]

Arguably, globalized perspectives in the tradition of the Stanford School – although rarely explicitly referred to – have had a significant influence on Middle Eastern studies. By any account, Middle East studies have traditionally been state-biased and have leant heavily on assumptions about rational and self-interested actors. This has led to a multitude of studies focusing on state emergence and consolidation as well as inter-state relations.[96] But rather than focusing on the domestic constellations which have brought about the current states in the Middle East, the Stanford School emphasizes the way in which individual states have to be understood from the perspective of the world polity. More dramatically spoken, world society 'allocates responsible and authoritative actorhood to nation-states', and there is hardly a place in the world where this authority is as jealously guarded as in the Middle East.[97] As far as the domestic dimension of Middle East states is concerned, there are various studies which have identified the isomorphic adaptation of nationalism and rationalism in the Middle East,[98] that is, world models which 'licence the nation-state not only as a managing central authority but also as an identity-supplying nation',[99] based on a model which was originally 'invented' in nineteenth-century Europe. As both historians and political scientists have equivocally pointed out, 'nationalism' has had a powerful role in state emergence and consolidation in the Middle East by providing the anti-colonialist movement and its political leaders with a shared norm, namely Arabism – ironically often picked up by Arab leaders and intellectuals, such as Michel Aflaq, educated in the West.[100] Similar arguments have also been made with regard to the nationalist norm of 'Zionism' in the Jewish diaspora, the Yishuv and, later, Israel.[101] The Middle East state not only consolidated and enlarged its organizational grip on society – for example, by founding state institutions, improving education and infrastructure and establishing finance authorities and secret services – but also provided an identity-anchor on the basis of which political actions could be justified but which – as

Michael Barnett has shown – also provided a powerful constraint for political leaders who risked falling outside such cultural frames.[102]

World polity approaches stretch further, with their enrichment by an analysis of the way in which primary institutions of international society, as defined by the English School, have permeated Middle East inter-state relations.[103] The literature on the centrality of sovereignty, diplomacy, great powers, war and balance of power in the Middle East – still owing to the underlying realist hegemony in Middle East studies in IR – fills entire libraries.[104] Moreover, an (implicit) orientation on world cultural models also characterizes many studies on economic development in Middle East states, with their heavy emphasis on (the lack of) socioeconomic development and progress in the region.[105] Finally, the mushrooming of studies since the 1990s on the rise of non-governmental organizations and 'civil society' in the Middle East bears witness to a world polity 'filled with associations'.[106] Thus, notwithstanding the more or less successful attempts by many Middle East states to circumscribe and limit their societal and political impact, the emergence of countless non-governmental organizations in the region – on a national, trans-national and global scale – in 'science, education, the economy and economic development, human rights, and medicine'[107] indeed draw attention to the emergence and consolidation of a 'shared modernity'.[108]

Finally, mirroring attempts in Middle East studies that argue that modernity cannot adequately be understood as a Western programme but has long, indigenous cultural traditions,[109] theories of multiple modernities, as developed by Shmuel Eisenstadt, are helpful in detecting historical trajectories, differentiations and processes of heteromorphization without abandoning a world societal focus.[110] While the Stanford School argues that the 'rationalized modernity is a universalistic and inordinately successful form of the earlier Western religious and post-religious system', thereby sharing the theoretical focus on Europe in world-systems analysis and modern systems theory, theories of 'multiple modernities' have developed a polycentric notion of modernity.[111] In a nutshell, modernity becomes structurally coupled with cultural variables and distinctions and can, therefore, be regarded as a specific code which unfolds in various ways with regard to different cultures and civilizational contexts. As a result, modernity as the 'blank slate' of globalization[112] becomes translated into different forms of modernity. While Eisenstadt does not dispute the historical origin of modernity within a Western context, he nevertheless breaks with the prime focus on isomorphization in the Stanford School or cultural hegemony in

world-systems analysis. This is well summarized in a highly instructive
remark by Eisenstadt, where he has argued that:

> the various programmes of modernity that developed in these socie-
> ties have been continuously cristallized through the process of a
> highly selective incorporation and transformation in these civiliza-
> tions of the various premises of Western modernity. These cultural
> programmes entailed, among others, different emphases on the
> various components of the 'original' Western programme of moder-
> nity – such as man's active role in the universe; the relation between
> Wertrationalität and Zweckrationalität; the conceptions of cosmolo-
> gical time and its relation to historical time; the belief in progress;
> the relation of progress in history as the process through which
> the programme of progress develops; the relations to the major uto-
> pian visions; and the relation between the individual and the collec-
> tivity, between reason and emotions, and between the rational and
> the romantic and emotive.[113]

Ultimately, such a focus on heterogeneity, path-dependent cultural,
religious and civilizational trajectories which transform and shape
distinct regional and cultural forms of modernity is a highly valuable
tool for all theories of globalization, which aim to focus simultaneously
on 'isomorphization and heteromorphization in an inter-connecting
world'.[114] Without going into detail at this stage, the literature on
the Middle East, with its emphasis on regional and cultural peculiarities
builds strongly – but again generally implicitly – on such a perspective
on the relationship between global models and their selective transformation in the region, as we have observed above. This relates, *inter alia*,
to the literatures on the relationship between state and religion and
regional forms of leadership as well as the execution of political
power, and, in particular, the impact of regional values and norms on
Middle East politics.[115] In that context, it is somewhat unfortunate
that in order either to counter Western hegemonic domination or
reject one-dimensional applications of isomorphic concepts onto
Middle Eastern histories, the focus on regional and cultural subjectivity, as mentioned above, often goes hand in hand with a *sui generis*
approach to Middle East politics and society. In contrast to theories
of multiple modernities such an approach is ultimately hardly able to
account for the obvious structural and cultural global embedding of
the Middle East.

A world society perspective on the Middle East

This overview on several key theories of globalization should be helpful in identifying key aspects which any theory of globalization related to Middle East politics must take into serious consideration. Thus, a comprehensive approach to the place of the Middle East in world society must not only state the obvious, namely that there are today virtually no places, people or processes in the region which would not in one way or the other be affected by worldwide political, economic and cultural developments and interconnections. Seen from that perspective, and to borrow from a James Bond movie title, the world is not enough; the approach requires a more systematic and explicit theoretical underpinning. Accordingly, by transcending generally under-theorized notions of global interconnections, the aforementioned theories of globalization all offer important and theoretically dense perspectives on politics in the Middle East within a globalized setting. Theories of cobweb models direct attention towards de-territorialized communicative networks. As a result, the world no longer appears as a one-dimensional space but rather as a network of complex and multi-dimensional overlapping and intersecting societal constellations on the functional, cultural, geographical, economic and political levels. Moreover, world-systems analysis is alert to the way in which the globalization of production integrates the entire world into one world-system. While this system comprises all societal spheres it is dominated by economic production and the latent structural hegemony of Western regions in global economic, political and cultural relations. Further, world polity approaches, while also focusing on the role of Western culture and organizations, emphasize the integrative but not necessarily harmonious dimension of globalization which becomes visible as a result of worldwide processes of isomorphic diffusion, in particular the diffusion of notions of rationality and progress as well as organizational structures such as the state and related institutions. Finally, theories of multiple modernities highlight that such isomorphic processes should not be equated with global homogeneity but have to be understood against the background of culturally and regionally distinct interpretative frames of modernity. This comparative overview on various comprehensive theories of globalization suggests that rather than adopting *one* of these forms of observation of world society, their various perspectives should rather be integrated into a theoretical framework which combines at the same time the focus on communications and de-territorialized notions of regionalism, global systems of production and hegemony, processes of isomorphism and homogeneity as well as the dynamics of heteromorphism and heterogeneity. As this section argues the theory of world society in modern systems theory is a useful candidate for such an endeavour.

This book does not aim to provide a systematic overview on the theory of world society in modern systems theory and neither does it aim to discuss its general applicability to IR or specific issue areas dealt with in the discipline.[116] The aim here rather is to identify some key components of the theory of world society which are relevant for this particular study on Middle East politics. As a welcome side effect, it will be argued that world society theory is also helpful in integrating the individual strengths of the aforementioned theories of globalization within the framework of a comprehensive and critical theory of society. It will then be up to the subsequent chapters of this book to dig deeper into the ways in which world society theory tackles more specific issues related to Middle East politics, such as regionalization, power, inclusion/exclusion, identities, conflict and peace. The purpose of this section is more general in the sense that some basic tenets of world society theory will be discussed here in order to identify why it offers a useful starting point for analysing Middle East politics within a comprehensive globalized *and* societal framework. In brief, this section argues that world society theory offers a comprehensive basis for analysis of Middle East politics because it allows the addressing of societal phenomena that seem at first sight contradictory and paradoxical but are, in fact, two sides of the same coin, and, from an IR perspective, equally relevant to a systematic understanding of politics and society in the region. This relates, in particular, to seemingly contradictory processes of globalization versus regionalization/localization, integration versus fragmentation, homogeneity versus heterogeneity and, finally, construction versus deconstruction.

First, on the dimension of globalization versus regionalization/localization, world society theory can make a useful contribution in overcoming the alleged contradiction between these processes, thereby focusing on the unity of this distinction. By showing that society is constituted by 'communication all the way down',[117] world society theory not only leaves behind rather outdated sender-receiver models of communication but allows for the replacement of such models with a radical constructivist understanding of communications. The main insight of this communication-theoretical starting point is that there is no social order (and disorder) beyond communication. More precisely, society consists only of communication. Following on the linguistic turn in the social sciences, regions cannot be regarded as distinct geographical places but rather as communicative orders which are, in a sense, placeless. In other words, the Middle East is constructed wherever it is communicated and a glance at the literature on Middle East diasporas or global media reporting already provides a hint of the conceptual consequences which such a focus on communications entails.[118] Translating this focus in world society theory on communication as the basic unit which constitutes society into IR demands that we start not with specific actors – such as states, domestic interest groups or international organizations – nor with the assumption of specific pre-existent structures, such as an anarchical inter-state system, an international society or normative/ cognitive frames. In both models communication exists, but is treated in terms of sender-receiver models, which regard communication as a material object exchanged between autonomous actors within the overall context of an ontologically presumed international system. In contrast, world society theory emphasizes – thereby being close to similar lines of argument in poststructuralism – that rather than actors or structures producing communication, in fact communication generates all social orders, actors and societal processes in the first place. In the tradition of modern systems theory, communication can be described as the unity of a threefold contingent and placeless selection of information (some information must be selected by Alter at the expense of other potential information), utterance (it must be 'visibilized' as such an information by Alter, for example, as a demand in a direct oral interaction or a written request, at the expense of other possible utterances, for example, shouting, begging, claiming and so on) and, finally, understanding (that is, Ego observes the unity of the difference between information/utterance and 'understands' this – at the expense of other possible forms of understanding, including misunderstandings).[119] Any 'response' in the form of selecting information and utterance by Ego, followed by understanding by Alter is already connective communication. Such chains of interconnected communications over time put in place emergent orders and regularities, but also disjunctions and contradictions.[120] What are the effects of this basic, yet highly consequential centrality of communication for a study on the Middle East? For example, the Middle East can no longer be conceptualized as a region which is simply 'there'. As Pinar Bilgin has, from another theoretical angle, shown in her study on the genealogy of the term 'Middle East' in historical and contemporary security paradigms, this concept does not merely carry geographical connotations but various social, cultural and political meanings, too.[121] While it might well be that we observe a particular density of communications within a specific geographical region, the Middle East is also all communications which constantly recreate this region in globalized (political) discourses not only in the Pentagon or the Elysée palace. While not embarking further at this stage on the various connotations of communication in world society theory (see also the following chapters), it suffices to emphasize here that putting communication first necessitates a renewed survey of issues and concepts central to IR and Middle East studies, such as regionalization processes (Chapter 2), political orders (Chapter 3), issues of exclusion (Chapter 4) and identities and conflict dynamics (Chapter 5). This will be done by conceptualizing the Middle East as a placeless spatial attractor which is constituted on the basis of (political) communications in and on the region on a world societal scale.

Second, as a result of world society theory's polycontextual perspective on 'society', too narrow a focus on distinct social orders (such as politics in classical IR theory or the economy in world-systems analysis and much of the globalization literature) is avoided. By addressing the unity of the distinction between functional systems (such as politics, economics, law and others) and their environments (referred to above as the contradiction between integration versus fragmentation), world society theory can make a contribution to transcending the somewhat limited focus on states and geopolitical constellations which still dominates much research on the Middle East in IR. More precisely, as particularly chapters 3 and 4 will discuss, such a polycontextual perspective on integration within distinct orders/functional systems and fragmentation into various social orders allows a specification of the reach and also the limits of politics and power in the region. In other words, these theoretical premises shift the spotlight not only onto the complex interrelation between different functional spheres, referred to here as functional differentiation, but also onto the manifold power constellations that exist within and between these spheres.[122] More precisely, dealing with politics in the Middle East from a world society perspective requires putting politics into a wider societal and historical perspective. While the concept of functional differentiation is central to sociology, it is striking that it has only half-heartedly (if at all) been embraced by political science and IR, which either normatively assume that there is a primacy of politics in relation to other societal spheres or simply deny the relevance of the impact of non-political spheres on society, for example, by hypothesizing that the focus on elite political actors and their interests would suffice to account for the main dynamics of regional politics.[123] In contrast, this book aims to show that an accurate account of Middle Eastern *politics* requires a complex model of *society* into which politics is structurally embedded as one amongst many functional systems. The systems/environment conceptualization of a polycontextual world society is a useful candidate for this endeavour since it simultaneously allows us to address integration of and fragmentation between functional systems. This is based on the observation that while society cannot accurately be described from the perspective of one distinct social sphere, societal operations (which are based on communications) always mark a distinction and, recurrently, establish a demarcation between different social orders. Each of these social orders, then, cannot but observe world society through the prism of its own systematic operations. As a result, what emerges is a world society characterized not only by constant communications which ensure the continuation of distinct social orders but also by various border demarcations, distinctions, fragmentations and patterns of heterogeneity within and between these social orders. The primary borders in world society are those between different functional orders, however, as particularly Chapter 5 will discuss, they also comprise symbolic borders between different collective identities.

Third, the focus in world society theory on processes of internal border demarcation *within* world society (such as between different functional spheres) allows the observation of the unity of the distinction between homogeneity versus heterogeneity.[124] This focus on bordering processes will be particularly helpful in addressing the various inequalities, fractions, fragmentations and patterns of inclusion versus exclusion which characterize world society (and certainly the Middle East). At the same time, however, a world society framework also draws attention towards the powerful unifying dynamics of global interrelations in the context of world society formation and an emergent order of world politics.[125] As in particular chapters 4 and 5 will discuss, world society theory allows us to approach differences on the symbolic/identity dimension without recourse to problematic notions of 'culture' or 'civilization' which often operate as residual yet heavily under-theorized variables when accounting for obvious regional and cultural peculiarities. By way of addressing such symbolic bordering dynamics on the identity level, chapters 5 and 6 will discuss conflict and cooperation dynamics in the Middle East on the basis of a communication-theoretical framework which helps to avoid such static simplifications.

Finally, a world society perspective is helpful in addressing the emergence and stabilization of specific political orders without attributing any stable and permanent status to such orders. This observation points to the manifold similarities between world society/modern systems theory, on the one hand, and post-structuralist and deconstructivist theories, on the other.[126] More precisely, the focus on the processes of permanent deconstruction and (re)construction sheds light on the paradoxes which underlie (and bedevil) all political orders. As will be argued in subsequent chapters, this simultaneous focus on deconstruction and construction proves particularly useful in avoiding the reification of existing power relations and conflict dynamics in the Middle East, for example, by relating these dynamics to specific and allegedly stable identity patterns of Middle Easterners, Muslims, Israelis or Arabs. As will be elaborated further below, the deconstructive fundamentals of world society theory provide a sound basis for writing constructively about the obvious centrality of identity and conflict in the region, that is, without essentializing these identities and conflict orders (see chapters 4 and 5). In other words, the simultaneous focus on deconstruction/construction allows us to account for the structures of regional politics, in general, and regional conflicts, in particular, without unconsciously transforming the region into a zone of intervention.[127]

Outline of the book

The book is divided into three parts. Embarking on the communication-theoretical framework outlined above, Part I focuses on the unity of the distinction between globalization versus regionalization/localization. Building on what has already been said in this chapter, Chapter 2 looks in much greater detail at the way in which patterns of global communicative interconnectivity affect Middle East politics, focusing in particular on the interplay between functional and territorial differentiation. By addressing several case studies, this chapter shows that the construction of the Middle East is of necessity a globalized enterprise. In a first step, it relates the literature on Middle East diaspora communities and other forms of transnational interconnectivity to a world society framework. However, as argued above, globalization is more than mere interconnectedness and cannot adequately be comprehended without a parallel focus on processes of functional differentiation. Therefore, this chapter addresses the way in which the Middle East is constructed in various functional spheres. It argues that taken together these various 'framings' of the Middle East allow the specification of what Burton meant by de-territorialized notions of regionness. Regions are, according to this analysis, understood as the merging of shared forms of observations (for example, as a problematic 'perennial conflict region') across a variety of functional spheres on a world societal scale – in other words, the Middle East (and territories, identities and actors therein) as a meaningful societal 'object' results from (structurally debordered) political communications in and on the Middle East. It is in that sense that this book advances a communication-theoretical approach to the study of all territories in world society while at the same time assuming that observers (such as those reading this book) know which territory (for example, Syria, Lebanon, Jerusalem, Amman) is actually meant. In systems-theoretical parlance, there might indeed be a structural coupling between society and distinct spaces on the globe. Yet, as socially meaningful (political) semantics and structures these territories always remain empty spatial attractors insofar as their relevance in political (and other functional) discourses crucially depends on the impossibility of arriving at a static and holistic understanding of their very identity: what these spaces are (on the issue dimension), where they begin and end (both on the spatial and temporal dimensions) and what relations between people they produce (on the social dimension) remains subject to ongoing spatial negotiations and it is in that sense that territory as a socially-generated structure has no corresponding and fixed reality beyond communication.

Part II discusses the main dynamics of regional politics, addressing the unity of the distinction between construction (of concrete power constellations) and deconstruction (of the contingency of these orders). It focuses in particular on the role of power as well as the patterns of inclusion/exclusion in the Middle East. More precisely, it looks at the manifold manifestations of (crude) power constellations in the region as well as the ways in which the inclusion/exclusion paradigm constantly undermines any permanent reification of such settings. Chapter 3 focuses in detail on the main dynamics of regional politics, in general, and the role of power, in particular. It provides a fresh perspective on regional politics, which allows us to overcome the heavily state-centred and status quo-oriented focus of much IR and Middle East studies literature. By focusing on politics as the communication of power, it argues that the global 'problematization' of the Middle East, as identified in Chapter 2, is nurtured by the 'frozen' character related to the crossing between communications of power and powerlessness with regard to political communications in and on the region. In several case studies this chapter looks at the difficulties in the contestation of power in various Middle Eastern countries, for example, with regard to the role of Islamists, national minorities – and at times majorities – and democracy movements. This focus on 'frozen crossings' and 'hot contestations' in political communications in and on the Middle East is exemplified by addressing the tight linkages between politics and the security apparatus (army, secret services, militias) which serves the function of stabilizing what are in fact highly fragile political orders. 'Frozen crossings' thus refer to distortions in code-oriented communications which significantly hamper the ability to shift between both sides of the code (in the case of politics the crossing between power and powerlessness). With regard to Middle East politics, this becomes obvious in the somewhat problematic overlap between these two sides of code-oriented communications, on the one hand, and the relatively stable relegation of specific persons, groups or political programmes to either side of the distinction, on the other. More precisely, the ability to experiment with alternative persons, groups or political programmes (that is, the possibility of crossings and re-crossings between power and powerlessness) is severely hampered in many instances of political communications in and on the Middle East. However, the world societal embedding as well as the general structural features of a functionally differentiated world society ensure that even seemingly entrenched political orders in the Middle East, which are based on severe manifestations of frozen crossings, do not reify in the sense that they become taken-for-granted, quasi-stratificatory orders. Within a primarily functionally differentiated world society, contestations are an inherent feature of all political communications. It is because of this that orders of frozen crossings invite constant opposition by those who, for whatever reason, find themselves permanently located on the side of powerlessness. Note that these arguments do not suggest that the distribution between power and powerlessness is reified in any objectivist sense. The key point here is that *communications* and not actors observe themselves on the basis of 'frozen crossings' between power and powerlessness. Thus, in many conflict settings, such as for example, in Israeli-Palestinian relations, the dynamics of 'frozen crossings' underpin political communications which emanate from both sides. The arguments in this and subsequent chapters on 'frozen crossings' and blunt relegation dynamics, do not therefore suggest that this distribution of power constellations necessarily relates to specific actors, but rather that these dynamics affect the logic of political (and other functional) communications in and on the Middle East which produce these actors as meaningful societal addresses operating within the discursive confines of 'frozen crossings' in the first place.

Since in that context opposition has only a faint chance of crossing the lines between powerlessness and power, such contestations do not easily evaporate but rather augment into peaceful or violent but always power threatening constellations. Henceforth, they are referred to here as 'hot contestations'. As a result of these dynamics, power has constantly to underpin and defend its concrete manifestations against structurally-given and ubiquitous 'hot contestations' through an inflationary recourse to highly visible symbols of power and the use of overt violence. By failing to (temporarily) obscure the founding paradoxes which accompany all political orders, these dynamics then ironically undermine the very fundamentals of power in Middle East politics. This argument is further elaborated in Chapter 4, which addresses the dynamics of inclusion/exclusion in the region. By putting observations made by, *inter alia*, the Arab Human Development Reports into a more comprehensive theoretical perspective, it argues that the crisis of power in the region – identified in Chapter 3 – extends to other societal spheres, too. Hence, the blunt relegation dynamics of power communications (that is, the way in which specific groups of persons are often systematically and permanently relegated to either side of code-oriented communications such as powerful/powerless) extend to other societal spheres. This chapter studies such extended frozen crossings in scientific communications as well as with regard to the status of women in the Middle East. The key argument is that due to the inclusion/exclusion paradigm these extended frozen crossings do not reify but are constantly observed and represented in scandalous terms as highly contingent and unjust societal and political orders. Inclusion/exclusion is thus the form which allows constant opposition – but not fundamental alteration – to the overall dynamics of frozen crossings in regional politics. Thus, frozen crossings, on the one hand, and the form of inclusion/exclusion as the observation of the contingency of these frozen crossings, on the other, exist in parallel but ultimately are uneasy bedfellows – nurturing what is, therefore, referred to throughout this book as the creeping antagonization of Middle East politics.

By focusing on the unity of the distinction between integration and homogeneity (through conflict dynamics) and fragmentation and heterogeneity (through practices of de-securitization), Part III, finally, accounts for the way in which this creeping antagonization plays out in Middle East politics. This perspective also allows us to address the main function of social conflicts in Middle East politics, namely constantly to translate this creeping antagonization into tangible societal structures – thereby preventing the reification of concrete orders of frozen crossings, as solid as they might appear. Chapter 5 argues that the creeping antagonization of Middle East politics makes the explicit thematization of (antagonistic) identities a necessary and central element of political communications, since knowledge about 'identity' carries too much informational meaning to be ignored. This constant thematization of antagonistic identities facilitates lock-in effects of social conflicts because communication offers are regularly interpreted against the background of this taken-for-granted context and, consequently, are seen to originate from an antagonistic (and threatening) Other. This analysis of the 'deep perturbation' of Middle East politics by conflict dynamics[128] allows the focus to shift from an alleged disintegration through conflicts to the question of how conflicts, understood as social orders in their own right, constantly solve the problem of their own continuation. This focus on how conflicts in fact integrate (antagonistic) identities into shared conflict settings underlines the argument that the centrality of identities and conflicts in Middle East politics is not a unique characteristic of the region but already part of the operations of structurally debordered world societal communications, in general, and broader patterns of conflict emergence and conflict change, in particular. These arguments are studied here by drawing from various conflict settings in political communications in and on the Middle East at local, national, regional and global levels, for example, in Lebanon, Israel, the Palestinian-Israeli conflict as well as with regard to conflict constellations involving the Middle East on a global scale. However, and relating to what has been said above, there are indeed many dynamics of cooperation, coexistence and even peace in the region which are, unintentionally or for strategic purposes, often downplayed in scientific and political discourses. This study, therefore, closes with some concluding reflections on the place of peace in the Middle East (Chapter 6). It argues that (actualized or potential) dynamics of cooperation and narratives of peace continuously challenge the conflictive and antagonistic moments in Middle East politics, thereby preventing any permanent reification of conflicts as the taken-for-granted order of political communications in and on the region. The totalizing identity of the creeping antagonization of Middle East politics is, therefore, always incomplete.[129]

2
Regionalization and Debordering: the Middle East between Global Interconnectivity and Functional Differentiation

لنا بلد من الكلام / *We have a homeland of words*
محمود درويش / Mahmoud Darwish[1]

Relocating the Middle East

Many analyses that address the impact of globalization on the Middle East start from the assumption that the 'global' and the 'regional/local' are opposite and frequently even contradictory dynamics.[2] Thus, according to a widespread analogy, the Middle East witnesses in the contemporary era the uncontrolled collision between the tectonic plates of global, Western-dominated practices and an entrenched local/regional culture. In more abstract terms, this collision is also conceptualized as the simultaneous confrontation between 'modernity' and 'tradition' on Middle Eastern territory.[3] It is this simultaneity of un-simultaneity[4] which then renders the Middle East the epicentre of a major global clash between the 'modern' forces of globalization, on the one hand, and 'traditional' forms of local and regional resistance or (angry) acquiescence, on the other.[5] According to this perspective, Middle Easterners reclaim their distinct traditions, subjectivities and localities in direct opposition to external forces of globalization and modernity.[6] This analytical narrative relates closely to a more general sentiment in the Middle East, reaching beyond Islamist and Arab nationalist quarters, of an unjust structural dependence on and suppression by a politically and economically hegemonic yet culturally shallow West.[7] As Bassam Tibi consequently summarizes this widespread perspective, 'Muslim fundamentalism is a cultural answer to the globalised, techno-scientific modernity of the West',[8] and similar things can be said about the impact of norms of Arabism and how these affect the structures of opposition between both Arab states and citizens and Arab states and the West.[9] However, this narrative is not limited to Western-Muslim and Western-Arab relations. Thus, as Avi Sagi and Yedidia Stern argue with a view to Israel's allegedly problematic position as a Jewish-Zionist state in the context of a perceived *external* globalization, 'the global post-modern mood is not suited to the State of Israel's complex existential reality. It should not be denied that we are in this mood, but neither should we surrender to it'.[10]

This and the following chapters challenge the usefulness of this distinction between 'modernity' and 'tradition' in accounting for the ways in which globalization relates to local/regional developments in the Middle East.[11] As will be argued in this chapter by drawing from a range of empirical manifestations in Middle East politics, a theoretically more demanding notion of globalization, as advanced, *inter alia*, by world society theory, requires as a first step modifying the very notion of the Middle East's 'regionness', thereby overcoming the simplistic 'territorial container perspective'[12] which shapes the perception of an external, Western and modern form of globalization versus an internal, traditional and authentic local/regional Middle Eastern culture, be it Arab, Christian, Muslim, Shi'i, Jewish, Syrian, Israeli, Palestinian, Sephardi, Bedouin, Druze or another.[13] Thus, rather than constituting territorially separated entities with distinct cultures, regions in world society are, first of all, the *result of* global debordering processes which draw from a worldwide horizon of communicative interconnectivity. Due to the communicational foundations of (world) society, which have been outlined in Chapter 1, all attempts to define major developments in Middle East politics on the basis of the modernity/tradition dichotomy or attempts to pin down its precise territorial shape and borders are a futile exercise.[14] They ultimately only reproduce the *problematique* of classical sender-receiver models of communication in which the Middle East is a concrete substance (that is, territory) with one [sic] corresponding reality in space and time.[15]

In contrast, as modern systems theory posits, territories are not given objects which simply exist outside society. In order to become social and political realities, territories as meaningful semantics depend on their societal emergence and consolidation on the basis of communication as society's basic unit. At this stage it should be recalled what has already been said in Chapter 1 about communication as the unity of the three-fold contingent selection of information, uttering and understanding as well as about the continuous processing of such single instances of communication which create social structures in the first place. Thus, the

'location' of each of these three selections, which only together constitute an instance of communication, cannot be confined to a single corresponding place or, for that matter, individual persons or groups.
Communications, which constitute the Middle East and other spaces
in the region as territories in world society, can, thus, draw from live
information on a demonstration in Beirut by supporters of Hezbollah
and General Aoun, uttered by an Al-Jazeera news-caster in Abu Dhabi
and understood by a student of Arab (or, indeed, Spanish) politics in
London, Bielefeld or elsewhere – and only taken together do these
three elements constitute an instance of communication, thereby gener-
ating spaces as de-territorialized results of communications. Moreover,
the connectivity of communications on this demonstration is not
restricted to certain territorially confined spaces and, therefore, the
Middle East as a sense-making 'localization' necessarily has the world
as its permanent and ever-unfolding horizon. It is from this perspective
that world society theory maintains that the Middle East and other territories are 'placeless' spatial attractors for and within various societal
spheres.[16] There are two main theoretical considerations which under-
score this perspective.

First, the continuous reproduction of these spatial attractors is not
restricted to communications within distinct territories but is structurally dependent on the global interconnectivity of communications
across various functional spheres. Building on complex notions of systems,[17] which emphasize the operational autonomy *and* cognitive openness of systems in relation to their environment, it becomes immediately
apparent that there are no specific Middle Eastern codes of communication that would ensure such operational autonomy of the Middle
East.[18] In other words, territorial borders do not constitute *regions as systems* as would be held by many IR approaches that conceptualize the
Middle East as a sub-system of the international system.[19] Adopting an
alternative standpoint, this chapter contends that territorial borders
demarcate *regions as spatial attractors* for various globalized functional
systems – such as, for example, politics. In other words, not territories,
but various functional spheres are the prime systemic differentiation
in world society.[20]

Second, as far as the corresponding ascriptions of meaning of spatial
attractors are concerned, they too draw from a necessarily global horizon
of sense-making communications, thereby rejecting all notions of
cultural essentialism in which there are real internal (for example, the
famous 'situation on the ground') and deficient external (for example,
Orientalist) understandings of the Middle East. As this chapter will

argue on the basis of these theoretical premises, the Middle East is a global spatial attractor which emerges and continuously reproduces itself as a result of world societal communications – in other words, the Middle East 'is' whenever and wherever it becomes communicated in world societal communications. In order to highlight this crucial theoretical and empirical insight, this book refers to (political) communications both in *and* on the Middle East in subsequent chapters.

Of course, being subject to constant debordering and rebordering processes,[21] neither shape and borders nor the corresponding ascriptions of meaning of the Middle East are fixed – and herein lies the inherent political significance of such bordering dynamics.[22] Mirroring some of the arguments by John Burton on de-territorialized notions of 'region-ness' introduced in Chapter 1, regions must consequently be understood as the temporary stabilization of spatial convergence between bordering processes across several functional spheres. Therefore, regions cannot be conceptualized in spatial terms, that is, characterized by a single corresponding border and territories demarcated by such borders, but rather as multi-dimensional, functional spheres which overlap, cross-cut and intersect each other. As this chapter will argue by drawing from the theory of functional differentiation,[23] bordering processes, which lead to the emergence of regions in world society, are primarily structured by various global functional divisions and their interrelations rather than segmentary (territorial/centre-periphery and so on) or symbolic (cultural/religious/ethnic and so on) divisions in which globalization is almost always perceived as an external and alien imposition. Moreover, the polycontextuality of these simultaneous bordering processes across various societal spheres (primarily functional, but also segmentary and symbolic) generates regions as fuzzy and heterogeneous spatial attractors which comprise at times overlapping, at times cross-cutting economic, political, religious, legal, ideological and other borders. Thus, territory matters, but it has to be understood against the background of func-tional differentiation as the prime form of internal differentiation in world society.[24] This then is also the reason why the formation of regions and their territorial borders is necessarily a result – rather than the negation – of (world societal) communications and functional differ-entiation. It is, finally, the way in which regional borders are observed in, say, politics, academia or mass media,[25] which gives rise to specific (yet, contingent and often contradictory) ascriptions of meaning with regard to different regions of world society. These ascriptions of meaning will subsequently be referred to as 'scripts', for example, various and often contradictory notions of the Middle East as a 'perennial conflict region', a place 'lacking human development', a 'realist political space', 'the cradle of civilization', a 'place of unique cultures', 'a place of resistance' or others. Due to this book's focus on the place of the Middle East in IR, this chapter addresses primarily the 'location' of the Middle East in politics, thereby narrowing down the analysis to one functional sphere. However, from a theoretical and empirical perspective, it might indeed be worthwhile to extend this analysis in the future to a wider comparative study on 'localizations' of the Middle East across a wider range of functional contexts since this would enable a fuller picture to emerge of the polycontextual and complex borders which constitute the Middle East as one of world society's main regions.

In order to elaborate in greater detail on how these arguments are helpful in conceptualizing a theoretically and empirically rich understanding of the 'regionness' of the Middle East in world politics, this chapter is divided into four sections. The next section provides some more theoretical considerations of why the political meaning of the Middle East and territories within the region are always the result of world societal deliberations. This analysis builds on concepts of debordering in world society, that is, the ways in which the structural permeability of territorial borders for globalized (functional) communications shapes distinct localities in the Middle East. It looks in particular at the global communicative interconnectivity of the Middle East, thereby underlining the argument that the Middle East and other spaces within this region are not objective territories but rather debordered, global spatial attractors which serve a specific role for societal communications in various functional spheres. This section addresses the ascriptions of meaning of the Middle East and other territories within the region in political communications, thereby focusing on those communicative dynamics which aim to ensure the legitimacy of specific ascriptions of meaning to the Middle East in world politics. By way of applying these theoretical considerations to concrete empirical manifestations, the following section then addresses the way in which global political interconnectivity and functional debordering equip one specific territory in the Middle East, namely Palestine, with concrete (and often opposing) meaning(s). The focus is laid, in particular, on the role of global Palestinian diaspora communities as well as international organizations in such processes. This analysis shows that the global 'bordering' of Palestine is neither restricted by territorial/regional nor symbolic/identity boundaries. The world societal horizon against which all territories and borders must be understood is, of course, not limited to such (contrasting) spatial semantics but relates to concrete structures in world society as well.

Consequently, the next section looks at the way in which the city of Jerusalem becomes a topical form for political communications in and on the Middle East at the global level by being framed as world cultural/ religious heritage. More specifically, it is argued here that referring to Jerusalem as a world city can be understood as an element in the (nascent) emergence of concrete structures of (inclusive) world statehood which parallels rather than replaces ongoing exclusive sovereignty claims on Jerusalem.

The concluding section addresses the multiple forms of interconnectedness between such world societal semantics and structures of 'regionness' and discusses the question of how the ensuing role of the Middle East as a global spatial attractor within and across various societal spheres translates into a theoretically rich notion of the formation of the Middle East as a distinct region in world society. For that purpose, this section critically refers to a central argument in world society theory, namely that functional differentiation and region-specific forms of structural coupling between various functional spheres foster territorial forms of observation in world society, thereby, *inter alia*, consolidating the 'regionness' of the Middle East.[26] This chapter concludes that in order to arrive at a full understanding of the regionness of the Middle East and other territories within the region, the world societal horizon against which spaces are permanently renegotiated must systematically be taken into consideration, thereby overcoming the segmentary-territorial and symbolic-cultural bias which still shapes, often implicitly, many accounts on territoriality in world society, in general, and the Middle East, in particular – including the somewhat problematic notion of region-specific forms of structural coupling referred to above, which ultimately risks reifying the notion of a distinct identity of different regions. In contrast, the focus on manifold different spatial constructions of the Middle East in politics and other (functional) spheres might provide a better route since it forms the basis for widespread global *political* semantics on the Middle East, which often translate into powerful – yet contradictory – 'scripts' on the Middle East in global political communications, such as the observation of the Middle East as a dangerous location ('perennial conflict region'), a place of unique cultures ('cradle of civilisation'), a heroic territory ('place of resistance') a place of de-development ('lack of knowledge society) and others. This analysis underlines a central conclusion of this chapter, namely that regions are a topical form of observation in several functional systems in world society. The Middle East and, by the same token, other spaces within the region are territorial signposts for world societal communications and, therefore, always have an inherent political dimension since the associated ascriptions of meaning highlight specific forms of observation, while neglecting others.[27]

Debordering the Middle East

Following the theoretical arguments set out above, all territorial borders and, consequently, all territories in world society must necessarily be understood as being the result of global (communicative) dynamics. Accordingly, the very notion of the 'regionness' of both the Middle East and territories within the region must be shifted from a positivist, spatial and cultural understanding to a concept of territory as a world societal and communicatively generated phenomenon. It is on the basis of these theoretical premises that this and the following sections trace the ways in which world societal communications generate the Middle East and spaces within this region as politically meaningful territories. Notwithstanding their contingent, dynamic and fuzzy character, spaces and borders nevertheless serve a specific and important function within various functional spheres – such as *inter alia* politics and conflicts[28] – by acting as territorial signposts for societal communications within these respective social contexts.

In order to study such a de-territorialized understanding of (communicating and politicizing) the Middle East, this section builds in particular on the concept of debordering, as developed in constructivist IR theory and critical geography.[29] Thus, while it is true that territorial units, and particularly state authorities in the Middle East, often seek to insulate themselves from their spatial environment through manifold practices of securitization, which aim to de-legitimize or limit the reach of alternative spatial representations,[30] the pervasiveness of functional differentiation in world society renders such attempts largely futile.[31] Thus, as Mathias Albert and Lothar Brock argue, functionally-induced 'debordering within the world of states is understood as an increasing permeability of [territorial] borders together with a decreasing ability of states to counter this trend by attempts to shut themselves off'.[32] These dynamics of debordering – that is, the secondary status of territorial vis-à-vis functional borders – become obvious on a more fundamental level when addressing the actual attribution of (political) meaning to distinct territories in world society, which is not a state affair but a world societal process of deliberations on the highly political meaning of distinct spaces. More precisely, the concept of debordering highlights the permeability of territorial borders but also the way in which both these borders and the spaces demarcated by them are the result of world societal communicative dynamics in the first place. These processes then turn borders and territories into empty (and placeless) spatial attractors[33] – which necessarily need to be 'filled' with various and often contradictory ascriptions of meaning in various functional contexts, thus underlining the structural de-territorialization of territories as a social, political and potentially conflictive spatial attractor.

As already briefly observed, these communication-theoretical fundamentals are also the reason why the Middle East cannot be conceptualized as a *system*, as many approaches in IR – both positivist and constructivist[34] – hold. In order to qualify as a system, regions (or states) would have to be constituted by clearly demarcated systemic borders which, in turn, produce sharp, systemic inside/outside distinctions. However, in contrast to functional borders, which indeed establish such clear demarcations between the operations of different social systems, territorial borders are not able to produce an 'internal' logic of operations within a specific region, thereby separating these internal operations from an external environment which obeys different operations and, ultimately, is structurally distinct from the internal space. Thus, in opposition to widespread notions in IR and area studies of the Middle East as a territorial (sub-) system[35] or a unique cultural space,[36] this section looks at the world societal linkages between communication, power and space in an attempt to identify the debordering dynamics which ensure that the Middle East and territories within the region 'are' whenever and wherever the Middle East emerges as a topic of world societal political communications. Invocations of territorial or identity-related inside/outside distinctions do not correspond with systemic forms of observation but are already political re-inscriptions into notions of space in world society.

In other words, the Middle East must be relocated from a spatial to a functional understanding of regionness, which addresses the question of how the shape and borders of this region, its political relevance as well as claims and contestations between conflictive territorial narratives are permanently negotiated and renegotiated on a world societal scale.[37] This focus on functional debordering also allows us to identify the ways in which the Middle East operates as an empty and, consequently, powerful spatial attractor in different (global) functional spheres. This de-territorialized understanding of regionness strips territories of all primordial, natural and positivist denotations and turns the spotlight onto the political (and, likewise, economic, religious, scientific or legal) communications in world society that continuously bestow territories and borders with specific (and often contradictory) meanings.

As a result, this perspective on the role of space in world society undermines any neat, one-dimensional understanding of spaces as separate and static territorial entities. More precisely, it directs attention toward both the functional and polycontextual contexts within which territories gain their societal relevance. An adequately complex notion of space thus comprises the observation of how borders and spaces overlap and intersect, thereby underlining the uncountable ascriptions of meaning as well as fuzzy borders of territories within and across functional spheres.

Such world societal deliberations on space and spatial orders with regard to the regionness of the Middle East will be addressed on the following pages in greater detail. The focus will be laid on three dimensions of *political* debordering which are of direct relevance to the regionness of the Middle East. First, the role of diaspora communities and international organizations as an example of how global interconnectivity and functional debordering ensure that the processes of ascribing political meaning(s) to Palestine always operate against the background of a world societal horizon; second, the way in which notions of space inherent in the concept of world religious/cultural heritage, as evident in the case of Jerusalem as a world city, can be understood as (nascent) emergent structures of world statehood; finally, the polycontextual processes through which regions as a crucial form of observation in world politics are the result of multi-dimensional bordering processes related to manifold framings of the Middle East in politics and other (primarily functional) spheres. Re-inscriptions of territorial exceptionalism can, on the basis of the analysis in this chapter, be understood as securitizing practices attempting to invisibilize the global horizon of all borders and territories in world society. Paradoxically, however, by doing so, they only underline the world societal and functional embeddedness of space.

Bordering Palestine

This section argues that Palestine as a politically meaningful territory has to be understood against the background of functional debordering and global communicative interconnectivity. More precisely, in order to be recognized as socially relevant, spaces must be equipped with functional (for example, political) meaning. Due to the dynamics of functional debordering outlined in the previous section, such 'spatial negotiations' are necessarily held against the background of a world societal horizon. Thus, the functional context within which territories such as Palestine acquire meaning demands a communicative interconnectivity between

all global representations of Palestine. However, the (open) world societal horizon also ensures that such representations are subject to constant
change and ongoing competition between 'legitimate' notions of territory.[38] Against the background of these theoretical premises, the choice
of Palestine as an example of world societal representations of territory
might be criticized. The fact that occupied Palestinian territories in the
West Bank and Gaza Strip lack formal recognition as a state means
that Palestine might be seen as too simplistic a case for tracing the way
in which global horizons structure borders and territories in world
society. What follows from this line of argument is that since a Palestinian
state has not yet come into existence and that, as a result of this, state-
sponsored securitization practices limiting the scope of 'acceptable' territorial narratives are considerably less developed, notions of Palestine
might be comparable to global patterns of spatial negotiations on fragmented states such as Lebanon,[39] but differ significantly from spatial
practices in allegedly more powerful and unified states such as Israel,
Jordan and Syria. However, on closer inspection this argument seems
less compelling. Thus, while it is reasonable to assume that state authorities indeed have a powerful role in affecting territorial narratives, there
is no plausibility to the assumption that they would have a monopoly in
negotiations on spatial orders. A glance at the manifold and often contradictory representations of Israel, Jordan, Syria or, for that matter,
the Middle East[40] at the domestic, regional and global levels points to
the structural embeddedness of official spatial narratives in (political)
global spatial deliberations that always undermine the discursive borders
erected by governmental narratives.

The observation that global interconnectivity and functional debordering are indispensable elements in endowing spaces with distinct
meanings has been an underlying theme in the literature on Middle
East and, in particular, Palestinian diaspora communities. In that context, it is a central argument that the 'geosocial space of Palestine in
exile'[41] is crucial in explaining domestic struggles over the Palestinian
homeland in political, economic, religious and cultural spheres.[42] The
process of equipping spaces with distinct meaning is, thus, not constrained by regional boundaries. Therefore, 'Palestine' not only includes
Palestinians in the 'near abroad', such as Palestinians in refugee camps
throughout the region, the 'internally displaced',[43] or Palestinian citizens of Israel, Lebanon and Jordan, but also the Palestinian diaspora
community in, say, the US or the EU. However, notwithstanding the
remarkable insights into the transnational linkages of ethno-religious
communities, the focus on homeland/diaspora relations might also

produce some theoretically imprecise classifications. Thus, when distinguishing between homeland and diaspora, these relations are primarily observed through the prism of territorial (that is, transnational) divides. The contribution of diaspora communities in endowing meaning to 'local' spaces then becomes conceptualized as an 'external' – yet legitimate – interpretation of an internal space (that is, the homeland), thereby advocating a theoretical primacy – and ontological status – to territorial borders. While sharing with world society theory its focus on the permeability of territorial borders, transnational studies do not emphasize to the same degree the *functional contexts* within which territories and homelands emerge in the first place. This might also be the reason why such studies are often characterized by a culturalist bias. Hence, by primarily focusing on diaspora/homeland relations, the general world societal processes in the construction of the homeland, which not only transcend territorial but also kinship boundaries, acquire only secondary status. As will be outlined further below, the processes of attributing meaning to spaces are, however, structurally open to all communications, independently of whether they originate from within or beyond specific territorial or symbolic-cultural confines.[44] By focusing on the global political processes through which Palestine acquires meaning, this section embeds its focus on the Palestinian diaspora community into a wider functional perspective. In other words, it advocates a systematically debordered perspective on 'global Palestine',[45] thereby stressing the de-territorialized communicative processes of equipping Palestine with specific political meaning across spatial (for example, Middle Eastern) and symbolic (for example, Palestinian) boundaries.[46] This focus on the twofold dynamics of debordering, that is, across territorial and kinship divides, underlines the argument that a world societal perspective on the functional processes through which spaces such as Palestine (or Israel, Lebanon, Syria – the Middle East for that matter) acquire and constantly change their meaning is ultimately required for a comprehensive account of the role of borders and territory in world society. However, it should be stated from the outset that any 'full' understanding of territoriality would require observation of the countless linkages, overlaps and intersections of spaces within and across a wide variety of functional spheres – an argument which will be returned to towards the end of this chapter.

Another caveat seems appropriate here. This chapter is not concerned with the question of *which* notions of Palestine (or other territories) emerge as a result of world societal deliberations. While such arguments on the political leaning of, for example, diaspora communities are indeed often made, any generalizations of whether radical and exclusive or moderate and cooperative attitudes abound are not the concern of this chapter. From both a theoretical and an empirical perspective, such generalizations are hardly convincing. Thus, the observation that functional debordering and global communicative interconnectivity ensure that Palestine as a meaningful political territory becomes constructed against a world societal horizon already presupposes that territorial and symbolic boundaries do not determine the content of political communications. In other words, the primacy of functional spheres in world society, amongst them politics, is also on that level not constrained by geographical or kinship proximity. This is not to say that territorial or symbolic confines might not operate as amplifiers and 'legitimizers' of specific spatial representations but this already is a secondary question of how politics, as a self-referential system, operates.[47] To put it into more systems-theoretical parlance: global interconnectivity and functional debordering ensure that all political communications on space and spatial orders are made against the backdrop of a structural world societal horizon. There is, thus, more to debordering than a mere permeability of territorial borders. It not only relates to the movement of ideas or goods across borders, but equally covers the very process of equipping borders and demarcated spaces with concrete societal meaning, thereby emptying territory of all material content. This functional perspective then allows, in a second step, the deconstruction of the political mechanisms of invoking legitimacy and power with regard to certain spatial representations, for example, by claiming better knowledge due to territorial proximity (permanent confrontation with the 'situation on the ground'), kinship linkages or functional (for example, academic or journalistic) expertise.

A central political semantic which structures attempts to limit 'legitimate' spatial representations is the equation between territorial spaces and national governments, for example, using 'Damascus' and 'Amman' (or 'Syria' and 'Jordan', for that matter) to denote the governments of Syria and Jordan. This is more than merely an innocent spatial simplification.[48] It is, therefore, not surprising that the Oslo agreements of 1993, which formally established the Palestinian Authority (PA) as the (civilian) government for parts of the West Bank and Gaza Strip, make use of this world societal political script[49] and, consequently, state that the Palestine Liberation Organization (PLO) – which was meant to constitute the backbone of the PA – is the 'sole representative of the Palestinian people'.[50] Of course, from an empirical perspective, this has from the outset been a legal-political, rather than a factually convincing statement. After an initially positive perception of the agreements amongst most Palestinians, the lack of a 'peace dividend' soon led to a much more sceptical attitude towards both the Oslo process and the ruling PLO leadership.[51] Thus, the widespread critique of 'Oslo' amongst Palestinians – in Palestine and the diaspora – as well as beyond kinship circles documents the limits of this noteworthy attempt to securitize Palestine in accordance with the principles of a world polity in which governments claim a privileged role in defining borders and territories. Somewhat ironically, therefore, the victory of the Islamist Hamas party in the national parliamentary elections of January 2006 is in a paradoxical way interlinked with this founding mythology of Oslo, as Hamas took control of the PA while refusing to recognize the agreement which established it.[52] Seen from this perspective, the opposition by Hamas to the Oslo process has to do with more than its confrontational attitude towards Israel. Thus, an acceptance of the Oslo agreements would not only challenge its concept of Greater Palestine but also undermine its claim that as the government of the day, Hamas and not the PLO represents the Palestinian people. Notwithstanding these considerations, the election victory – and the fact that these elections corresponded with democratic standards unique amongst most Arab countries – equipped Hamas with enough political legitimacy to claim that for the time being it is the representative of the Palestinian people and, indeed, Palestine – arguably in *cohabitation* with Palestinian President and chairman of the PLO, Mahmoud Abbas. However, from a theoretical perspective on spatial orders, such power struggles are a second step, being preceded by political processes through which territories acquire meaning in the first place – independently of the question of which territorial representations ultimately succeed in claiming legitimacy.

The world societal horizon of such territorial ascriptions can well be studied when addressing the role of the global Palestinian diaspora in demarcating Palestine as a de-territorialized space. More precisely, global interconnectivity and functional debordering allowed Palestinians successfully to circumvent local restrictions in the critique of the Oslo agreements. To cite one example, one of the main Palestinian newspapers, *al-quds al-arabi*, is located and published in London and has, since 1993, taken a critical stance on the Oslo agreements and the role of the PLO.[53] What matters here is that *al-quds al-arabi* not only relied upon but actually profited from its spatial detachment, thereby undermining the PA's 'monopoly of meaning'.[54] Attempts by the PA to censor 'internal' Palestinian media, which 'reflected the official understanding of the new political reality',[55] provided 'outside' Palestinian voices from the outset with an aura of credibility. Diaspora media could not only claim to be independent from the securitization practices pursued by the PA but, more importantly, it could claim to remind the government of what 'real' Palestine actually entailed.[56] What renders this and other episodes on homeland/diaspora relations interesting for the purpose of this section is not so much the obvious global distribution of and competition between varying notions of Palestine but rather the observation that territories are empty spatial attractors – not given objects – which acquire their full meaning only through functional deliberations in world society.

Functional debordering is, however, not limited to such structural global interconnectedness. Thus, the twofold securitizing effects of neo-patrimonial policies by the PA and Israeli occupation, each of which proposes specific (contested) representations of Palestine, actually attracted such 'external' interventions in localizing Palestine unhindered by domestic constraints. Consequently, the impact of the Palestinian diaspora was not limited to Palestinian and wider Arab media, but covered a larger constituency, for example, interventions by famous intellectual 'Palestinian dissenters such as Edward Said [and] Joseph Massad',[57] both from Columbia University in New York. Playing on the theme of functional debordering, for Said exile not only meant a philosophical and moral condition, but also comprised a central element and, ultimately, a political tool in the process of arriving at full – yet always contrapuntal – notions of space and identity.[58] Seen from this perspective, living in the diaspora even works as a 'spatial amplifier' by providing 'outside' representations of territory with particular legitimacy – at least for those successfully claiming symbolic belonging to the homeland. This central role of the diaspora in bordering Palestine has, however, not been limited to sophisticated academic reflections on the relativity of space: through addressing representations of Palestine in Palestinian refugee camps the relevance of debordering in attributing meaning to spaces in more mundane contexts immediately comes to the fore. More precisely, the widely-held view amongst Palestinians that any territorial arrangement with Israel needs to include a right of return for Palestinian refugees, equipped refugees with a powerful semantic tool which enabled the claim that refugee camps literally are Palestine, thereby de-legitimizing any political initiatives based on 'the notion that justice – from a Palestinian perspective – can be found in any solution that denies some refugees the right of return'.[59]

What matters here is not merely the observation that Palestinian refugees indeed have their own practices of memorizing space,[60] but also the fact that these ascriptions of meaning to Palestine gain political relevance in the context of functional debordering in world society. Randa Farah's analysis of the notions of homeland held by Palestinian women in refugee camps is an intriguing example of such processes. Farah underlines the fact that notions of Palestine held by Palestinian women in refugee camps serve a double purpose. On the one hand, they re-inscribe refugee camps as Palestinian places, thereby underlining the de-territorialized character of space in world society. On the other hand, these re-inscriptions are also part of a functionally debordered process in which these notions of Palestine compete with alternative spatial-political conceptions. It is on the basis of these two parallel processes of de-territorialization and debordering that Palestinian women 'played an active role in re-inscribing refugee camps as *Palestinian* places and in opposition to humanitarian practices and policies, the objectives of which are to maintain the camp as a "humanitarian space"'.[61] Such a focus on the contribution of Palestinian refugees in spatial negotiations in world society also proves helpful in avoiding a too simplistic conceptualization of the powerlessness of non-state actors in Middle Eastern identity formation processes. Thus, it is a common claim in the literature that the responsibility for demarcating refugee camps as Palestinian places primarily lies with Arab states unwilling to grant Palestinians (full) citizenship status.[62] In contrast to this claim, various empirical studies on refugee camps have pointed to the interrelationship between Palestinian and non-Palestinian voices in spatial representations of Palestine, thereby shifting the lenses of observation from the state level to a functional perspective on the interplay between manifold global political/spatial negotiations on Palestine. Thus, like other diaspora groups,

> Palestinian refugee women are actively engaged in appropriating places and discourses in ways that prompt their struggle and sense of self . . . More significant for Palestinian women is the political struggle, wherein their reproduction of the 'home' as a Palestinian domestic sphere in the context of the Diaspora has political significance in resisting integration in host societies and maintaining a sense of peoplehood through common cultural references.[63]

Of course, the role of the Palestinian diaspora in spatial representations of Palestine, at least since the second half of the twentieth century, has always been pronounced, as a result of its structural entanglement with the Palestinian national movement. In a sense, the 'lost years' – dating from Al-Nakba in 1948 until the emergence of the PLO in 1964 – which were at first sight characterized by a 'disappearance' of Palestine instead constituted the overture for a powerful 're-emergence' of Palestine as a global spatial attractor.[64] Moreover, from the 1960s until 1993, the PLO, independently of whether it operated from Amman, Beirut or Tunis has always had a pivotal share in spatial representation of Palestine, as has nowadays the Hamas leadership in Damascus. Edward Said summarized this observation on the centrality of exile well, when making the emphatic point that it was 'the Palestinian diaspora, which produced Arafat in the first place: it was from Kuwait and Cairo that he emerged to challenge Shukairy and Hajj Amin'.[65] In this context, it is interesting that the Draft Palestinian Constitution of 2000 foresees a bicameral system in which the second chamber consists entirely of representatives from the Palestinian diaspora community.[66]

By shifting the space of the 'internal' from the spatial to the symbolic level, representing all those who successfully claim to be Palestinians, Palestinian refugee camps are a particularly interesting example of the political dynamics related to functional debordering and global communicative interconnectivity. Thus, the distinction of Palestinian vis-à-vis other representations of Palestine already points to the world societal political context within which these various representations of Palestine compete with each other. In other words, the horizon against which Palestine emerges as a meaningful territory transcends all spatial and symbolic divides and includes all (political) communications in world society – claiming legitimacy of specific notions of Palestine then already is a connective, self-referential operation of the political system meant to counter alternative forms of spatial representation. Seen from that perspective, Dan Tschirgi's doubtlessly accurate remark on the 'internationalization' of Palestine, due to which 'it is therefore not only inevitable but also legitimate that "third-party" voices figure in the discourse over a final settlement of the Palestinian refugee problem' and, ultimately, about what Palestine actually 'is', might need some theoretical recalibration.[67] This quote seems to imply some uneasiness concerning the legitimacy of 'external' representations of territory. However, following the argument developed above, claiming legitimacy is already a semantic tool structurally independent of prior world societal political processes through which borders and territories emerge in the first place. Or, to rephrase Tschirgi here, the internationalization of Palestine (and any other territory) is indeed inevitable, while there is no theoretical plausibility to the claim that 'outside' representations (seen from a territorial or symbolic perspective) would be more or less legitimate when compared with 'internal' perspectives. To put this into systems-theoretical terms: since there is no independent observer who could ultimately decide which spatial representations are to be considered acceptable and which are not, the political legitimacy of competing representations of Palestine is self-referentially decided in the context of world societal, functional spatial deliberations.

This argument is sustained by addressing the claims of legitimacy related to the tremendous number of third-party interventions in Palestine – from the EU, the United Nations Relief and Work Agency (UNRWA), Saudi-Arabia, evangelical groups, Egypt, Israel, Hezbollah, the US, the IMF, Syria, Iran and many others. While all these parties certainly contribute to the various and often contrasting attributions of meaning to Palestine, claims for the legitimacy of such 'outside' interventions serve only to document the structural world societal horizon within which strategies sustaining or limiting the reach of specific spatial representations are embedded. To cite two examples of such processes of legitimizing and de-legitimizing 'external' interventions: claiming that the promotion of democracy is an outside (Western) intervention into Palestine is a common practice in securitizing Palestine, but one that de-legitimizes those Palestinian individuals and NGOs – both in Palestine and the diaspora – who also pursue democracy agendas[68] rather than constituting an accurate observation of the world societal processes of attributing meaning to territories which transcend territorial and symbolic boundaries. Second, Stéphanie Lodo has highlighted successful strategies for legitimizing 'external' contributions in bordering Palestine. Thus, by looking at the relationship between the Palestinian diaspora community and non-Palestinian groups in the UK, she detects 'the emergence of transnational political spaces in relation to Palestine [which are based on] the rise of new forms of Palestinian activism and a national struggle anchored in global activism, anti-globalisation movements, and based on an increased grassroots participation'.[69]

Notwithstanding the frequency of those spatial representations in politics that stress the temporal endurance of specific territorial re-inscriptions – for example, Hamas stating that it will *never* accept Israel occupying 'historic Palestine' or the common reference in Israeli politics to Jerusalem as the '*eternal* and undivided capital' – it should have become clear by now why notions of space cannot be understood from a static and material perspective. Lacking any primordial status, territories need to be permanently reproduced self-referentially through societal communications and this also includes the (sometimes dramatic) change of spatial inscriptions, independently of whether or not they once had hegemonic status. Of course, in order to claim legitimacy for such changes, new spatial ascriptions are often historically contextualized, that is, they are connected with previously dominant spatial narratives. This can, for example, be seen when looking at the widespread spatial discourse of Palestinian supporters of a territorial compromise with Israel. References to a Palestinian state within the 1967 borders tend to be garnished with the insistence that this alternative notion of Palestine – adopted for the sake of a peaceful future – in any case represents only '22 percent of historical Palestine'.[70] In other words, the future Palestinian state within the 1967 borders becomes in itself a multilayered territory which merges the ongoing actualization of an allegedly primordial, historical space with an acquiescence of contingent, political imperatives. This territorial narrative not only signals that a further drawback is unthinkable but also operates as a semantic mechanism connecting this new and controversial notion of Palestine with remembered and seemingly uncontroversial spatial representations. These arguments, finally, point to even more encompassing shifts in spatial representations in which previous forms simply dissolve. In that context, Bernard Rougier's analysis of the role of the Salafi movement in the Palestinian refugee camp Ain Al-Hilwah in Lebanon is a particularly telling example for the futile character and radical contingency of all territorial representations. Rougier argues – and laments – that internal political dynamics within this camp have over time significantly undermined its seemingly entrenched Palestinian character – in other words, Palestine has been transformed from an 'internal' to an 'external' space. Thus, in Ain Al-Hilwah, internal rifts, which reached the brink of civil war, have 'undermined solidarity among the refugee population, because certain segments of this population no longer belong to the national Palestinian *universe*'.[71] By 'investing in conflicts that are removed intellectually and geographically from Palestine', the Salafi groups have led to a '*displacement*' of these camps from Palestinian spaces into Sunni-Lebanese spaces, thereby 'undermining the foundations of Palestinian national sentiment from within'.[72]

While Rougier's analysis underlines the volatile status of territorial representations in the light of ongoing identity or subordination conflicts,[73] conflict and the spectre of a creeping dissolution of refugee camps operated more often as a powerful securitizing device in ensuring that refugees camps are *Palestinian* spaces – and recognized as such by both the PA and the global donor community. A case in point was the

UNRWA financial crisis in 1997. UNRWA announced in the summer of 1997 that it had run into considerable financial problems and, consequently, proposed budgetary cutbacks. While this proposal was initially received positively amongst the mainly Western donor community, it raised, from the outset, serious concerns in Palestinian refugee camps. What is interesting for the purpose of this chapter is that these concerns transcended a mere opposition to financial cutbacks. In fact, the financial issues, highlighted by both UNRWA and the donor community, received only minimal attention in Palestinian refugee camps. Within the camps the main concern centred on the suspicion that these financial issues were no less than a cover for a sinister plan to alter the very definition of refugee camps as Palestinian spaces. This perspective was well summarized by a commentator in the *Jordan Times*, who argued that UNRWA's real aim was to redefine refugee camps as local spaces through 'settling the Palestinians in Arab countries, as provided for in the peace agreements with the Zionist enemy, in the course of liquidating the Palestinian problem and cancelling the Palestinian people's right to return to their homeland'.[74] As Robert Bowker explains, 'Palestinian refugee mythologies caused the 1997 crisis to be understood amongst Palestinians refugees in very distinct terms', namely as a joint approach by UNRWA, Israel, the donor community and – initially – the PA to ultimately 'accept the irrevocable compromising of Palestinian refugee aspirations central to their political mythologies and collective memories'.[75] Moreover, the UNRWA crisis also threatened an originally negligent PA and PLO leadership, which was accused from within refugee camps of not sufficiently opposing these plans, thereby implicitly subscribing to this spatial redefinition of Palestine. By taking up this powerful criticism, the PA, however, quickly jumped on the bandwagon of refugee mythologies and 'skilfully moved the focus of the Palestinian refugee reaction toward blaming the donor countries'.[76] This example nicely underlines the active role of Palestinian refugees in territorial representations of Palestine, thereby challenging the argument that territorial re-inscriptions of Palestine in refugee camps are primarily the result of 'external' policies by UNRWA, which constructs Palestine through surveillance practices,[77] 'unrelated to its initial and honourable mission'.[78] In direct contrast to this reasoning, the UNRWA financial crisis highlights the 'subjectivity' of Palestinians within and outside refugee camps in world societal spatial representations of Palestine, as a result of which the status of refugee camps as Palestinian spaces had once more been reaffirmed – the financial crisis was then, in fact, solved through an increase rather than a cutback of UNRWA's budget.

To summarize, the analysis in this section on world societal processes of bordering Palestine cautions against assuming a primacy of territorial borders in spatial re-inscriptions, in which either internals have a more accurate knowledge of the 'real' situation 'on the ground' or externals are more objective. Similarly, the re-inscriptions of symbolic borders, that is, assuming a primacy of kinship relations in defining spaces, is also problematic, since it equally neglects the global and functional context within which Palestine becomes a politically meaningful space in the first place.[79] Seen from that perspective, Ehteshami's observation that the 'role of NGOs in Palestine cannot be understood without recourse to interrelation between Palestinian NGOs and the donor community',[80] gains an additional dimension, which transcends this somewhat obvious reference to global interconnectivity. Thus, the very shape and borders of Palestine cannot be understood without addressing this structural interrelationship between the 'local' and the 'global'. It is on the basis of this argument, that this section has focused on the world societal horizon against which Palestine and all other territories in the Middle East are constantly negotiated and re-negotiated in political communications in and on these spaces. This focus on the global processes of spatial representations, which permeate territorial and symbolic borders, then shows that claiming legitimacy for specific framings (for example, by erecting territorial or symbolic borders) is an operation of an already debordered world political system. Seen from that perspective, Rashid Khalidi's statement that 'the centrality of attachment to place [is] characteristic not only of Palestinians, but also of others in traditional and semitraditional societies', is somewhat problematic.[81] Thus, attachment to space is not a prerogative of 'traditional' societies, but occupies a central role in a 'modern' world society, too. More precisely, borders and territories operate as powerful attractors and signposts within various functional spheres, in which the erection of borders and the demarcation of territories, such as Palestine, are not primordial spatial manifestations but de-territorialized, communicatively generated semantics and structures whose various – and often contrasting – meanings are self-referentially reproduced against the background of a world societal horizon.

Jerusalem as a world city

As argued above, spaces in world society are not constituted by territorial distinctions, but must be understood against the background of de-bordered global political (or, indeed, other functional) communications.

Neither are they demarcated as a result of deliberation in symbolically !confined discourse communities, since this would only shift the untenable notion of regions-as-systems to a focus on identity groups as systems.[82] Territories in the Middle East are, thus, global and de-territorialized spaces insofar as their full – and contradictory – meaning(s) only materialize in debordered, global communications in and on these territories. Such a world societal perspective on territory is, of course, not suggesting that world societal representations translate particularistic notions of territory into a peaceful and universalist Kantian space. Being subject to constant change within various functionalist spheres, territories are polycontextual and multidimensional entities which necessarily relate to different (functional) world societal horizons and, accordingly, attract different – and often opposing – ascriptions of meaning. Indeed, in global political communications, territories in the Middle East often acquire fundamentally opposing ascriptions, for example, when referring to Israel as the 'light upon the nations', a 'besieged and threatened nation', the 'only democracy in the Middle East' or an 'apartheid state' or to Palestine as a 'suppressed nation', a 'disenfranchised people', a 'severe security threat' or a 'zone of turmoil'. None of these ascriptions are political attributions onto pre-existing spaces but rather constitute these territories in the first place – and the same holds true for 'emancipatory', 'progressive' and 'global civil society' perspectives on Israel and Palestine. This section further develops this observation and argues that the world societal and functional horizon of Middle East territories even transcends such semantics of territory. More precisely, spaces are not only the result of debordering, which indeed shapes the global semantics on these spaces, but can also operate as world societal structures. In order to exemplify this claim, this section addresses the way in which spaces in the Middle East attain such a structural status, focusing particularly on notions of Jerusalem as a world city. As this section argues, the status of world religious/cultural heritage site, as provided for, *inter alia*, by UNESCO declarations, renders Jerusalem an interesting example of such a world city.[83] Moreover, this section argues that the designation of Jerusalem as a world religious/cultural heritage site is one example of (nascent) emergent structures of world statehood. A word of caution is, of course, pertinent. Thus, the concept of world statehood is not implying an analogy with the principle of Westphalian statehood and neither is it a normative plea for introducing global democracy in conflict areas.[84] As Mathias Albert elaborates, 'world statehood is a form of inclusive statehood. It emerges only if no exclusive claims on sovereignty juxtapose each other. In particular, such a form of statehood appears without the formal attributes of statehood and (for the time being) without a significant semantic of a world state.'[85] In other words, world statehood does not replace national, ethnic or confessional sovereignty claims on specific spaces. Consequently, world statehood, which expresses itself in notions of world religious/cultural heritage, is not accompanied by a Weberian monopoly on territory but can rather be detected when tracing 'the emergence of an accompanying semantic, picking up the notion [of world statehood] in the self-description of the political system of world society'.[86]

What matters here is not the obvious and frequently cited religious attachment of Jews, Christian and Muslims to Jerusalem – for this would only highlight particularistic and often exclusive claims on sovereignty – but rather the observation that in the case of Jerusalem as world religious/cultural heritage site, these different religious bonds are intertwined within a single inclusive political framework explicitly located at the global level. Thus, reference to all three monotheistic religions in the context of world religion/cultural heritage establishes an inclusive sovereignty over Jerusalem as a world city, in parallel rather than as a replacement of ongoing confessional and national demands. This section is not concerned with sophisticated reflections on the sacredness of Jerusalem in religious discourses over the past three millennia; such an exercise, intriguing as it is, is obviously far beyond the scope of this analysis.[87] Nevertheless, it investigates how the city's religious status not only provides the basis for exclusive national projects but at the same time consolidates Jerusalem's status as a world city.[88] Designating Jerusalem as a world cultural heritage site, as embodied in UNESCO documents since the 1980s, can then be understood as establishing an inclusive sovereignty over Jerusalem as a world city in the shadow of powerful claims on exclusive sovereignty. Addressing such nascent structures of world statehood for the case of Jerusalem – that is, a heavily contested city – would then also require some recalibration of Albert's argument that inclusive statehood only emerges if there are no opposing claims on sovereignty.

As with other elements of world statehood, the problem with the notion of Jerusalem as a world city lies in the lack of an adequate vocabulary for such global political structures, which might be the reason for the ubiquitous, yet theoretically imprecise invocation of Jerusalem's importance to all three monotheistic religions. It might also be the reason why many social scientists tend to view the issue of Jerusalem through the lenses of an allegedly 'new religiosity' in IR and why 'as a result of this radical religiosity, the holiness of Jerusalem has acquired a new centrality that secularists cannot afford to ignore'.[89] In contrast to this perspective, addressing the status of Jerusalem as world religious/cultural heritage site does not need to make recourse to an alleged re-awakening of religious primacy but is able to show how such recourse to the sacredness of Jerusalem, ironically, forms the basis for the status of Jerusalem as a world city, which is characterized 'by its void, the emptiness of the space and the depth of understanding' rather than from concrete confessional meaning.[90] Studying the religious dimension of Jerusalem for Christians, Muslims and Jews is more than a flirtation of modern social scientists with spiritual concerns, rather it acquires a fundamental meaning in global political communications.[91] As Rashid Khalidi notes, 'indeed, where Jerusalem is involved, the need to consider the concerns of a broad range of constituencies is more urgent than with any other issue in the Arab-Israeli conflict, because of Jerusalem's profound resonance for so many people'.[92]

Seen from this perspective, Jerusalem not only emerges as a place of competition between particularistic political and religious projects, but simultaneously enables the addressing of inclusive claims on sovereignty over Jerusalem as a world city, which equally draw on invocations of sacredness and notions of world religious heritage. Or, as a Vatican spokesman argued, admittedly having a Catholic constituency in mind, 'first of all, Jerusalem has world relevance'.[93] Addressing the way in which Jerusalem is referred to as a part of world religious heritage shows how the city operates as a semantic form for world statehood, and the fact that various organizations – ranging from the Islamic Conference, to the Vatican, the EU or the UN – explicitly evoke such cross-confessional perspectives on Jerusalem, underlines the pervasiveness of the semantic of Jerusalem as a world city in global political communications. Thus, there is more to evocations of sacredness in politics than a mere mechanism to ensure particularistic claims on sovereignty, as has been argued by Guy Ben-Porat when stating that 'religion serves an indispensable role in consolidating and demarcating territorial boundaries and legitimating the exclusionary practices of the nation-state within the ostensible secular national system as well'.[94] Of course, when addressing the political rhetoric of the PA or the Israeli government, it is immediately evident that declaring a state of holiness of Jerusalem to the three monotheistic religions can also be part of a strategy to ensure the legitimacy of particularistic national projects. However, when adopting notions of world religious heritage, national governments cannot control for all 'dynamics of the sacred'.[95]

In other words, in order to sustain particularistic claims, they have to pay the price of operating within the semantic confines set by notions of Jerusalem as a world city, which consequently is more than mere 'cheap talk'.[96] For example, the status of Jerusalem as a world cultural heritage site provided the basis for a mission by the UNESCO Technical Mission to Jerusalem, after contested excavation works by Israeli authorities in February 2007 at the Mughrabi Gate of the Haram As-Sharif/Har Ha-Bait. The report of the Technical Mission documents the degree to which the notion of Jerusalem as a world city, in which UNESCO claims inclusive sovereignty, impacts political considerations. Thus, the report emphasized that the National Mission of Israel to UNESCO declared that 'the World Heritage Centre will be consulted on the professional process before proposing the recommendations to the IIA [Israeli Antiquities Authority] and [Jerusalem] Municipality' and calls for a future supervision of any building activities concerning the Mughrabi Gate by 'an international team of experts coordinated by UNESCO'.[97]

There is, thus, more to the semantic of Jerusalem as a world city than an additional way of ascribing meaning to the city in world societal political communications. The semantic of Jerusalem as a world religious heritage site also provides the basis for concrete political structures which consolidate the status of Jerusalem as a world city in parallel to ongoing national/confessional structures, for example, by the Israeli government or the Islamic Waqf. More precisely, the semantic form of Jerusalem as a world religious heritage city formed the basis for the 1981 decision to assign to the (Old City of) Jerusalem the status of world cultural heritage site. Based on a request by the government of Jordan, the International Council on Monuments and Sites (ICOMOS) proposed in 1981 to include Jerusalem on the World Heritage List, following the UNESCO World Heritage Convention of 1972. ICOMOS explicitly based its decision on the fact that 'Jerusalem is directly and materially associated with the history of the three great monotheistic religions of mankind, Judaism, Christianity and Islamism', thereby evoking the semantics of world religious heritage. As Mike Turner elaborates, the status of Jerusalem as world cultural heritage site not only transcends exclusive sovereignty claims on the city, but directly leads to the question of 'how [Jerusalem's] boundaries [are] redefined and how this can allow us to reappraise and contemplate the city from an entirely new perspective'.[98] By translating the semantics of world religious heritage into the structure of world cultural heritage, Jerusalem acquires a tangible status in world politics which leaves behind religiously inspired world semantics, such as *axis mundi*, 'the navel of the earth [or] the cradle of religions'.[99] Declaring Jerusalem as part of world cultural heritage, therefore, renders Jerusalem into a concern for a global 'public realm'[100] as a result of which the city no longer is Muslim, Christian or Jewish, 'no longer east and west or north and south but a heritage for all', and is thereby turned into a concrete manifestation of world statehood.[101]

Such a focus on the status of Jerusalem as a world city does not, of course, neglect the obvious political reality that Palestinians and Israelis, Jews, Christians and Muslims have each acquired great mastery in linking Jerusalem to their respective political claims vis-à-vis a global political public. However, what becomes evident is that in their pursuit of claiming partial/exclusive sovereignty, the parties 'on the ground' do not only have to confront the claims of the respective other side(s) but also to (rhetorically) relate to the status of Jerusalem as a place of world religious and cultural heritage. This was evident in the peace negotiations during the Camp David summit in the summer of 2000. Facing a final settlement for Jerusalem, the Christian churches in Jerusalem directly referred to the relevance of Jerusalem as a world city in an attempt to oppose an Israeli proposal to divide the Old City. While the Israeli proposal foresaw a division of sovereignty between Israel and Palestine, the former gaining control over the Jewish and Armenian quarters, the latter taking over the Muslim and Christian quarters, the Christian churches – for particularistic reasons – had a more inclusive form of sovereignty in mind. These 'fears that Israel was bent on an exclusivist vision of Jerusalem' shattered the traditional perception amongst church leaders 'of Israel's commitment (and ability) to enforce an open city' for Jerusalem in its entirety.[102] Dumper's observation that 'Israel's proposals for Jerusalem at Camp David appear to confirm the failure and the definitive abandonment of Israel's earlier policy aimed at co-opting the church leadership in its drive to gain international recognition for control over the city' then only covers parts of the political significance of this development.[103] Thus, while the proposal was regarded in Israel as a dramatic sea change and a remarkably 'generous offer',[104] it nevertheless was based on a continuity of exclusive sovereignty claims (now divided between two governments) inapplicable to a more inclusive notion of Jerusalem as an open city for a world (religious/cultural) public. Hence, while it is true that, *inter alia*, as a result of the developments at the Camp David summit, the widespread notion in Israel of Jerusalem as the eternal and undivided capital ultimately 'failed as a hegemonic project',[105] the status of Jerusalem as a world city thwarted subsequent attempts to find a political solution based on the execution of exclusive sovereignty over parts of the city. In other words, the Israeli proposal in Camp David – which from the Israeli perspective is perceived as a historical concession – not only failed because of opposition from the Palestinian side but also because of the semantic pervasiveness of invocations of Jerusalem as a world city, to which this proposal turned a blind eye by ignoring that 'Jerusalem's physical and social landscape is criss-crossed by multiple political and symbolic boundaries'.[106]

From this perspective, the Palestinian negotiating team at Camp David only made a virtue out of necessity when linking their own exclusive understanding of sovereignty over (parts of) Jerusalem with the notion of Jerusalem as a world city. This is well summarized by a remark which was reportedly made by Yassir Arafat to Bill Clinton at the summit: ' "Jerusalem is not only a Palestinian city", he would say. "It is also an Arab, Islamic, and Christian city. If I am going to make a decision on Jerusalem, I have to consult with the Sunnis and the Shi'a and all Arab countries, I have to consult with many countries starting from Iran and Pakistan, passing by Indonesia and Bangladesh, and ending with Nigeria" ' – and one could add with the Vatican, Greece, Armenia, Ethiopia and other states – or (state) churches – as well.[107] In a similarly pronounced manner, the global (albeit symbolically confined) status of Jerusalem was evoked by Edward Said when objecting to a monopoly of the PA in deciding the final status of the city. As a result of the limited political capacities of the Palestinian leadership, 'it therefore falls to the diaspora Palestinians, who constitute the majority of Palestinians in the world and who produced the PLO in the first place, to take the initiative on Jerusalem'.[108] To avoid misunderstandings: there is no doubt that reference to Jerusalem as a world city, of direct relevance to all monotheistic religions, is often made by Palestinians in an attempt to establish a powerful exclusivist counter-narrative to the Israeli notion that 'Jerusalem, complete and united, is the capital of Israel', as the Jerusalem Law of 1980 states.[109] In other words, an alleged asymmetry 'on the ground' is challenged by invoking a worldwide reference point for the purpose of a national programme, however, thereby paradoxically revealing the significance which the notion of Jerusalem as a world city has already acquired.

The political relevance of inclusive world sovereignty over Jerusalem can then be detected in the famous Clinton proposals, which also were issued at the summit. While it is true that on most accounts Clinton's idea to divide Jerusalem according to demographic 'realities' rests on the notion of exclusive sovereignty, it nevertheless includes some rudimentary, yet politically significant, elements designating

Jerusalem as a world city. Thus, while the Palestinians have succeeded in gaining responsibility for the Islamic sites in the Old City, the Clinton proposal simultaneously foresees a rudimentary global structure, when proposing that a 'committee made up of the UN Security Council and Morocco would grant the Palestinian state "sovereign custody" of the Haram, while Israel would retain "residual sovereignty"'.[110] While not included in the Clinton proposals, the extension of a similar form of inclusive sovereignty for the Christian sites in the Old City to the UN and church bodies follows the logic of the intervention by several patriarchs to Clinton when they insisted that in order to accept a final agreement on Jerusalem they – and not only the Israeli and Palestinian secular leaderships – should 'send representatives to the summit and any other fora concerned with the future of the city'.[111]

Reference to Jerusalem as a world city, finally, also figures prominently in other attempts to reach a final settlement for the city. The Geneva Accord of 2003, which is one of the main peace proposals jointly drafted by leading Israeli and Palestinian politicians since the Madrid Peace Conference of 1991, refers directly to the status of Jerusalem as a world cultural heritage site and links its proposal to establish a (temporary) International Verification Group (IVG) in Jerusalem – consisting of the Quartet, the Organization of the Islamic Conference and others – directly with the obligations of the states of Palestine and Israel arising from the World Heritage Convention. Hence, the main task of the IVG is not only to oversee the continuous preservation of the Convention but also includes a rudimentary global sovereignty-dimension in the form of policing tasks in the Old City. While this role of the IVG certainly does not amount to exclusive 'world' sovereignty as, for example, foreseen in the *corpus separatum* provisions of the UN partition plan of 1947, it moves, in a sense, much closer to the concept of world statehood referred to above. Thus, by proposing an inclusive sovereignty at the 'global' level alongside ongoing exclusive sovereignty by Israel and Palestine, Jerusalem's status as a world city gains further institutional recognition. This argument should not be misunderstood in the sense that the status of world city could be equated with a peaceful Jerusalem, in which multi-religious harmony abounds. As with all political projects, inclusive sovereignty can also stir opposition and provoke conflict and it is, in consequence, not an inherently peaceful solution for the healing of societal rifts. However, what is maintained here is the observation that the semantics and structures designating Jerusalem as a site of world religious/cultural heritage point to the emergence of (nascent) structures of world statehood in parallel to ongoing national/religious claims on sovereignty, which ironically often tend to cloak their respective exclusive demands with the draperies of Jerusalem as a world city.

Rebordering the Middle East

In the previous three sections this chapter has focused on the way in which functional debordering and global interconnectivity in world society lead to an alternative perspective on the meaning of borders and territory in the Middle East on the level of both spatial semantics ('global Palestine') and spatial structures (Jerusalem as a 'world city'). However, in order to shed light on the centrality of borders and territory in world societal communications in and on the Middle East across functional spheres some further comments on the processes of spatial rebordering in world society are needed. In that context Rudolf Stichweh has suggested that the focus should be laid on 'the structural coupling of society with specific spatial differences'.[112] In order to trace such structural couplings of society with spatial differences, this concluding section focuses on the notion of the Middle East as one of world society's main regions. What will be argued, in particular, is that the polycontextual features of world society and the pervasiveness of functional differentiation necessitate a complex understanding of regions as characterized by multidimensional and fuzzy borders, which overlap and intersect, thereby undermining all one-dimensional, neat territorial distinctions between world regions (or other territories, for that matter).

In other words, the order of observation is reversed – rather than taking regions for granted and, therefore, seeing them as autonomous from societal communications, a functional perspective maintains that regions and other territories are first of all the result of global communicative dynamics within several functional spheres. Yet, while the previous two sections have addressed the structural embedding of the Middle East into global *political* communications, there is no reason to assume that the world societal horizon would be different for global scientific, economic, religious or art-related communications. Taking this polycontextual perspective on borders and territory seriously, it becomes obvious that in order to be recognized as a world region within a distinct functional sphere, such as world politics, it might not suffice for regions to be global spatial attractors in only this single functional context. In order to render the notion of regions as prime forms of observation in world politics plausible, these regions must accumulate enough 'critical mass', that is, being observed as a region across various functional and other societal spheres. At the same time, these manifold functional and symbolic borders in world society ensure that territories as placeless global attractors are always characterized by fuzzy and intersecting borders which undermine any clear-cut territorial division between spaces.

Thus regions are not characterized by neat borders but rather by (communicatively generated) observations of these regions within and across various functional spheres which then turn regions into crucial territorial signposts in world politics. Indeed, such linkages – and contradictions – between different discourses of regions and territory are a central theme in the literature on the Middle East in IR and area studies.[113] This is not the place to elaborate on these region-specific discourses on the Middle East in great detail, although it is noteworthy that central denominations of the Middle East in world politics are exactly located at the intersection of various functional spheres. For example, references to the Middle East as a rentier-region directly link such regionalization discourses in politics and economics; the detailed analysis of Middle East knowledge society – or the lack thereof – in the 2003 Arab Human Development Report underlines a coalescence between politics and science; moreover, the observation of the Middle East as a 'perennial conflict region' in academic writing or media reporting points to region-specific links between politics and conflict; finally, the widespread reference to the centrality of religion in the region highlights the entanglement between the functional spheres of politics and religion in world societal communications in and on this region. Of course, this list should not be limited to linkages between functional spheres only. As the Middle East literature amply illustrates, there are notions of the Middle East's regionness which transcend a functional logic, for example, when addressing the regional linkages between politics, on the one hand, and territory, ethnicity and gender, on the other. What matters here, however, is not elaborating in detail the countless world societal framings of the Middle East within and across various societal spheres. What is probably more central is the observation that when taken together, the heterogeneous regional borders generated by these – and the manifold other – discourses of the regionness of the Middle East necessarily lead to an understanding of regions which are characterized by cross-cutting, overlapping, polycontextual, non-essentialist and constantly changing borders. Moreover, a comprehensive understanding of the Middle East as a world region must, of course, equally address linkages between functional discourses beyond the sphere of politics, for example, by addressing notions of regionness which stem from linkages between art/religion or social assistance/religion to pick but two examples.[114] It is on this basis that the notion of world regions formulated in this chapter comes close to John Burton's plea for a de-territorialized understanding of regions as 'global cobwebs', referred to in Chapter 1.

Notwithstanding the complexity of regions as polycontextual, debordered spatial attractors, the aforementioned linkages between spatial framings across various functional spheres have an inherently political dimension insofar as they render specific ascriptions of meaning to the Middle East plausible. These dynamics then translate into powerful – yet often contradictory – 'scripts' on the Middle East in global political communications, for example, referring to the Middle East as a 'perennial conflict region', the 'cradle of civilization', a 'place of resistance', an 'authoritarian space', a place of the 'ubiquitousness of the sacral', a 'rentier-state' region, an area characterized as 'lacking human development', a region which 'best fits the realist view of international politics' or, alternatively, an area subject to normative negotiations on regional order between key local actors which create 'a world of their own making and unmaking'.[115] What matters then is not primarily the accuracy of each of these regional narratives – all of which certainly describe *facets* of the complexity of the Middle East as a world region – but rather that only when taken together, these and the manifold other ascriptions of meaning to the Middle East, many of them located at the intersection of functional spheres enable an observation of the Middle East as a polycontextual region which evades all attempts to pin down its borders, territorial scope and ascriptions of meaning to a single and static 'reality'. Moreover, such scripts of the Middle East are, of course, not neutral. They often either problematize or idealize the region and gain an inherently political dimension by highlighting specific forms of observation, while neglecting others. Thus, labelling the Middle East in world societal communications always provides the basis for securitizing practices which justify interventions, the establishment of institutions and the implementation of distinct governance projects.[116] It is an interesting side note here that such labelling practices often stand in direct competition with each other, for example, contrasting scripts of the Middle East as a place of ancient civilizations versus a place of sectarian strife (at the intersection of politics/identity); the home of the great monotheistic religions versus an area of religious fundamentalism, lacking secularization (at the intersection of politics/religion); or as a perennial conflict region versus a place of resistance to Western hegemony (at the intersection of politics/conflict).[117]

The focus on such region-specific linkages comes with an important caveat. It is essential to bear in mind that none of these linkages is unique to the Middle East. To pick only a few examples, linkages between politics and religion figure prominently in other world regions too, for example between Catholicism and politics in Latin America or Southern Europe or politics and the various strands of Protestantism in North America. The same holds true for linkages between politics/identity (caste system in India, 'tribal' systems in Africa) and politics/conflict (sub-Saharan Africa, structural violence in Central and Latin America and so forth). What ensures the formation of distinct regions in world society are not so much allegedly region-specific forms of structural coupling between various functional systems[118] but rather the accumulation of several, often highly heterogeneous framings of such spaces within politics and other societal spheres. Only taken together do these manifold framings provide enough critical mass to turn regions into plausible signposts of world societal communications across functional divides. The distinction between world regions does not disrupt the countless communicative filaments which structurally embed these regions and their fuzzy, constantly changing borders in a shared world societal context and neither does it require the conceptualization of regions as neatly separated territories. These arguments caution against any essentialist reading of the conceptualization of regionness in this chapter. This would only risk reifying culturalist understandings of the role of, say, politics, religion, culture or identity in 'creating' the Middle East.

We do not live in a borderless world. Yet, in order to arrive at a sufficiently sophisticated understanding of borders and territory in world society, one-dimensional notions of territory and accompanying ascriptions of meaning must be left behind. Observing regions from the perspective of functional debordering and global interconnectivity shows that spaces cannot be seen in isolation from the specific functional contexts to which they relate. It is on this level that rebordering constantly takes place, always operating against the background of fuzzy, overlapping and cross-cutting spatial divides as well as manifold and often contradictory spatial ascriptions of meaning. That is also the reason why the demarcation and labelling of places in world politics is always a 'moral grammar that underwrites and reproduces power', as Julie Peteet has noted.[119] And it is to these dynamics of power in political communications in and on the Middle East that the next chapter turns.

Part II

The Creeping Antagonization of Middle East Politics

3
Power and Contestations: Crossing the Lines between Power and Powerlessness in the Middle East

Doesn't matter what you see/Or into it what you read/You can do it your own way/If it's done just how I say
Metallica – Eye of the Beholder[1]

Mystifications of power in the Middle East

Power is an omnipresent point of reference in the study of the Middle East in IR and neighbouring disciplines. Echoing a widespread sentiment in both academic and political circles, what distinguishes the Middle East from other world regions is the overt and blunt occurrence of interest politics, strategic thinking, zero-sum calculations, force, violence, conflict, insurgencies, war and suppression. As Louise Fawcett summarizes, the Middle East 'provides, for some, an illustration of the international state of nature described by Thomas Hobbes, a world which, in the absence of a Leviathan, sees the prevalence of anarchy, greed and power struggle'.[2] Interestingly, this centrality of (bare) power dynamics bridges otherwise quite opposite theoretical strands in the analysis of Middle East politics. To borrow from Fred Halliday's classification of the main theoretical categories on the study of the Middle East in IR, within various dominant theoretical traditions power politics indeed occupy a central space. For example, historical analyses on state emergence in the Middle East refer to the processes through which colonial powers, in particular Great Britain and France, have shaped regional borders, thereby institutionalizing ongoing border disputes in the region.[3] They also point to the linkages between state formation and armed struggle by nationalist movements, be it the Lebanese national movement around Charles Corm, the factions within the Jewish Yishuv in the 1940s or the PLO since the 1960s.[4] Moreover, the focus on the

Middle East 'as the last world region, whose theory-guided analyses are still dominated by realist schools of thought'[5] also renders power the central category in accounting for the dynamics of Middle East politics in this intellectual tradition. Thus, the Middle East is observed as an unfriendly, anarchical environment in which states and, occasionally, other (rational) actors, such as, for example, Hezbollah, are obsessed with 'security and the maximisation of power'.[6] Likewise, through their focus on elite decision-making, foreign policy analyses shift the focus on rational actors, self-interest and zero-sum power games from the (anarchical) level of the inter-state system to the interplay of 'a diversity of forces within a shifting complexity of contexts within and without' the state.[7] Finally, by addressing domestic power struggles below the state level as well as the power of norms and ideas, both liberalist and social constructivist approaches add another nuance to this centrality of power in the Middle East.[8] Thus, the Middle East is the playground of 'an ongoing struggle in the region between multiple competing identities that can throw light on the process of identity formation' and, indeed, account for regional political dynamics more generally.[9] This social constructivist outlook is thereby often conceptually linked with liberalist accounts of Middle East politics,[10] since the patchwork of religious, ethnic and political identities across all states in the region requires subtle deliberations (and, at times, violent interventions) in the relationship between the political centre and actors/structures at the periphery, be they – to take two examples – local communities and pious religious movements in Syria and Jordan or the Palestinian population in Jordan and Israel.[11]

If there is one connecting theme in the literature on the Middle East in IR and other social science disciplines, it is the assumption of the centrality of 'power' in accounting for Middle East politics at the domestic, regional and global levels. The Middle East is conceived of thus as one of the last purely Machiavellian terrains in world politics, a space par excellence of power politics, rational calculations and ruthless assertions of interest. In short, the region is primarily characterized by political actors aiming to secure their tenuous survival vis-à-vis equally ruthless contestations nurtured by 'the violent nature of the region'.[12] While it is true that this narrative particularly attracts and renders plausible realist accounts, it also underlies several of the aforementioned alternative conceptual perspectives, be they liberalist analyses on domestic power struggles or social constructivist approaches on the power of exclusionary norms and identities in the region.[13] This chapter does not aim to contradict the observation that 'power' has a central place in accounting for the dynamics of Middle East politics. Indeed, how could there be a social, let alone a political setting in which power would not be an essential resource? However, this chapter argues that without a clear theoretical elaboration on what 'power' as a crucial source of societal evolution entails, accounts of 'power' in Middle East studies risk falling into the trap of a 'mystification of power'. This mystification of power shapes studies on Middle East politics on at least two dimensions. First, power relations are often merely described in terms of alleged power resources and interests of states and other political actors, for example, the autocratic *mukhabarat* system in Syria, the military superiority of Israel vis-à-vis its Arab neighbours, autocratic structures in the Palestinian Authority, the possession of arms and political capital by sectarian groups in Lebanon or the violent confrontations between Hamas and the Al-Aqsa brigades in Palestine.[14] However, such a focus on resources and interests mystifies power insofar as it does not specify how 'power' as a central medium of communication in society depends on both the assertion of power *and* the acceptance of and acquiescence to power(lessness).[15] In other words, power is not an objective category – tanks, ideology, troops, secret service personnel and leadership capacity – which simply exists and is 'exchanged' between actors[16] but is first and foremost the result of societal communications.

Second, possible changes in power relations – such as those envisioned by Islamists or regional/extra-regional democratization efforts – are regularly problematized in the literature, thereby often indirectly reifying official securitization discourses and power relations. For example, such securitizing practices by state authorities in Syria, Lebanon, Israel, Jordan and Palestine are regularly implicitly justified in the literature by pointing to the threats posed by Islamist fundamentalist groups – thereby however more often than not replicating first-order narratives on legitimate and illegitimate power.[17] In a similar way, the widespread and often well-meaning reference to 'cultural dialogue' between the Middle East and the West ironically supports the labelling of specific political concepts, such as democracy and human rights, as being part of an external, Western culture, notwithstanding the existence of countless individuals and groups (as well as historical traditions) in the Middle East linked to democratization and liberalization.[18] It is also these accounts which, in consequence, risk consolidating official securitization practices. In a nutshell, the mystification of power in the Middle East relates to all those instances in which power structures are observed through the lenses of (powerful) first-order observations rather than from a more general theoretical perspective on what 'power' as a key medium of communication in world society actually entails.

Based on this observation this chapter maintains that without a clear elaboration of the theoretical fundamentals of 'power', studies on power politics in the Middle East risk reifying existing power relations and securitization dialogues. In more systems-theoretical parlance, 'power' needs to be observed from a second-order perspective that is able to transcend 'the ontology of the present' in the analysis of actual power relations, to borrow here from Derridaean terminology.[19] This shift of perspectives allows us to detect the paradoxes, the 'unmarked spaces' and the excluded 'traces' of power inherent in all political communications in and on the Middle East. Power is, thus, not a material capacity (for example, specific actors such as states, presidents and troops or specific structures and semantics such as oil-resources and nationalism) but an *empty signifier* for all those world societal communications which observe themselves on the basis of the distinction powerful/powerless. Transcending positivist notions of power as a material resource allows us to address power as a global medium of communication. In that context, the distinction between different spatial levels of analysis – such as domestic, regional and global – might have some heuristic value[20] – but is ultimately theoretically problematic. Not only because it contradicts the non-territorial status of all communications, but also insofar as such distinctions often go hand in hand with specific legitimization strategies, such as the replication of securitization discourses or the reification of symbolic (culture, identity) and territorial borders.[21]

In order to elaborate on the role of power in Middle East politics, this chapter is divided into five sections. The next section further outlines the key theoretical premises underlying the way in which power is conceptualized in this book, while the third section addresses region-specific manifestations of power, focusing in particular on the symbolization and use of violence by power-holders, defined here as 'frozen crossings'. The final section puts these 'frozen crossings' into relation with the 'hot contestations' by, *inter alia*, Islamists and democracy/human rights movements. To reiterate what was said in Chapter 1, 'frozen crossings' relate to distortions in code-oriented communications in the form of an overlap between the two sides of code-oriented communications (that is, power and powerlessness) and the relatively stable relegation of specific persons, groups or political programmes to either side of the distinction. Yet, the double world societal horizon of all (political) communications structurally prevents any reification of even seemingly entrenched political orders in the Middle East. Contestations are an inherent feature of *all* political communications and, therefore, frozen crossings invite rather than prevent constant opposition by those who for whatever reason find themselves permanently located on the side of powerlessness. However, in such orders of frozen crossings, contestations do not easily evaporate (by crossing the lines between powerlessness and power) but rather transmute into peaceful or violent but always power-threatening forms of opposition and can, thus, be referred to as 'hot contestations'. The main argument of this chapter is that the freezing of the (easy) crossing between power and powerlessness is, paradoxically, undermined by the structural world societal context in which all political communications in the Middle East are embedded. However, these frozen crossings not only lead to excessive use and inflationary excesses of power, but also to an increase in the intensity of contestations to existing power relations. To put it in post-structuralist terms, it fosters a multiplication of antagonistic moments in Middle East politics and a creeping transformation of politics towards antagonism and conflict. In a nutshell, the two main features of these region-specific forms of power are, first, a profound crisis of power as the medium of political communications in and on the Middle East, and second, a de-politicization of Middle East politics.

Readdressing cycles of power and powerlessness

There are several possible strategies through which to demystify power and, thereby, reconstruct our understanding of the role of power in Middle East politics. Independently of the precise starting points, it is necessary to elaborate on the theoretical location of 'power' as a meaningful scientific concept in the first place, rather than taking 'power' as a taken-for-granted or even objective category as is often done in Middle East studies (and IR) with its reproduction of official or 'realistic' power semantics and mystification strategies referred to above.[22] Following this premise, a key argument of this chapter is that what can be observed in the Middle East is not so much a particular centrality of power but rather a crisis of power and a de-politicization of politics as a result of the clash between region-specific antagonistic transformations of power and the operative logic of politics as a global functional system.

Modern systems theory is helpful for such an envisaged demystification of power for at least three reasons.[23] First, by adopting the communication theoretical perspectives outlined in detail in Chapter 1, it becomes apparent that power as a societal phenomenon needs to be emptied of all stable properties and objective content, thereby avoiding the risk of being blinded by the omnipresent symbolic displays of power in Middle East politics.[24] In contrast, modern systems theory stresses the dynamic and contingent communicative processes through which power and powerlessness constantly have to reproduce themselves. Power is not an objective category, based on charismatic leadership capacities, various forms of legitimacy, weapons, money or other positivist ornaments of power but solely the result of communication as the basic unit of society.[25] Yet, if communications – and not actors, structures or actions – are society's basic unit, the question is how power becomes a topical point of reference in world society in the first place. Moreover, what also has to be specified is the precise relationship between power as a topical form of communication, on the one hand, and politics as a central sphere of societal differentiation, on the other. As will be argued further below such a focus on power and politics proves particularly helpful for an identification of the processes responsible for the (always contingent and temporary) consolidation or loss of power.

Political communications that use the medium of power are those communications which constitute and qualify themselves on the basis of the distinction between power/powerlessness. As modern systems theory postulates, this binary coding of power as a medium of communication underlies all political communications. One side of the distinction (power) has the function to ensure connectivity between communications, while the other side (powerlessness) enables contingency reflection.[26] This unity of the distinction between power (order) and powerlessness (alternatives/contestations) in every single political communication immediately directs attention towards the *problematique* in the relative neglect of powerlessness in Middle East studies with its strong positivist (and objectivist) focus on one side of the distinction, for example, powerful actors and securitization practices. More precisely, the relative neglect of powerlessness falls into the trap of what Derrida has referred to as the 'traditional version of metaphysics as the ontology of the present',[27] thereby favouring the observation of the connectivity of hegemonic power communications at the expense of the in-built contingency and fractures of all power. This essentialization of power is, for example, evident in the mystification of the agenda-setting power of those actors in the Middle East who can, actually or potentially, successfully claim to exert power and physical forms of violence vis-à-vis others, be it the aforementioned *mukhabarat* apparatus in Syria, Lebanese faction leaders with their alleged disposal over peace or civil war, the domination of Palestinians by the Israeli army and Jewish settlers in the occupied territories or the ability of Hamas and the Al-Aqsa brigades to send suicide bombers or rockets into Israeli heartlands. This is, of course, not to deny that all these actors possess power. Yet, what also becomes visible when adopting a systems-theoretical perspective is that power as a medium of communication only emerges as a result of the constant presence of the (often unobserved) side of powerlessness and, consequently, the shadow of contingency and fragility accompanies all actual manifestations of power. As Luhmann puts it, 'all peculiarities of the medium power rest on this presence of the excluded (or, in the words of Jacques Derrida: on the *trace*, which is left behind by the absent)'.[28]

The role of power – as of all other media of communication such as truth, money and love – is to render the unlikely (that is, the acceptance of or acquiescence to contingent communication offers in the light of countless alternatives) likely by establishing a specific medium of communication, namely power, which privileges one side of the code over the other.[29] However, since power is based on communications, other potentialities and alternative power constellations always lurk on the horizon. While ensuring connectivity, power always remains fragile and open to contestations. This structural contingency of all power communications 'implies that *both* sides have alternatives, the realization of which they however want to *avoid*'.[30] Alter prefers anticipatory obedience by Ego but must have credible threats at her disposal in case Ego voices opposition. Similarly, Ego might or might not be aware of his possible contestations to Alter's powerful demands, but prefers – for whatever reason – acquiescence over opposition. This is also the basis for Luhmann's claim that within all communications of power lies 'the information that the power-holder rather wants *not* to realise his avoidance alternative – but is ready to do so'.[31] This stands in marked contrast with the powerless side which is less inclined to resort to her avoidance alternatives.

Modern systems theory's focus on power as the asymmetrical communication of avoidance alternatives, referred to as the power of negative sanctions, has received some criticism in being too narrow a definition of power.[32] Thus, power does not only comprise 'power to' (negative sanctions) but also operates via incentives (positive sanctions) and other, often more subtle forms of exerting influence ('power over').[33] Yet, on closer inspection it becomes evident that modern systems theory does not claim that political communications are unable to resort to incentives and subtle forms of influence, such as, *inter alia*, Foucaultian structural practices of governmentality, diffuse and relational forms of power in international relations as analysed by Michael Barnett and Raymond Duvall, or Steven Lukes's third dimension of power in which 'the dominated acquiesce in their domination'.[34] However, what happens if incentives, structural imperatives or taken-for-granted practices are not successful in convincing Ego to pursue Alter's agenda?[35] This is the basis for Luhmann's argument that 'a second-order observer sees that every political communication is based on threat communication. Thus, on the willingness to threat and force if need be; since otherwise this would not be political action but an academic discussion, a seminar, a beauty competition … with indirect political consequences at best'.[36] What matters for the discussion in this chapter is the observation that power, understood as the communication of asymmetrical avoidance alternatives, does not need to be implemented and in fact tries to avoid the implementation (and even the explicit visibilization)[37] of its threat alternative, for example, by offering positive incentives, relying on structural conditions or referring to established notions of legitimacy. To summarize, while both sides always have avoidance alternatives at their disposal, the side with the higher avoidance interest is subordinate and, consequently, power is a binary coding based on the distinction between powerful/powerless. To caution against any positivist reading of this distinction, the actual processing of the code powerful/powerless always remains a communicative affair and neither side can thus be attributed to a specific structure or actor. Similarly, the powerful cannot be sure whether the other side would not, for whatever reason, follow a more costly avoidance alternative. Thus, power and powerlessness are not static categories but communicative artefacts constantly open to change, thereby underlining the contingent and fragile character of each creation and stabilization of (political) order.[38]

This argument points to another central observation in modern systems theory, namely that power actually increases if there are alternatives. Thus, power as an available resource of societal communication grows if it is able to assert its status 'vis-à-vis attractive alternatives … And power can only be increased in parallel to an increase in the freedom of those subject to power', that is, if Ego subordinates himself in spite of *attractive* alternatives.[39] Accordingly, power dissolves 'when it comes to the realization of the avoidance alternative'.[40] In this case power either 'switches' sides as a result of the successful challenge by the previously powerless side or is replaced by conflict and, possibly, violence in the case where power resorts to implementing its avoidance alternative of threat and force. This might also be the reason why the functionally differentiated world society, 'which requires much more power than traditional societies', tends to relegate the blunt and violent implementation of power to its edges (war zones, prisons and so on) and why the 'carceral continuum' of power in modern society usually appears in its structural rather than open and violent form, that is, without the need to implement the avoidance alternative of the underlying threat to use force and violence.[41] These arguments once more caution against being dazzled by the often unvarnished symbolic display and rough execution of power in the Middle East. Part of any demystification of power is, hence, to observe the proportionally high recourse to the (forceful and violent) avoidance alternative in Middle East politics not as an argument in favour of a particular 'powerful' status of power in the region but rather as an indication of a crisis in the operation of power as a medium of communication, on the one hand, and politics as a social system, on the other – an argument which will be returned to with more empirical data below.

The second reason why modern systems theory is helpful for a demystification of power is related to the notion that power – like all other media of communication – unfolds in society through paradoxical and cyclical operations.[42] More precisely, the paradox of power lies in the moment of the constitution of the code. Thus, in order for power to be established as a medium of communication, a decision has to be made to distinguish power/powerlessness. But how can this powerful [sic] decision be made *prior to* the very establishment of the code power/powerlessness? This long shadow of the founding paradox is then 'remembered' in every subsequent operation of the code.[43] Consequently, one of the main problems of power is to ensure that the paradox of the code – and the daunting question of whether the distinction powerful/powerless and its subsequent empirical manifestations really are powerful – becomes temporarily invisibilized in each actual operation of the code.[44] While such deparadoxification strategies are necessary for all system-specific codes (for example, invisibilizing the question of whether the legal code legal/illegal is legal or whether the scientific code true/false is true) power, arguably, occupies a central role. Thus, while each social system has established its own, code-related practices of invisibilization, the initial constitution of any code ultimately is a political act, a paradoxical 'decision of writing' in a moment of fundamental undecidability, thereby underlining the 'double inscription' of power and politics in society.[45] As Slavoj Žižek notes in a somewhat flowery way, 'the "political dimension" is thus doubly inscribed: it is a moment of the social Whole, one among its subsystems, and the very terrain in which the fate of the Whole is decided'.[46]

The mere fact that power communications can be related to one or the other side of the code is not sufficient to capture the complexities of power as a medium of communication in world society. Being based on its founding paradox, the code alone does not indicate how to decide power and powerlessness or what side should be attributed with which. Consequently, specific programmes and legitimization strategies are needed in order to invisibilize the paradox of the code and ensure the actual operation of the code on the basis of cyclical processes of self-referential connectivity of those communications which perceive themselves on the basis of the distinction power/powerlessness. In that context, the code functions as an empty signifier, deprived of all objectivist and stable content. While programmes and legitimacy strategies – as well as other forms of governmentality – ensure the actualization of power in society, the code of power always has constantly to oscillate between (systemic) closing and (environmental) openness. Thus, code-oriented 'communication reproduces in its operative execution ... the closeness of the system. Through the characteristics of its observations ... it [however, also] reproduces the difference between closeness and openness. And that is how a system emerges that is open to its environment because of its closeness, because its basal operations are set to observe.'[47] As Luhmann concludes, if a system that ensures closeness on the basis of self-referential operations interrupts its openness towards the environment, and thereby towards the uncountable potentialities to current actualizations of power, this 'no-longer communicating' would lead to 'the end of the operations of the system'.[48] In other words, ensuring the undistorted operation of the code depends on two key requirements. First, the invisibilization of the code's founding paradox; and second, the emptying of the code so that the code is able to ensure the ongoing operation of the code (closeness), on the one hand, and the flexibility of the code towards (unforeseen) potentialities and environmental perturbations (openness), on the other. Power, as all other media of communication, hence crucially depends on the dislocation of the code, that is, the emptying of the code from all a priori commitments which would only limit the flexibility and openness in the way power operates in society. This disposition (and vulnerability) of the functionally differentiated world society towards contingencies and potentialities then explains the natural drift of code-oriented communications towards operational closeness and cognitive openness vis-à-vis its environment. Even more important for the purpose of this chapter, 'coding is powerful in particular if the change between the two code-values, the crossing of the border between them, happens quasi-technically, without being e.g. socially or psychically particularly conditioned' for this dramatically increases both the operational closeness and the cognitive openness towards environmental information and other potentialities of any system, such as, *inter alia*, politics.[49] In a sense, in its very operation a system always communicates its dislocation since potentialities always threaten the fragile unity established through the hegemonic initial constitution of the code and its subsequent re-articulations. Ernesto Laclau rightly relates this impossibility of total closure to the constant dislocation of the system, that is, the failure of each hegemonic order of discourses in the light of the impossibility of establishing immaculate discursive systems.[50]

In that context, programmes and legitimacy strategies have a double function. They not only (temporarily) invisibilize the founding paradox of the code but also provide for a concrete mechanism of crossing between the two sides of the code, thereby supporting the cognitive openness and flexibility of the system towards its societal environment.[51] However, if the programmes and legitimacy structures do not allow easy crossing – such as in Middle East politics – this distortion leads to an inflation of the code and, ultimately, growing antagonisms. 'The crossing of the code becomes more difficult since the antagonism of negation, which was implicit in the "original" code, becomes radicalised and thereby prevents technical and automatic crossing of sides.'[52] Recall that in each communication of power 'both sides pursue selections while being aware of these selections by the other'.[53] Yet, even in situations of frozen crossings, both sides still have countless (potential) alternatives and the very contingency of all selections structurally 'increases the temptation of negation', independent of the roughness of power to ensure obedience.[54] In other words, frozen crossings run in parallel with a decrease of alternatives for both the powerful, who has to maintain visible threat structures in order to ensure obedience in any case – thereby permanently displaying her actual or potential ability to resort to the monopoly of violence – and the powerless, who either has to acquiesce or to enter into open (and costly) antagonism and conflict with the established power.

The price paid for such frozen crossings between power and powerlessness is the constant visibilization and display of the naked paradox of the code. In a sense, cementing power by erecting frozen crossings overburdens and undermines power at the same time. Since challenges to power are ubiquitous in a world society based on communication as its basic unit, the most likely result of frozen crossings is an increase in hot contestations and antagonisms, that is, communications which cannot evaporate due to the enduring grip on power of specific actors or structures. This freezing of the code leads to a crisis of the system in which power *as* structurally debordered power[55] is constantly challenged, while the proper operation of the code can no longer be organized by the system and its programmes. Thus, the naked visibility of power and the decrease of alternatives, in particular for the powerful, ultimately lead to a de-politicization of politics. As Urs Stäheli has elaborated in detail, in such situations of frozen crossings and hot contestations, the politics of deparadoxification are no longer based on programmes and other smooth strategies of invisibilization. The code powerful/powerless itself becomes rearticulated in an antagonistic fashion and, thereby, 'filled' with material content, such as, *inter alia*, sharp distinctions between Self and Other, solid structures of inclusion and exclusion and, ultimately, the usurpation of politics – and other social systems – by conflict dynamics.[56] With dramatic societal consequences, crossing can no longer be assured.

Third, the continuous communicative interconnectivity between those communications which recognize themselves on the basis of power leads to the establishment of politics as a global functional system. The world, as outlined in detail in Chapter 1, is always the double horizon of all (power) communications, by ensuring structural global interconnectivity, on the one hand, and by constituting an open horizon of potential communications, on the other. Hence, frozen crossings are, for basic structural reasons, not able to shut off contestations. As a result of the world societal embedding of all political communications, there are always possible alternatives and alternative power constellations which doze at the world societal horizon. This is precisely the context of frozen crossings and hot contestations in Middle East politics, and a world society framework consequently allows us to address these dynamics better than state-centred or multi-level approaches or notions of regional exceptionalism.[57] Finally, power also has a specific function in world society as well as vis-à-vis other systems, in particular to provide societal capacities for collectively binding decisions, and more generally to determine situations of undecidability.[58] In other words, the system of politics is not a closed, quasi-institutional segment of society, consisting of actors or organizations, but an open, decentralized and debordered system which self-referentially constitutes itself anywhere and at any time that communications perceive themselves on the basis of the distinction between power and powerlessness. Theoretically speaking, politics is one of many systems which constitute world society as a primarily functionally differentiated society. Empirically, it is of course evident that politics – in some world regions more than in others – aims to reach out to other systems, thereby claiming a privileged position vis-à-vis other societal spheres. The price for these hierarchical practices of domination is, however, either a malfunctioning of other systems – as has been well documented in various Arab Human Development Reports – or a replacement of functional differentiation by antagonistic structures of inclusion/exclusion and severe structures of conflict.[59]

Frozen crossings: the naked visibility of power in Middle East politics

This and the following sections address in greater detail the place of power in Middle East politics. This section takes as its basis the systems-theoretical framework developed above and uses it to consider the centrality of 'frozen crossings', that is, the impediments to a quasi-technical crossing between power and powerlessness in political communications in and on the Middle East. It starts with a discussion on the overall limited effect of liberalization and peace processes in the Middle East since the 1990s in fundamentally altering these dynamics. There are two main consequences of 'frozen crossings' for political communications in and on the region, namely the inflationary symbolization of power, on the one hand, and the ubiquitous implementation of the threat of force and presence of violence, on the other. Yet, rather than consolidating power in Middle East politics, these dynamics point to a deep crisis of power and, consequently, politics in the region. Thus, power is forced constantly to take recourse to extraordinary means in order to ensure the maintenance of the existing borders between power and powerlessness. The resulting securitization of political communications in and on the Middle East deprives the system of politics of much of its required openness and flexibility. Moreover, the general world societal embedding of all political communications further contributes to this fragility of 'frozen crossings'. On this basis, the final section briefly assesses the role of Islamist and democratic movements and looks at the world societal horizons of 'hot contestations' in the Middle East, that is, the peaceful or violent, but always power-threatening contestations to these 'frozen crossings'.

The various political and societal reforms and changes in the region since the 1990s initially fed the expectation that after decades of enmity between and authoritarian governance within Middle Eastern states, at last a gradual 'defrosting' of political communications in the region would take place. This was based on the observation that in the wake of cautious reform efforts in Arab countries, economic liberalization had led to the emergence of a new, and politically conscious middle class, while the extension of press freedoms and other basic rights, such as the right to association, had increased the space for civil society movements, legal political opposition and less confrontational public debates.[60] This positive assessment was encouraged by the rise to power of a young and allegedly more reformist generation of new leaders in countries such as Jordan and Syria at the turn of the century. Moreover, various peace processes in the region, such as the 1989 Ta'if agreement, which formally ended the Lebanese civil war, or the 1993 Oslo accords between Israel and the PLO raised hopes that established structures of conflict would give way to normal political competition and even cooperation in the region, both within and between Middle Eastern states.[61] This went in parallel with a marked increase of elections and constitutionalization processes in the region, such as in Palestine, but also in Jordan and Lebanon.[62] Finally, there was the hope that these regional changes would also have global repercussions and decrease tensions and mutual suspicions between the Middle East and outside powers, in particular the EU and the US.[63] However, while it is true that all these developments are evidence of some limited increases with regard to the openness of political communications in and on the Middle East, they cannot conceal the pertinence of those forms of political communication which continue significantly to obstruct the crossing between power and powerlessness in regional politics. Thus, the overall societal effects of political and economic reforms, leadership changes or peace processes have been relatively meagre. The Arab countries still suffer from a tremendous democratic and reform deficit; structures of domination and violence still characterize relations within and between Middle Eastern states; Israel still resembles more an ethnic democracy than a fully-fledged polyarchy;[64] and, in the context of the 'war on terror', interregional and global relations involving the Middle East have soured.[65] Thus, the changes of leadership and the promise these entailed for greater liberalization soon made way for the observation that the traditional firm grip of leaders and the neopatrimonial governing style of ruling elites remained the defining feature of politics in the region even after this 'false spring'.[66] As Glenn Robinson has argued with a view to developments in Jordan, political liberalization efforts in the region are often no more than the 'defensive' reactions[67] of beleaguered political elites hoping to foster their political domination (and survival) through tactical concessions with regard to some limited economic and political freedoms.[68] Moreover, the honeymoon between conflict parties, be it between Israel and Palestine, between Lebanon and Syria or between ethno-religious/political factions in Lebanon and Palestine (but also in Jordan, Syria and Israel) soon gave way to disillusion. Thus, the potential of peace accords to reshuffle the distribution of power in the region and to overcome the deep alienation between identity groups within the region as well as between the Middle East and outside powers remained low.[69] In sum, despite manifold liberalization efforts, rudimentary forms of greater interregional cooperation and various peace processes, political communications in and on the Middle East remain heavily securitized and so do the borders between power and powerlessness.[70]

Consequently, the reform debates and peace efforts of the early 1990s did not succeed in altering the main dynamics of Middle East politics. As a result, the borders between power and powerlessness are not regulated by quasi-technical, institutionalized mechanisms of crossing, but rather by solid structures which continue to impede on the open and flexible crossing between both sides in political communications in and on the Middle East. Liberalization in the region can, thus, be regarded as 'not an end in itself; rather its purpose is to maintain the regime's hold on power'.[71] However, these 'frozen crossings' ensure, paradoxically, that power in the Middle East is fragile and precarious. Thus, the 'frozen crossings' underpin the status quo orientation of Middle East politics, the lack of societal development in the region and the asymmetric distribution of power to specific societal groups both within and between Middle Eastern states. Theoretically speaking, power in the Middle East does not operate as an empty signifier but is locked in with regard to the power of specific programmes, ideologies, charismatic and traditional leaders or identity-groups. This close linkage between political communications, on the one hand, and a remarkable inflexibility of the code, on the other, has led many scholars to argue that there is a profound de-politicization of Middle East politics inherent in these dynamics. Katarina Dalacoura's observation that these dynamics contribute 'to the emergence of "rhetorical" politics which pays inordinate attention to morality and high principle, to the detriment of actual workings of power and domination' is not only true for the study of Islamist politics but also characterizes Middle East politics on a more general level.[72] Power communications are 'frozen' insofar as they are based on a profound status quo orientation which necessitates the upholding of a solid distinction between the concrete manifestations of power and powerlessness in the region. As Mehran Kamrava explains, power-holders 'have succeeded in depoliticising society through repression and enticing fear of political endeavours among the population. Inclusionary states, having turned streets and neighbourhoods into political theatres, have successfully diverted popular political energies into projects that actually sustain the very basis of the regime.'[73] In other words, political communications are not based on operative closeness and cognitive openness of the code of power but on 'frozen crossings' that hamper the regular operation of the code and the system of politics in the region.

As convincing as this narrative on the problems of crossing in Middle East politics is, there is also a problematic dimension to it, namely its inherent reification – and overestimation – of existing power relations and subtle securitization strategies in the region. Thus, too close a first-order perspective on the rigorous borders between power and powerlessness, as is characteristic of many mainstream approaches to the Middle East, privileges one side of the distinction, namely the side of power, when accounting for the main dynamics of regional politics. This becomes particularly evident when power is attributed to specific actors rather than being analysed as a form of communication as the basic unit of society. As, for example, Raymond Hinnebusch argues with a view to political dynamics in the Middle East, 'robust modernized forms of authoritarianism' – or more generally, massive power asymmetries – on the national and regional levels are the 'local form of governance' which enables power-holders to 'manage their societies' in 'a political process in which a relatively autonomous state elite has the last word'.[74] While such mainstream perspectives are ready to acknowledge that as a result of these 'frozen crossings' power-holders are in a precarious situation insofar as they are forced to adopt various Machiavellian techniques in order to secure their fragile political survival against more or less ruthless contenders, this reification and overestimation of power nevertheless shapes the power-bias of mainstream accounts on Middle East politics on at least two crucial dimensions.[75] First, as far as the analysis of domestic politics is concerned, there is a heavy focus in mainstream approaches on elites, decision-makers and rulers, suggesting that an understanding of the main dynamics of Middle East politics primarily requires an assessment of the strategic rationales of these concrete actors. Thus, Volker Perthes notes that notwithstanding some rudimentary pluralisation in the region, such an elite perspective is central to understanding the main dynamics of regional politics since these elites 'wield political influence and power in that they take strategic decisions or participate in decision making on a national level, contribute to defining political norms and values … and directly influence political discourse on strategic issues'.[76]

Second, as part of this elite bias, such perspectives also stress the ways in which incumbents and rulers control political processes – and the status quo orientation in the distribution of power – both in their countries and in regional politics more generally. This relates, for example, to the way in which politics in Arab countries become 'competition over patronage' rather than competition over power.[77] On a different level, these dynamics also shape the 'frozen crossings' in a democratic state such as Israel, primarily but not exclusively between Israel's Jewish and non-Jewish citizens.[78] This reification of power relations is, however, not only characteristic of state-centred perspectives. While it is true that notwithstanding the significant features of an 'ethnic democracy',[79] Israel is the only democratic state in the region, the mantra-like insistence on this narrative invisibilizes existing power relations on the supra-national level. Thus, it blanks out the domination by Israel of those territories it has occupied since the Six Days' War and the people who inhabit them. As an interesting aside, the equally widespread reference to a Palestinian right to resistance does not only then bear the *problematique* of blurring the border between violence and political opposition but, more interestingly for the purpose of this chapter, actually underpins this first-order observation of allegedly absolute Israeli power – to which only extraordinary (and violent) means of resistance by the disenfranchised can respond. Finally, as we have seen in previous chapters, this narrative of asymmetric and permanent (and unjust) power distribution also features prominently in widespread discourses amongst many Arabs on their domination and subjugation by the West.[80]

This book does not want to deny the political prevalence of all these dynamics. Neither does it suggest ignoring the obvious power asymmetries in the region. Indeed, while there are both ruthless and enlightened authoritarian rulers and regimes in the Arab countries in the region, when push comes to shove, all these regimes keep a firm grip on power. Moreover, despite the reference to shared Arabness, bilateral relations between most Arab countries in the region, whether between Syria and Lebanon, Syria and Jordan or Jordan and Palestine, have traditionally been tense. On another level, Israel struggles with the contradiction between its democratic and Jewish character in domestic politics; it occupies Palestinian land and dominates Palestinian people; and its bilateral relations with its neighbours are characterized by suspicion and regular threats. At the same time, Israel is largely excluded by its

Arab neighbours from even rudimentary forms of regional cooperation on both governmental and societal levels and is subject to frequent violent attacks on its population – which is not a very hopeful environment for triggering significant de-securitization. Finally, there are massive stereotypes of Muslims, Arabs, Jews and Israelis held in the region itself, in the West and elsewhere, which often constitute powerful political narratives and contribute to the overall status quo orientation of Middle East politics, not least because such narratives provide the background for Western support of authoritarian elites in Arab countries and specific conflict parties in the region.[81]

Yet, what is problematic about such mainstream perspectives is that, to varying degrees, they all build on a positivist understanding of power which equates power either with a classical Weberian enforcement of power against opposition or with objectivist materializations of power with regard to specific rulers, political institutions or structures of domination and control. Thus, they reify rather than critically deconstruct first-order observation on power in political communications. Playing on a theme by Nazih Ayubi, Middle East studies in IR should, hence, not only be wary of overemphasizing the Middle Eastern state,[82] but also of implicitly empowering power in the Middle East. What these approaches fail to observe is the way in which this alleged centrality of power in Middle East politics actually inhibits the constant emptying as well as the necessary flexibility of the code of power, thereby de-politicizing and undermining power in political communications in and on the region. A systematic second-order observation on the actual workings of power in the Middle East not only adds another account on the institution of and contestation to these widely acknowledged 'frozen crossings' but enables an identification of the fundamental crisis of power and politics in the region which accompanies them.

The necessity of such a deconstruction of power for a systematic analysis of Middle East politics becomes particularly evident when embarking in greater detail on the two main consequences of 'frozen crossings' for this crisis of politics in the region, namely the inflationary symbolization and open display of violence in Middle East political communications. While it is true that the inflationary symbolization and violent display of power at first sight solidifies the borders between power and powerlessness, it simultaneously reifies both sides of the border, thereby depriving power as a medium of communication of much of its potential flexibility and openness.[83] More specifically, these two dynamics do not only limit the alternatives of the powerful – thereby undermining the power of politics to constantly threaten but not to resort to force – but also invite constant opposition, either by peaceful or violent but always power-threatening means. It is in that context that Kamrava has referred to the 'politics of weak control' in the Middle East; thus, power holders are able to play the 'theatre of power' but because of rather than in spite of the reality of violent domination and suppression in the region, they ultimately fail in successfully lowering the avoidance interests of the powerless.[84]

The inflationary symbolization of power in the Middle East

In order to counter omnipresent power-threatening challenges, power in its concrete empirical manifestations in the Middle East has constantly to have recourse to extraordinary means in order to ensure the maintenance of its borders. This securitization of political communications in and on the Middle East has two main dimensions. The second of these is the centrality of violence, which is discussed below, the first concerns the way in which, to a much greater degree than in other world regions, power needs to make recourse to inflationary symbolizations of power. Such symbolizations should, however, not be mistaken for the widely studied visibility of material symbols, such as flags, mythologies of the nation, the clan and the religion or narratives of charismatic and traditional forms of legitimacy of specific rulers and political orders in the Middle East.[85] The systems-theoretical understanding of symbolizations of power, as it has been outlined in this chapter, goes one crucial step further and highlights the inflationary and code-oriented symbolization of the threat of force in political communications in and on the Middle East. One clarifying remark is essential at this stage. Such an understanding of symbolization does not refer to the distinction between the production and the presentation of politics, in which production relates to the 'tangible' results with regard to collectively binding (and effective) decisions while presentation relates to the symbolic politics of spin-doctoring and selling politics to an audience in order to ensure (temporary) legitimacy for specific political programmes.[86] Indeed, identifying this distinction as a central feature of Middle East politics is crucial for a wide range of literature on the region, for example, when talking about the aforementioned Middle East 'political theatres' in which rhetorical politics are insufficient to cover the Middle East 'state's limited capacities to fulfil the tasks it sets for itself'[87] or Yazigh Sayigh's observation that 'the state is the source of patronage and is the prize for social contenders, for whom control over power rather than production remains the key asset'.[88] However, notwithstanding the obvious inadequacy of politics in the Middle East to provide society with effective collectively binding decisions and (social) security,[89] this distinction between tangible results and rhetorical, symbolic theatres is misleading insofar as politics as a functional system is *always* based on the unity of the distinction between production and presentation, as has been emphasized by Klaus Japp and Isabel Kusche.[90] In other words, the symbolization of politics is an integral part of (the self-description of) all political communications. It is, thus, not merely the overemphasis on 'Byzantine' ornaments of power vis-à-vis 'occidental' rationality in decision-making that underpins the crisis of power and the de-politicization of politics in the Middle East. Following the theoretical reflections at the beginning of this chapter, this crisis of power rather relates to the increased visibility of the violent moment of the institution of the founding paradox of all political orders in the context of this inflationary symbolization: in other words the 'noise of the founding paradox' echoing in Middle East political communications.[91] To recall what has been said above, the functional objective of quasi-technical programmes and other strategies of deparadoxification is to (temporarily) invisibilize the founding paradox of political orders rather than to highlight it. This mechanism is significantly hampered in the Middle East since the 'violent inception of the code' is visibilized by the specific types of symbolizing the threat of force in political communications in and on the region, thereby allowing a more precise identification than is possible in other approaches of the reasons behind the underlying crisis of power in regional politics.

This is, of course, not to argue that there are no successful strategies of deparadoxification in Middle East politics. To pick two examples from the field of educational politics, narratives of leaders and ruling families in Jordan and Palestine serve a powerful role in invisibilizing the founding paradox of political orders in both countries. As Betty Anderson has shown in her study on history textbooks in Jordan, the Hashemite monarchy's strategy of deparadoxification not only builds on the ancestral links of the family with the prophet Muhammad and its negotiating-skills with tribal leaders,[92] but, more importantly here, on the fact that political narratives in Jordan attribute the foundation and survival of the country solely to the Hashemite kings, who historically came from territories located within the Arabian peninsula. Hence, 'the only actors the Hashemite kings recognize are themselves. As the Hashemites are the only players in this tale, they appear as larger-than-life embodiments

... Thus, their activities serve as the *point of origin* for the Jordanian nation.'[93] In a similar way, Nathan Brown has argued that the main purpose of history-telling in the Palestinian educational system 'goes beyond inculcating a sense of Palestinian identity to supporting the *authoritative structures* in Palestinian society', foremost the personal rule of Yassir Arafat and of the PLO leadership, but also a much wider understanding of authority and political order relating to clan structures and family models.[94] The point here is not to argue that there are no successful strategies of deparadoxification in Middle East politics, of which there are countless other examples,[95] but rather that due to the 'frozen crossings' in Middle East politics many of these strategies simultaneously need to resort to an explicit and constant visibilization of the underlying threat of force, in order to keep the specific political orders intact. This 'noise' of the underlying threat of force can then be detected in many instances of political communications in the Middle East. Take, for example, analyses on Alawite rule in Syria, where even presidential amnesties for political dissidents are not so much an expression of occasional clemency on the part of the ruler[96] as a constant reminder of the enormous powers of arbitrary arrest held by the Syrian president and the Syrian state elite. The public knowledge and visibility of – and the 'noise' of the collective silence on – the powerful role of the Syrian army and the Syrian secret service are thus a central theme when studying the question of 'who's afraid of Syrian nationalism?'[97] The literature stresses 'the relevance of institutions that have been established within the last three decades', that is, since the rise to power of Hafiz Al-Assad, which consolidated Alawite rule by constantly visibilizing the threat of force communicated by power-holders rather than embarking on political programmes which *successfully* invisibilize the founding paradox of Alawite rule.[98] This 'public memory' of the violent potential, that is, the echoes which past violence produces in political communications, is then also the deeper background of Volker Perthes' remark on the long-term impact on Syrian politics of the raid by the Syrian army against Islamist movements in the city of Hama in 1982, when more than 10,000 inhabitants were killed. Thus, 'Syrians remember too well the events of 1979–82, when a series of violent confrontations between the regime and the Islamist opposition shook the country, and nobody wants a replay.'[99] Yet, the way this replay would look is precisely communicated through the inflationary symbolization of the threat of force in Syrian politics; it has become the omnipresent noise of political communications.

Such an explicit visibility of the threat of force also relates to more pluralistic states, such as Jordan, and the kingdom's subtle mechanisms of communicating to the opposition where the 'red lines' of opposition lie.[100] But it also affects the politics of a democratic country, such as Israel. As Uri Bar-Joseph explains, the 'paradox of Israeli power' is 'primarily the product of an erroneous national security concept in which military force is regarded as an almost exclusive answer to external threats',[101] for example, with regard to the territories conquered in 1967 or Israel's constant reminders to Syria (and vice versa) that it is prepared for war. It is also exposed in collective identity politics, in which the symbolization of the underlying threat of force occupies a central place. Take, for example, the public display of martyrdom myths, such as the Massada-narrative, which symbolizes Israel's willingness to resort to force to counter *all* fundamental challenges, even if the price of resistance is total annihilation.[102] Seen from this perspective, the unofficial nuclear potential of Israel increases – rather than minimizes – the 'noise' of the explicit threat of force in political communications in and on the region precisely because of its unofficial and nebulous status. But it is not only with regard to outside powers that this explicit symbolization of the underlying threat of violence gains prominence. As Yoav Peled has argued with a view to the riots in northern Israel in October 2000, where Israeli Palestinians protesting against the killing of Palestinians in the Al-Aqsa Intifada fought the Israeli police – and during which 14 Israelis were killed, 13 of Palestinian and one of Jewish origin – the Or Commission, which had the task of investigating this outbreak of violence, unintentionally reified the 'frozen crossings' between Jewish and non-Jewish Israelis. Thus, while the commission report elaborated in detail on the various levels of discrimination against Israeli Palestinians, in general, and criticized the behaviour of Israeli authorities and police in the riots, in particular, it also subtly 'restored ethnic democracy' by suggesting that in order to enjoy full citizenship rights, Palestinian Israelis need first to 'adhere to their obligation to protest this violation within the narrow confines of the law'.[103] As Peled outlines in detail, the Or report provided the basis for a subsequent solidification of the distinction between Jewish and non-Jewish Israelis in Israeli legislation and, as a consequence, challenges to this political order could now more easily be framed as security threats to which the Israeli authorities would have the right to respond forcefully.[104] The report did not provide answers to the question of how protest against 'frozen crossings' would be possible at all, if the 'narrow confines of the law', on the one hand, and these 'frozen crossings' between Jewish and non-Jewish Israelis, on the other, were to coalesce. Thus, the naked visibility of the underlying threat of force serves a central function not only in legitimizing the specific case at hand, but also in projecting the need forcefully to guard and uphold the borders of ethnic democracy, as a specific political order, in the future.

In that context, a comment by Yezid Sayigh on the linkage between state formation and armed struggle in Palestine is highly intriguing. Sayigh critically addresses the gap between the ambitious political rhetoric of the PLO, on the one hand, and the overall meagre concrete political results, on the other.[105] While Sayigh's argument closely resembles the critique by Amal Jamal and others on bad governance and corruption by the PLO and the absence of socio-political development in Palestine after the establishment of the PA,[106] it is intriguing for another reason. 'The fact that the Palestinian movement was able for so long to accommodate such a marked discrepancy between rhetoric and reality, between slogans and capabilities, and between nationalist myth and social requirement suggests that performance was not measured in conventional military terms and that armed struggle served other primary functions',[107] namely to uphold the frozen crossings between the PLO leadership, on the one hand, and its various contenders in Palestine and the diaspora, on the other. Consequently, Palestinian politics relied to a large extent – and not only in order to counter Israeli occupation – on the constant visibilization of the threat of force. This constant presence and visibility of the founding paradox of political order is then amplified – rather than softened – by the fuzzy borders between political and military factions in Palestinian politics. The debate on whether the 'political' or 'military' wings of Fatah and Hamas inside and outside Palestine are more central for a solid understanding of Palestinian politics misses the crucial point that it is precisely the nebulous form of this distinction which ensures the constant symbolization and societal noise of the threat of force in political communications. A similar argument has then been made by Mona Harb and Reinoud Leenders on the role of Hezbollah in Lebanese politics. They argue that the question of whether Hezbollah is in a process of moving from a 'professional guerrilla to a political party', is misleading.[108] Different framings of Hezbollah as a 'terrorist organisation' or a 'Lebanese factor' imply not only that both dimensions are needed adequately to describe Hezbollah's *political* role, but also that precisely this nebulous division amplifies the centrality of the threat to force as the central 'noise' in political communications involving Hezbollah. Thus, 'the *variety* of institutions Hezbollah has been carefully elaborating and readapting over the past decades' is the basis of Hezbollah's power, in which its 'social and political activities operate as an integrated and holistic policy network, disseminating the values of resistance while constructing a collective identity derived from the notion of the hala al-islamiyya, or "Islamic sphere"'.[109]

Two clarifying comments are central at this stage. First, the naked visibility of the founding paradox of the code does not correspond with objectivist or actor-centred readings of powerful and powerless. It would be premature to attribute the naked visibility of the underlying threat of force to the allegedly powerful actors in the region, such as, amongst others, the armies, secret services, police and governments of states like Israel, Syria or Jordan. As the arguments above on political-military factions such as Hezbollah, Fatah, Hamas or Islamic Jihad underline, the naked visibility of the threat of force extends to those actors who build large parts of their political capital on the claim that they represent the allegedly 'powerless', be it the Shi'i population in Lebanon, the Palestinian population in the West Bank, the Gaza Strip and Palestinian refugee camps throughout the region or the orthodox Muslim community in Jordan. Dag Tuastad's argument that 'Palestinians are victim of symbolic violence in two ways', namely due to allegedly external framings of Palestinians as 'terrorists' and 'traditional people' misses the point that the naked visibility of the founding paradox of the code (and consequently the symbolic violence of such political orders) relates to politics as the unity of the distinction powerful/powerless.[110] In other words, it not merely affects specific actors but characterizes political communications in their entirety, thereby relating to *both* sides of the borders. Second, building on the arguments of the previous chapter, this naked visibility of the founding paradox of all political orders does not only relate to political communications in the Middle East; this would only reify untenable notions of the Middle East as a regional container, or the notion of cultural exceptionalism of Middle Easterners, as has already been criticized in Chapter 2. A world society perspective allows us to observe the centrality of the explicit symbolization of the underlying threat of force in political communications in *and* on the Middle East – in other words, on the place of the Middle East in politics as a global functional system. Seen from that perspective, the widely referred to securitization and Orientalization of the Middle East by outside powers, such as the EU or the US, as, for example, in narratives of 'cultural' difference, the Middle East as a 'security threat' or a place of 'bad governance', only underlines the centrality of symbolizations of the threat of force in political communications in and on the region insofar as these discourses provide the basis not only for political, economic or military interventions but also for increased security measures against Middle Easterners in Europe, America and elsewhere.

The centrality of violence in the Middle East reconsidered

Closely related to this crisis of power induced by the inflationary symbolization of the threat of force is the widely documented centrality of open recourse to violence in Middle East politics: it is only necessary to recall the violent suppression of Islamist and democratic opposition movements in Syria throughout the last decades, the violent suppression of the Palestinian national movement in Jordan in the 1970s, or the establishment of the separation wall/fence, army checkpoints and road blockages by the Israeli army in the West Bank.[111] However, violence is not the *domaine réservé* of secular or monarchic leaders or state institutions. Recourse to violence equally structures large parts of intra-communal relations in Lebanon or Palestine and also shapes the rhetoric and actions of those groups claiming to be 'resistance movements' such as, to varying degrees, Fatah, Hamas or Hezbollah.[112] The open display of violence, finally, also relate to interventions by extra-regional powers, for example since the beginning of the so-called 'war on terror'. In that context, some authors have also referred to the more subtle and structural forms of violence shaping intra-regional and, in particular, Western-Middle East relations.[113] As Yasir Suleiman has explained in a related context, the subtle use of language, which puts in place specific cognitive frames, not only structures conflicts in the Middle East (what Suleiman refers to as a 'war of words') but also rationalizes and legitimizes recourse to open use of violence in the region.[114] This is, however, not the place to elaborate in greater detail on the rich literature on the centrality of violence in political communications in and on the Middle East. The narrower purpose of this section is to put this violence into a comprehensive theoretical perspective which allows us to address the linkages between power (that is, the medium of communication of the political system) and violence as representative of the symbiotic mechanism of politics.[115]

When addressing this role of open 'violence in the system' two main dynamics come to the fore.[116] First, the frozen crossings between power and powerlessness in Middle East politics render the entry of violence into political communications in and on the region more likely. Thus, the frozen crossings significantly facilitate the 'societal search for the actor',[117] since the attribution of actions – in other words the specific forms of causality attributions in regional politics – can relate to concrete *and* relatively stable (and, therefore, highly contested) addressees.[118] The cycle of violence in Middle East politics crucially builds on such interconnected attribution processes. As Dirk Baecker explains, 'violence is the communication of an unavoidability of an attribution to a [specific] action' in which 'this attribution is not left to communication but is enforced by action itself'.[119] This argument should not be misread as an action-centred deviation from the communication-theoretical framework of this book. The point here is not that violence is a situation in which naked action would replace communicative unpredictability but rather that the occurrence of 'violence in the system' leads to the emergence of communications which are based on the *communication* of an unavoidability of attributions to specific actions. In other words, 'as long as the communicative structure is characterised by violence, the reproduction of this [violent] situation orients itself alongside the almost tangible thread of the reproduction of actions' and the subsequent causal attribution of actions to concrete actors.[120] In such a situation, the usual systemic processing of (double) contingencies loses much of its power[121] and, as will be further outlined in Chapter 5, the ability to deconstruct notions of the Self and the Other by keeping the horizons of attribution in political communications relatively open and vague diminishes rapidly. Thus, the frozen crossings in the Middle East not only facilitate the entry of open violence into politics but also ensure the constant communicative reproduction of this violence. However, once actualized in the form of violence, power loses much of its flexibility as a medium of communication and it is for this reason that a creeping replacement of politics in the Middle East by antagonism and conflict can indeed be observed.

Second, the centrality of violence in Middle East politics not only constantly reifies the observation of frozen crossings and the associated power asymmetries between concrete actors. As already mentioned above, the massive occurrence of violence also leads to a decrease of alternatives in political communications. What is interesting here is that this decrease of alternatives and the subsequent 'communication of unavoidability' limits in particular the ability effectively to communicate power. Thus, responding to potential or actual challenges and contestations, power in Middle East politics not only makes recourse to the inflationary visibilization of the (un-actualized) *threat* of force. Additionally, and encapsulated in the aforementioned cycle of recurring causal attributions to specific actions (in which self-observations always frame actions as re-actions, while other-observations always observe actions as actions to which the Self is *forced* to respond), power needs to resort to the (actualized) implementation of violence in order to uphold the frozen crossings. Such an understanding of the linkage between politics and power in the Middle East cautions against a Weberian understanding of power in which power is merely equated with the successful realization of one's will against resistance. When looking at the linkage between power and violence from the systems-theoretical perspective developed above, it can be seen that this regular open recourse to violence in Middle East politics in fact limits the ability of power to operate as the code of the political system. The role of violence in 'deoptionalizing'– that is, in narrowing a range of options in – political communications[122] and, thereby, undermining the role of power in the Middle East, therefore provides a comprehensive theoretical underpinning to the often raised claim of a de-politicization of power in Middle East politics.[123] In other words, the powerful become entrapped in a heavily securitized atmosphere in which causal attributions for their own violent actions are communicated as *unavoidable* reactions to concrete actions forced upon them by specific Others. Such self-fulfilling prophecies are part-and-parcel of Middle East politics, in which there are countless semantics of reactive unavoidability which construct the region as a violent universe of its own which does, regrettably, not leave any space for more benevolent practices and in which the Other's violence is framed as onslaughts of 'random violence' in contrast to merely reactive and restrained violence by the Self.[124]

Analyses on the role of terrorism in Middle East politics are a prime example of this creeping encroachment of violence into the system of politics. From the outset it is crucial to emphasize that this chapter does not seek to establish a causality of terrorism, which either frames national or religious 'resistance' as a reaction to occupation and (structural) domination by, alternatively, Israel/Jews, the West/Christians or corrupt Middle Eastern state elites; and neither does it seek to identify the 'war on terror' as a reaction forced upon those states and entities physically attacked by 'terrorists'. Following the theoretical observations made above, the central point here is that the prevalence of the semantic form 'resistance/terrorism' in political communications in and on the Middle East is based on recurring communications which define themselves in relation to the aforementioned 'unavoidability of an attribution to a [specific] action' in which 'this attribution is not left to communication but is enforced by action itself'.[125] The frozen crossings in Middle East politics then structurally facilitate this deoptionalization of political communications because violence can much more easily be *causally* attributed to relatively time-consistent communications on asymmetries in the distribution of power.[126] These similarities in the semantic form of the resistance/terrorism distinction and how this distinction feeds into political practices have been analysed by Gertrud Brücher who has argued that the challenge of the terrorist attacks on New York on 11 September 2001 primarily lies in continuing to talk peacefully about peace, while escaping the vicious circle of responding to (and talking about) violence within a violence-prone, bivalent action/reaction scheme.[127] In a similar vein, Tamir Bar-On and Howard Goldstein have argued that 'far too often the tactics deployed to combat terrorism come eerily close to mirroring the very violence they seek to eliminate', thereby instituting a culture of violence at the expense of politics.[128] The fact that this is not limited to a simplistic Western/Muslim distinction becomes clear when addressing, for example, the violence between Islamists and autocratic Arab governments in the Middle East, public knowledge of which might, in particular outside the region, be constrained both by the lack of information on the scale of the violence and by its being superseded by the overarching Western/Muslim paradigm.[129] For example, 'when a December 1996 bomb blast [allegedly instigated by Islamists] killed eleven people in Damascus, the government press did not even report its occurrence, much less any associated communiqués from those responsible'. Public knowledge about this event – and subsequent government insurgencies against Islamists – remained low in Syria, let alone outside the country, and this is true for many other confrontations within the terrorism/resistance frame between autocratic Arab states and oppositional Islamist movements within Arab countries.[130]

This focus on the resistance/terrorism distinction is not meant to propagate any kind of equivalence between them, since such perspectives more often than not tend to belittle or legitimize violent excesses by the allegedly powerless in the Middle East. Moreover, when addressing the effects of violence by resistance movements/terrorists on political communications in and on the Middle East, a normative starting point would only obstruct the observation of the dynamics of both deoptionalized communications and unavoidable attributions within the reaction/action scheme.[131] While Western/Israeli observations often stress the immediate *physical form* of violence (for example, suicide attacks, marching militants, hijacked planes), Middle Eastern/Arab readings tend to stress the more structural notions of violence (for example, colonialization, dominance, conspiracies). While it should be noted that already the distinction Western/Muslim is problematic insofar as it easily reifies notions of a given and, therefore, *unavoidable* distinction between both sides, and therefore might indeed be a violent inscription itself, the empirical reality of the usage of this distinction in world politics, media and science can hardly be disputed. This distinction can then well be related to Dirk Baecker's third perspective on violence, which overcomes these more one-dimensional notions of violence as either physical or structural violence.[132] Thus, in contrast to this distinction, the communication-theoretical understanding of violence developed above allows us to address both dimensions simultaneously, without taking recourse either to non-communicational concepts of violence (physical violence) or to assumptions of world society as *generally* violent (structural violence), thereby ignoring the high incentives for non-violent communications in a functionally differentiated world society. In other words, a systems-theoretical perspective allows us to observe the dynamics of violence 'as the other side of communication' within the comprehensive framework of the communication and differentiation theoretical framework outlined in Chapter 1.

However, this also means,

> that terrorism must be put into the context of the political system of society. As much as politics tries to denounce terrorism as a mere criminal activity, and as much as it presupposes in recent times more religious and therefore allegedly cultural motives rather than political ones, so are both attempts of distancing-moves within the context of an already political game, which is not centring around murderers and criminals and not only around jihadists or cultural defenders but always about political opponents.[133]

It is from this perspective that Gary Gambill's claim that 'the centrality of terrorism to political conflict in the Middle East has tremendous implications for the study of international relations' – and one could now add, for the study of politics in world society more generally – becomes particularly plausible; thus, the 'study of the utility of terrorism is a small, but necessary, step toward the development of a more comprehensive theoretical paradigm that will reflect accurately the dynamics of modern international conflict. Such an undertaking has been severely impeded by "terrorism experts" who continue invariably to attribute the prevalence of terrorism in the Middle East to specific ideological, religious, or ethnic groups' – be they Muslim/Arab terrorists or Western/Israeli colonialists – rather than addressing the role of violence in the system from a more system(at)ic perspective.[134] The same is, however, also true with regard to self-justifications of (physical) violence by

Islamist movements and their discursive entrapment in political communications of alternativelessness and unavoidable attributions, for example, when Shaykh Muhammad Husayn Fadlallah from Lebanon argues that the confrontation between the 'West' and 'Islam' is 'a war of the arrogant against the downtrodden, a war of international [sic] interests against those who may threaten these interests'.[135] Seen from that perspective, suicide operations – as a widespread method of communicating an absolute and non-negotiable deoptionalized alternativelessness and necessity of attributions in the context of this confrontation – then appear as an 'ultimate form of communication'[136] insofar as they are firmly conditioned (and re-conditioned) within a violent reaction/action scheme.[137] Thus, those 'who annihilate themselves in order to kill would appear to face a condition in which their suicidal choice has become ontologically – and not only strategically – the only one available'.[138] Paradoxically, the upholding of frozen crossings becomes the main concern of political communications and, most interestingly, this applies also to those claiming to be (non-legitimately) located on the side of powerlessness. It is on this basis that Sheik Yusuf Al-Qaradawi, a leading Sunni scholar, makes a widely accepted argument in the Middle East, namely that 'if jihad for the liberation of occupied nations is considered "terrorism", then God raise me as a terrorist, and martyr me as a terrorist'.[139] Upholding the frozen crossings has become part and parcel of political communications in and on the Middle East and *both* sides of the border operate within and, consequently, stabilize its (violent) confines. These communicative dynamics are well documented in a statement by Sadiq Al-Azm, a liberal Syrian philosopher, who has voiced his amazement and embarrassment about his immediate reaction to the attacks of 11 September 2001. Thus, while on the one hand, he felt immediately repelled by this massive incidence of violence and while he realized that this event would in the end only solidify the power asymmetries between the West and Arab countries, he 'could not help experiencing a strong emotion of schadenfreude that I tried to contain, control, and hide'.[140] It is for this reason that 'the primacy of conspiracy' as a popular mode of observation in Middle East politics cannot be regarded as a mere misperception or misunderstanding, which could be resolved by more (emphatic) communications, but rather should be seen as a self-referentially produced mechanism which allows for a continuous re-inscribing of violence into the systems.[141]

To summarize, a systems-theoretical framework helps to show the ways in which politics is transformed by massive recourse to violence in the Middle East. Attribution processes, either to Western colonialist or to a specific religion such as Islam – what Dag Tuastad refers to as 'neo-orientalism and the new barbarism thesis'[142] – are already part of the creeping transformation of Middle East politics insofar as they fail to observe the communicative processes which continuously structure this incorporation of violence into the system up to the point at which violence, paradoxically, constantly challenges *and* (re)stabilizes the 'frozen crossings' characteristic of the region. This is not a moral judgement about the legitimacy of violent interventions and neither is it an 'objective' statement of who precisely is located on the side of the powerful and the powerless, but merely the observation of the extent to which political communications are characterized by violence and how this violence translates into the communication of a lack of alternatives and unavoidable attributions, thereby further undermining power as the code of the political system in its capacity to ensure a quasi-technical crossing between both sides.

Hot contestations: paradoxes of power and powerlessness

Notwithstanding this communication of a lack of alternatives in Middle East politics which directly derives from the effects of 'frozen crossings', both sides do, of course, have countless (potential) alternatives. As described in detail in Chapter 1, the double world societal horizon of all (political) communications ensures the structural availability of such alternatives. Yet, due to the effects of 'frozen crossings' this world societal horizon relates to both sides in a radically different way. As already alluded to above, 'frozen crossing' run in parallel with a decrease of power and a limitation of the alternatives, in particular those of the powerful. Since power has to constantly visibilize *and* implement its threat structures in order to ensure obedience – a dis-empowering of the role of power as the (empty) medium of communication in Middle East politics takes place. While contestations to power, of course, remain risky, and the powerless are confronted with the hardly attractive alternatives of acquiescence or open (and potentially dangerous) confrontation and conflict with the established power, 'frozen crossings' nevertheless do not to the same extent undermine the alternatives of the powerless. Recall that the very contingency of selections with regard to all (political) communications structurally ensures the prevalence of 'the temptation of negation', independent of the degree of force utilized by power-holders to ensure obedience.[143] Since challenges to power are ubiquitous in a world society based on communication, 'frozen crossings' limit in particular one side of the code, namely power, while the other side of the code, namely powerlessness, is structurally in a more advantageous position insofar as the double world societal horizon provides a constant template for (alternative) communications. More precisely, both the structural global interconnectivity and the inexhaustible possibilities of alternative (actualized or potential) power communications ensure that reduced alternatives on the side of power are confronted with an inexhaustible horizon of alternatives on the side of powerlessness.[144] However, since such contestations cannot evaporate as a result of the enduring hold on power of *specific* actors or structures, the freezing of the code leads over time to a crisis of the system, in which power is constantly challenged while the proper operation of the code (ensuring both temporary closure and structural flexibility between power/powerlessness) can no longer be organized by the system and its programmes.

At this point, it becomes again obvious why *sui generis* approaches that view the Middle East as a somewhat separate political universe operating according to allegedly regional logics of politics are highly problematic. They pay inordinate attention to the observation that as a result of the world societal horizon of *all* communications, the Middle East cannot be thought of as detached from world society in structural terms or from the inexhaustible pool of sense-making (actualized or potential) communications in the functional system of (world) politics. While the crossings in Middle East politics are indeed severely hampered, the system nevertheless constantly has to process contestations, either from within or from outside the region. Independently of whether they are violent or peaceful, contestations in Middle East politics are, therefore, regularly 'hot contestations', because they are always threatening power in its concrete and static manifestations rather than operating within the logic of power being the unity of the distinction between power/powerlessness. In other words, political communications always produce – and the political system depends – on contestations, while the facilitation of crossings as well as temporal closure ensure the operation of politics as a functional system in world society. The fact that these crossings are severely blocked in the Middle East turns almost all contestations into *hot* contestations which further amplify the aforementioned securitization of Middle East politics. It is, hence, hardly surprising that such hot contestations are widely documented in the literature, which focuses primarily on hot contestations to established power in the region emanating from both Islamist/orthodox religious groups and democracy movements.[145]

What is less often addressed, however, is how these hot contestations relate to a comprehensive theoretical perspective on power. This is not the place to analyse in detail the role of Islamist movements or democracy/liberalization-oriented groups in Middle East politics, for this would clearly go much beyond the narrower purpose of this chapter. To repeat what has been said above, this is also not meant to equate the democracy movement and Islamist/religious groups in the Middle East. Both movements are internally highly fragmented, they do overlap in part, as for example, the case of the Meimad-party in Israel illustrates,[146] but often they are mutually exclusive, with Islamists striving for politics subject to the encompassing rules of *shari'a* law or Orthodox Jews supporting a society based on Halacha law; moreover, both movements have a different relation to the use of violence in politics, with many religious (Muslim, Christian or Jewish) groups being linked to armed militias.[147] However, what contestations by Islamists (and other orthodox religious) or democracy movements share, is that they are regularly observed as directly power-threatening rather than as being part of the unity of the distinction between power/powerlessness and, therefore, part of the regular operation of politics. This is then also the deeper reason for the noteworthy securitization of oppositional movements in Middle East politics, not only in political discourses but, interestingly, also in many academic writings which, either implicitly or explicitly, uncritically subscribe to such securitizing strategies. This can, for example, be seen when addressing the role of democracy movements in the Middle East, which are often analysed against the backdrop of an alleged (violent) encounter between a Western concept and local tradition. The problem here is not only that such approaches fail to explain why there are indigenous Middle East democracy and human rights movements. More important for the argument of this chapter, such territorial/cultural framings implicitly legitimize powerful strategies by incumbents to uphold the 'frozen crossings' in Middle East politics by framing democracy either as an external intervention or as a threat to stability and, ultimately, peace. Similar observations can then be made with regard to the problematization of contestations by Islamist movements. Notwithstanding the often illiberal political agenda of such movements, the swiftness with which contestations by these groups become framed as a security threat, are indeed striking. This was, for example, evident in the immediate reaction of the PLO, the government of Israel, the EU, the US – but also many academic commentators[148] – to the election victory of Hamas in the Palestinian parliamentary elections of January 2006. The speed with which these and other contestations – for example, by Hezbollah in

Lebanon or by the Muslim brotherhood in Jordan[149] – become regarded as 'hot contestations', justifying extraordinary responses by national governments or the international community, only underlines the degree to which the 'frozen crossings' permeate political communications in *and* on the region and the ways in which political communications are actually gauged constantly to fortify these crossings.

It is precisely at this point that the distortion of the code of power in Middle East politics comes to the fore. Recall that both power (order) and powerlessness (contestation) jointly constitute the code. Earlier in this chapter it was therefore argued that the 'power of power' lies in its operation as an empty signifier of political communications. More specifically, while contestations challenge specific orders they are not a threat to power as the empty signifier of all political communications. These dynamics are constrained in Middle East politics, since the 'frozen crossings' overburden the code insofar as power becomes equated with upholding specific orders rather than the unity of the distinction between power/powerlessness. That is why contestations almost automatically resurge as power-threatening 'hot contestations' which only augment the crisis of politics in the region.[150] It is as a result of these dynamics that contestations to power in Middle East politics often tend to appear in a non-political form. Such an 'out-sourcing' of politics to allegedly non-political spheres – for example, the establishment of functionally-oriented services in the educational and health sectors by Islamist or Orthodox Jewish movements,[151] the rise of pietistic groups, such as the Salafi movement,[152] or the rapid growth of associational life with regard to the business community or the women's and environmental movements[153] – does not, however, solve the *problematique* of 'frozen crossings'. While such movements are at least to some extent successful in escaping constant surveillance by the powerful and while they do indeed fulfil certain societal tasks that the Middle East state is unwilling or unable to provide, the very fact that power remains wary of the activities of these groups – combined with the huge interest these movements attract in political science – casts serious doubts on the apolitical nature of these movements and whether they are ultimately able to overcome the 'frozen crossings' of Middle East politics. While such movements might feed into a romantic 'imaginary of autonomy'[154] of the modern life-world, it is less clear why they should constitute a sphere separate from 'real' political communications. Seen from a world societal perspective, the inherently political role of such developments can be seen on at least two dimensions. First, such allegedly non-political spheres enable an actualization of powerful narratives of powerlessness in world society, for example, of women in Arab countries, Palestinian refugees in Lebanon or pious Muslims in Jordan. Second, such frameworks also serve a crucial role in keeping the horizon of *alternative* political orders open, by imagining non-antagonistic and peaceful political spheres, be they in the form of a pure Islamic state or a polyarchic democracy. Seen from that perspective it becomes once more evident why the popularity of taking recourse to the Islamic (or Jewish) tradition is not a confrontation between modern and traditional worlds, but rather (one) possible way of imaging a less distorted operation of politics according to the requirements of a functionally differentiated world society.

To sum up, the main argument of this chapter was that a comprehensive theoretical perspective on power allows us to move away from the widespread mystifications of power (and states) in Middle East politics. This chapter has suggested that the freezing of the (easy) crossing between power and powerlessness is, paradoxically, shaped and undermined by the world societal context in which political communications in and on the Middle East are embedded. However, 'frozen crossings' not only lead to an inflationary symbolization of power and an increased use of violence in political communications, but also to an increase in the intensity of contestations to existing power relations, which have therefore been described as 'hot contestations'. To put it in post-structuralist terms, the prevalence of 'frozen crossings' fosters a multiplication of antagonistic moments in Middle East politics and a creeping transformation of politics towards antagonism and conflict. This process leads to a profound crisis of power and a subsequent de-politicization of Middle East politics. Hence, rather than viewing 'frozen crossings' as a manifestation of a particular centrality of power in regional politics, this chapter maintains on the basis of the theoretical framework developed above, that these dynamics underline the overall weak and fragile status of power in the region. Thus, the constant need of power-holders to visibilize and implement the threat of force significantly limits the alternatives of the powerful, thereby depriving power of much of its societal capacities. Moreover, the naked visibility of power, resulting from both the inflationary symbolization and the constant implementation of the threat of force, structurally undermines the invisibilization and, therefore, the successful deparadoxification of political orders in the Middle East. Power is overburdened by its symbiosis and association with concrete empirical constellations and, therefore, loses much of its necessary flexibility as the code of the political system. As a result, the code powerful/powerless becomes rearticulated in an antagonistic way.

It is this creeping transformation of politics – which, *inter alia*, relates to the extension of solid (frozen) structures of inclusion and exclusion across various functional spheres, the sharp distinctions between Self and Other, the centrality of identity in Middle East politics, and, ultimately, the usurpation of politics and other social spheres by conflict dynamics – which the subsequent chapters will address in greater detail.

4
Inclusion and Exclusion: Fragile Strategies of Deparadoxification in the Middle East

'There must be some way out of here', said the joker to the thief
Bob Dylan – All Along the Watchtower[1]

Inclusion and exclusion in Middle East politics

Classical approaches to inclusion primarily focus on the ways in which the modern nation-state and, more recently, the cosmopolitan level ensure the integration of the national (and global) population by means of institutional mechanisms and cultures of participation. As far as the former aspect is concerned, the role of citizenship in ensuring (formal) equality between all citizens of a state has been at the centre of focus of this research tradition, in particular by stressing the political and social rights associated with citizenship in the context of the republican model and the welfare state.[2] Moreover, transnational migratory movements and the settlement of significant 'alien' populations in foreign lands has enriched these approaches by analyses of dual and transnational forms of citizenship in the 'age of flexible sovereignty' and the changes these dynamics bestow on a traditionally state-centred understanding of citizenship.[3] From this perspective, institutional regulations in citizenship law are, arguably, part of a larger phenomenon in the process of the institutionalization of human rights as a central paradigm in the evolution of the global political and legal system. Consequently, human rights have been referred to as 'a new model of multicultural citizenship, legitimating the de-coupling of state membership, individual rights and national identities' since the end of World War II.[4] With a view to the participatory dimension of the integration/inclusion nexus, the role of 'civil society' has been central on three dimensions. First, in the context of the classical opposition between state/society in which scholars focused on the relationship between formal state institutions and 'their' distinct (civil) societies;[5] second, in the defence of a quasi-primordial personal life-world operating against systemic mechanisms through an institutionalization of deliberative politics;[6] and, third, in pleas for the role of a global civil society as a means of dialectic empowerment against the allegedly elite-driven forces of globalization and homogenization by local cultures, civilizations and identities, on the one hand, and universal rights and shared concerns of the subaltern, on the other.[7] In turn, exclusion figures prominently as the 'dark side' of these integrative and emancipatory practices. The study of exclusion dynamics, therefore, comprises diverse phenomena on both the national and the global levels, relating, *inter alia*, to significant inequalities in individuals' political and social rights as well as to structural and institutionalized impediments to a greater role in public affairs of individual groups of persons or of (global) 'civil society' more generally.[8]

The study of inclusion and exclusion dynamics in the Middle East has been closely linked to these important research traditions. Thus, the mechanisms of inclusion in the region have been addressed from various angles, discussing the impact of legal practices (such as citizenship, constitutionalization), political dynamics (general political rights, elections) and 'societal' spheres (role of NGOs, rights of participation) in shaping the regional outlook of inclusion/exclusion.[9] In this context, mirroring the state-centred perspectives in many studies on Middle East politics, inclusion has regularly been conceptualized as the ability of states in the region to integrate Lebanese, Israeli or Syrian 'society' by means of powerful norms and institutions, in particular nationalism and religion.[10] Given the often heavily particularistic nature of these projects of inclusion in the Middle East, the study of how these practices ultimately contribute to 'curtail freedom and fundamental rights and [how they] have weakened the good citizen's strength and ability to advance',[11] has made 'exclusion' one of the key words in the contemporary study of the Middle East. This relates, *inter alia*, to the study of topics such as engineered elections, significant impediments to freedom of press and association, denial of individual rights, but also to those exclusionary practices emanating from ethnocentric conceptualizations of citizenship, securitization policies and from various forms of conflict and occupation in the region, all of which negatively affect the status of distinct groups of persons in the Middle East.

Notwithstanding the crucial contribution of all these studies in fostering our understanding of Middle East politics, in general, and massive forms of inequality in the region, in particular, this chapter argues that addressing inclusion/exclusion from a world society perspective offers important insights into the role of inclusion and exclusion in the region on at least three additional dimensions. First, by integrating inclusion/exclusion into a comprehensive theory of globalization it is possible to avoid playing the 'local' and the 'global' off against each other. Thus, neither individual states, religions or cultures are the prime regulators of inclusion/exclusion, nor must the abandoning of such region-specific perspectives necessarily lead to the equally problematic alternative of merely shifting the focus of analysis towards the identification of homogeneous/universal principles which would, sooner or later, solve the regional problems of inclusion/exclusion. As has been outlined in chapters 1 and 2, a comprehensive theory of globalization – and, therefore, a comprehensive understanding of inclusion/exclusion – needs simultaneously to address homogeneity and heterogeneity and the local and the global rather than treating both dimensions as separate analytical levels. Second, a differentiation-theoretical perspective allows us to address the polycontextuality of inclusion/exclusion in (world) society. Hence, rather than being a unifying machine which locates individuals on one or the other side of the distinction – as might have been the case in pre-modern, stratified societies[12] – the problem of inclusion/exclusion in a functionally differentiated (world) society needs to be reformulated as the problem of many (sometimes converging, but most of the time cross-cutting) dynamics of inclusion and exclusion affecting all persons. Third, by firmly basing the analysis of inclusion/exclusion on the notion of communication as the basic unit of society, the inherent dynamism in the interrelationship between both sides of the distinction comes to the fore. Thus, inclusion/exclusion no longer appears as a static concept but rather as a (dynamic) form which depends on the possibility of crossing between both sides. Without embarking at this stage on these arguments in greater detail, they already underline the central concern of this chapter, namely to overcome an all too normative bias in prematurely equating inclusion with integration and exclusion with disintegration.[13] This chapter thus shifts the spotlight on to the question of what function the distinction between inclusion/exclusion actually performs in world society, in general, and Middle East politics, in particular.

It is on this basis that this chapter argues that the specific role of inclusion/exclusion in the region lies in particular in its (complex) relationship with the frozen crossings outlined in the previous chapter. More precisely, it is argued that the form of inclusion/exclusion provides a 'second-order perspective' on frozen crossings across a variety of societal spheres, thereby ensuring the constant problematization (and scandalization) of these impediments to a quasi-technical crossing in political (and other functional) communications. Hence, rather than reifying existing orders, the inclusion/exclusion nexus 'reminds' society of the contingency of these orders, thereby undermining all attempts at their (permanent) consolidation – yet, without being able to simply replace the central role of inclusion/exclusion in the (fragile) maintenance of these orders. In a nutshell, frozen crossings, on the one hand, and the form of inclusion/exclusion as the second-order observation of these frozen crossings, on the other, exist in parallel, but ultimately are uneasy bedfellows, nurturing what can be described as a creeping antagonization of Middle East politics (this is discussed in the first section below). In order to elaborate in greater detail on this argument the following section considers the main dynamics pertaining to the role of inclusion/exclusion in world society from a theoretical perspective. The next chapter considers the noteworthy centrality of inclusion/exclusion in the Middle East from an empirical angle. Two main dynamics are identified here. First, the frozen crossings previously discussed with regard to political communications range across a wide range of societal spheres thereby pointing to various distortions in code-oriented communications in the region. These extended frozen crossings are studied on the basis of the widely referred to 'crisis' of science and knowledge in the region. Second, these extended frozen crossings are accompanied by the relegation of specific groups of persons to either side of the inclusion/exclusion distinction across various societal spheres. As this chapter next elaborates , such chain exclusions can be well studied when addressing the status of women in the Middle East. The chapter concludes with a short discussion of the way in which the polycontextuality of world society relates to these dynamics. It argues that the world societal embedding of regional dynamics of inclusion/exclusion – in particular its embedding within the context of functional differentiation as world society's prime form of differentiation – provides the structural background for the antagonization of Middle East politics stemming from the simultaneous maintenance of frozen crossings and their constant thematization on the basis of the inclusion/exclusion paradigm.

Inclusion/exclusion and the creeping antagonization of Middle East politics

It is a widespread argument in Middle East studies that the exclusion of people from political, legal or economic participation is a powerful source of inequality, tensions and conflicts in the region.[14] Likewise, the ways in which certain normative frames and political orders, such as Zionism, Arabism, Islam and Judaism as well as other socio-cultural bonds and ethno-religious groups integrate (parts of) the populations of Middle East nation-states occupy an equally central place in the literature.[15] Yet, such approaches are primarily concerned with the (important) question of how specific organizations and groups (such as nation-states, religions, ethnicities, families and so on) regulate inclusion and exclusion via the form of membership/belonging, in other words by positively or negatively discriminating against people through assigning membership status to certain people and not to others.[16] This is, of course, not to deny the political salience and the grave societal costs associated with the generally strict and discriminatory patterns of inclusion/exclusion in the Middle East on which, for example, the Arab Human Development Reports and the Or commission have elaborated at great length with regard to Arab countries and Israel respectively. Notwithstanding the obvious empirical and theoretical relevance of such organizational dynamics of inclusion/exclusion, such a perspective is limited insofar as it fails to integrate these patterns of inclusion/exclusion into a wider communication-theoretical framework. More precisely, what is needed is a discussion on how the frozen crossings in political communications in and on the Middle East, which were identified in the previous chapter, affect the overall inclusion/exclusion dynamics in the region. In a nutshell, what needs to be addressed is the relationship between inclusion/exclusion, on the one hand, and functionally debordered political communications and functional differentiation as the prime form of differentiation in world society, on the other. This chapter argues that by complementing the manifold analyses on organizational dynamics of inclusion/exclusion in the Middle East with a systems-theoretical perspective on the communication-theoretical aspects of inclusion/exclusion, crucial insights can be gained into the dynamics of political communications in and on the Middle East, in general, and the antagonistic transformation of Middle East politics, in particular.

Initially, such a linkage between inclusion/exclusion and functional differentiation might seem problematic. The centrality of inclusion/exclusion in the Middle East might, at first sight, suggest that region-specific forms of solid stratification between persons rather than functional differentiation between social systems operates as the prime form of differentiation in the region. However, a closer inspection of the communicative dynamics of inclusion/exclusion in Middle East politics reveals that rather than undermining functional differentiation, the region-specific patterns of inclusion/exclusion actually sustain the pervasiveness of this form of differentiation in the region. In order to back up this argument, the ways in which inclusion/exclusion can be analysed from a communication theoretical perspective need briefly to be discussed. Thus, 'inclusion and exclusion ... point to the way psychic systems as persons are addressed or taken into consideration in the communication processes of social systems'.[17] And as Luhmann writes, 'inclusion occurs when within a social system a specific relevance of organic and psychic systems from the [social system's] environment is accepted in the form of "persons". We talk of exclusion in turn if a system presumes to be able to show indifference, ruthlessness or rejection against (socially constituted) persons.'[18] In other words, 'inclusion stands for communicative strategies of considering human beings as relevant. Inclusion is the social mechanism that constitutes human beings as accountable actors, as persons' within the context of system-specific communications.[19] Hence, when seen from a communication-theoretical perspective, the inclusion/exclusion of persons 'is not centring on the question whether individuals are part of society. They are not under any circumstances. The distinction inclusion/exclusion is a system-internal distinction which can only be used for ordering communications. But on this level it makes a difference whether persons are designated as relevant or not with regard to their participation. In the one case something depends on how they act and react; in the other case not.'[20] Having said this, it is important to note that communications in functional systems, such as, *inter alia*, politics, build on the structural expectation of full inclusion, that is, the structural expectation of a general relevance and addressability of all persons. The subsequent decision whether a person is regarded as relevant or not in concrete empirical manifestations is then regulated by system-specific operations and not by external, environmental considerations.[21] This postulate of full inclusion of all persons does not, therefore, contradict the obvious empirical occurrence of exclusions of and inequalities between persons. As Armin Nassehi explains, 'the postulate of access to all function systems is exclusively formulated on the issue-dimension, i.e. the issue-related distinction of functions is, from a functional perspective, insensitive towards forms of social inequality'.[22] Hence, the full inclusion of persons refers only to the structural expectation of a general addressability of all persons with regard to the issue-dimension of communications and not to the assumption of a formal equality between persons on the social dimension. Inclusion must not be mistaken for shared rights enjoyed by all people or the romanticist idea of a shared life-world unaffected by 'systemic rationality' but can, for example, also relate to inclusionary effects which firmly integrate conflict systems[23] or to discriminatory forms of inclusion (for example, the graduation of citizenship/social rights) within distinct societal spheres.

Notwithstanding this structural postulate of full inclusion, the continuous actualization of an inclusion of *all* persons at *all* times across *all* functional spheres is not possible – and neither is it necessary.[24] Exclusions are indeed a ubiquitous phenomenon in world society, but they are regularly balanced by both the simultaneous inclusion into other social spheres and the temporality of many forms of inclusion/exclusion. Accordingly, as single events, exclusions are most of the time unproblematic and might even remain unrecognized in ongoing communications. Moreover, the structural expectation of a full inclusion of all persons usually ensures the possibility of a crossing between inclusion and exclusion even within distinct functional settings. Against the background of the manifold different functional spheres and discourses in world society, what needs to be avoided is a perception of the distinction between inclusion/exclusion as a homogeneous and totalizing device. Thus, the inclusion/exclusion distinction needs to be adapted to the notion of a polycontextual, heterogeneous and internally highly differentiated world society. Warning against such totalizing perspectives, Luhmann accordingly maintains that 'every attempt to describe society with regard to a single distinction leads to a biased and unrealistic contrast. The difference between inclusion and exclusion is empirically never so clear that all persons can be attributed to one or the other side only.'[25] What matters is the observation that the inclusion/exclusion of persons is not regulated by society as a whole, but is decided autonomously through the self-referential communicative practices of each functional system.

Based on this notion of a polycontextual society, modern systems theory stresses the non-integrative character of inclusionary dynamics in world society.[26] Since the various forms of inclusion – that is, who is addressed as a person and in what ways – are decided by each functional system, the ties between inclusions across several functional spheres can be described as loose at best, and do not undermine the various interdependency interruptions which shape the relationship between different functional spheres.[27] For example, being addressed as a person in political communications (for example, as a voter, a president, a dissident, a terrorist or a freedom fighter) does not determine the forms of inclusion in, say, religious (a charismatic preacher, a believer, an infidel), economic (a customer, a debtor, an employer) or intimate (a lover, a friend) communications. It is on this basis that Luhmann has cautioned against any normative reading of the inclusion/exclusion distinction. Thus, any

> idealization of the postulate of full inclusion of all humans in society overplays grave problems. But this does not take salience from the issue. With functional differentiation of the societal system the decision of the relationship between inclusion and exclusion is transferred to the functional systems, and there is no central authority (as much as politics sees itself in this function), which supervises the subsystems accordingly.[28]

This is also the background to the observation that 'exclusion integrates to a much greater degree than inclusion' since permanent exclusions in one social sphere often extend to exclusions within other spheres as well.[29] Such structural (rather than loose) linkages between various forms of exclusion can be observed with regard to the exclusion of many Palestinian refugees from political participation in the Middle East and the effects this has on economic, legal, health-related and educational exclusions – and vice versa.[30] The problematic aspect is not the (temporary) exclusion of specific persons within one functional sphere – for example, politics – but stable chain exclusions across several functional spheres in which specific persons are for longer periods not considered relevant but might only be recognized as amorphous external perturbations, as moving bodies, passive objects or, ultimately, mere noise for ongoing communications. Without assuming a hierarchy between different functional systems, it is nevertheless fair to assume that politics occupies a particularly central place for the overall salience of inclusion/exclusion insofar as the function of politics to produce collectively binding decisions relies on the imagination (and addressability) of these collectives, that is, specific groups of persons, in the first place. As Nassehi explains, 'political power needs to produce visibilisations, social spaces of exclusive membership, internal/external borders' in order to uphold its functional specificities – and this includes the decision of who is addressed (and how) as a person belonging to a specific collective, and who is not.[31]

Against the background of a polycontextual world society it is somewhat surprising that Luhmann has repeatedly suggested that the (homogeneous) inclusion/exclusion distinction might replace functional differentiation as the prime form of (heterogeneous) differentiation in world society, at least in certain regions.[32] In that context, inclusion/ exclusion has been referred to as the 'prime form of differentiation' in the twenty-first century.[33] Thus, 'the variable inclusion/exclusion is in some world regions close to acquiring the role of a meta-difference and ... [mediating] the codes of the functional systems' and, at first sight, the Middle East seems to offer ample illustration for such an argument.[34] Following this understanding, the specific codes and functions of different societal spheres do not dissolve, but are increasingly mediated by inclusion/exclusion as the overarching distinction. Functional communications are overburdened by 'increasing expectation insecurity' which reduces the ability of different social systems to operate in a code-oriented manner and to convert to 'a continuous orientation at other factors' dictated by the totalizing effects of inclusion/ exclusion as the alleged new super-code.[35]

Yet, notwithstanding the obvious occurrence of grave forms of exclusion in world society, in general, and the Middle East, in particular, this assumption of a meta-difference is not really convincing. First, it is based on too static an understanding of inclusion/exclusion within the context of a polycontextual (world) society which no longer adheres to hereditary, life-long and stratificatory classifications of persons. This not only relates to the aforementioned polycontextual processing of inclusion/exclusion within and across various functional spheres, but also relates to more dramatic forms of systematic chain exclusions.[36] Following the communication-theoretical arguments already outlined in previous chapters, it becomes clear that 'even when exclusion spaces are territorially delimited, these are inner-societal spaces'.[37] Hence, favelas in Latin America, slums in the USA, cities next to abandoned coal mines in Wales, Palestinian refugee camps or isolated Palestinian villages surrounded by the separation fence/wall as well as impoverished Shi'i neighbourhoods in Lebanon necessarily are spaces generated by functionally debordered communications. This is also the background of Stichweh's observation that 'even if contact to function systems seems to be interrupted, the "parasites" of the function systems emerge, who nurture themselves from the unsolved problems of function systems, and reactivate for those persons living in exclusion spaces forms of contact ... to the functional systems'.[38] In other words, massively discriminatory chain exclusion of specific persons (and collectives) in the Middle East can, and indeed are, often thematized and scandalized by, say, religious communities, secular and pious political parties, artists, journalists, regional or global aid associations or, not least, Middle East researchers, thereby invoking the inclusion of persons into political and other functional discourses, paradoxically, by referring to these very chain exclusions. This paradoxical status of the inclusion/exclusion distinction, which Slavoj Žižek has translated into the catchy imperative 'include me out!/exclude me in!',[39] sustains the claim that notwithstanding the severity of chain exclusions, 'in modern society the differentiation principle is not based on the pattern of inclusion/exclusion; for this organizations are created (the nation-state is one such)'.[40] In other words, the inclusion/exclusion distinction is mediated by functional differentiation rather than the other way around. It seems, thus, more accurate to expect a paradoxical relationship between inclusion/exclusion, on the one hand, and functional differentiation, on the other, and to resort to a more compelling argument by Luhmann, namely that 'this difference between inclusion and exclusion has grave effects, because on the one hand it is triggered by functional differentiation of world society, while on the other hand it limits, if not prevents the regional production of the requirements for functional differentiation'.[41]

It might well be that these conceptual difficulties in reconciling the notion of functional differentiation as the prime form of differentiation in world society with the relevance of massive forms of inclusion/exclusion in the Middle East and other regions result from some avoidable contradictions in modern systems theory. Thus, the predominant understanding of inclusion/exclusion as the addressability and attribution of societal relevance to persons within functional discourses is indeed somewhat limited. As the aforementioned examples of polycontextual and paradoxical inclusion and exclusion dynamics reveal, excluded persons are often – albeit not always – directly addressed and considered relevant within and beyond the functional contexts which produce exclusion in the first place. Therefore, inclusion/exclusion does not necessarily refer to the overall issue of 'recognition' versus 'non-recognition', as most systems-theoretical accounts tend to emphasize, but rather to the ways through which, say, political communications relegate persons to demarcated, recognizable and *communicatively designated* spaces of exclusion. Such a perspective directs attention towards the dynamics which shape the inclusion in as well as the exclusion from communication possibilities in political and other functional communications – and this means in particular the mechanisms through which functional communications ensure that persons can, at least potentially, easily cross the borders between inclusion/exclusion, in general, and between the positive and the negative sides of all code-oriented communications, in particular.[42] It is precisely on this level that the close linkages between inclusion/exclusion and the frozen crossings in political communications in and on the Middle East, which were identified in the previous chapter, come to the fore. Inclusion then refers to the (relatively) stable relegation of specific persons to the 'positive'[43] side of the border, for example, the side of power in political communications, while exclusion refers to the relegation of specific (other) persons to the other side, that is, powerlessness. Such dynamics are, of course, aggravated by the extension of frozen crossings across various functional spheres, that is, those cases in which specific persons profit from the performances of different functional spheres (for example, education, rights, wealth, power),[44] while others hardly have access to these 'positive' performances of functional systems at all.

Consequently, it can be argued that it is the function of visibilizing (extended) frozen crossings which gives the distinction between inclusion/exclusion its particular relevance within a functionally differentiated (world) society. By thematizing frozen crossings in one or across several functional spheres, this distinction continuously directs attention towards the problematic relegation of relatively stable and fixed patterns of inclusion and exclusion to specific persons which run counter to the structural 'blindness' of social systems vis-à-vis persons on the issue-dimension. Moreover, by inhibiting this structural expectation of a full inclusion of all persons, these dynamics distort the potential to cross the borders between power/powerlessness in a quasi-technical manner, thereby pointing to distortions in code-oriented communications. Consequently, the distinction between inclusion and exclusion actually reinscribes functional differentiation into societal settings in which this form of differentiation is, for whatever reason, prevented from operating properly.[45] In systems-theoretical parlance it can, therefore, be argued that inclusion/exclusion functions as the second-order observation of (extended) frozen crossings insofar as it is the form through which observers observe how frozen crossings become established and maintained in political (and other functional) communications.[46] Second-order observations on frozen crossings, thus, relate to those mechanisms in political communications which enable a 'process of concentration on one medium of first-order observations', for example, how the distribution of power is regulated in the region.[47] As a result, by observing frozen crossings through the second-order lenses of inclusion/exclusion, the permanent relegation of persons to either side of the distinction can be systematically observed as a contingent rather than a 'natural' selection. Thus, while political communications in and on the Middle East often tend to observe (operate) on the basis of the distinctions established by frozen crossings, the two sides do not constitute separate, stratified entities which are quasi-ontologically given and presupposed in communication. In sum, inclusion/exclusion is the form through which (political) communications observe the tension between frozen crossings, on the one hand, and the structural expectation of full inclusion and quasi-automatic crossings in political and other functional communications, on the other. Through this, the form of inclusion/exclusion visibilizes the contingency of all political orders in the Middle East, thereby preventing their uncontested reification even in the context of conflict-laden political dynamics and often autocratic political orders, which forcefully sustain the manifold frozen crossings in political communications in and on the region.

The particular significance of inclusion/exclusion lies in its function to 'remind' political communications in and on the Middle East of the structural expectation of the full inclusion postulate of all code-specific communications and the subsequent *problematique* of permanently relegating specific persons to one or the other side of the inclusion/ exclusion distinction (for example, with regard to distinctions such as gender, ethnicity, religion, governmental/oppositional roles and so on). Note again that this does not mean that the 'exclusion prohibition of functional systems' requires the actual implementation of inclusion of all persons at all times.[48] While '*every* functional system reflects on the inclusion of *all* individuals', exclusions are a necessary side-effect of actualized inclusions and, as long as they do not result in chain exclusions or the establishment of frozen crossings, they are relatively unproblematic.[49] And, it is in that sense, that 'functional systems, then, are universalizing devices, trying to ignore particular identities'.[50] Of course, in the context of the actual operations of politics and other functional systems, inclusions and exclusions are permanently produced, but this remains acceptable as long as inclusion/exclusion 'cannot be reduced to something like a hereditary property' of specific persons.[51] This is, however, what happens in the context of (extended) frozen crossings in the Middle East which directly contradict the presupposition of each functional system that 'the population is a homogenous [sic] environment which can only be discriminated against according to its own criteria'.[52]

It is, thus, not merely the relegation of specific persons to either side of the inclusion/exclusion distinction – in other words specific first-order operations of (Middle East) politics – which fosters the creeping antagonization of (Middle East) politics. What is equally required is a communicative device which ensures the ongoing observation of how frozen crossings are constructed and upheld in (political) communications.[53] The function of inclusion/exclusion in providing a form of second-order observation of Middle East politics – that is, observations in the form of Žižek's postulate that the excluded is included, while the included is excluded – renders all attempts to attribute permanent, stratificatory and quasi-hereditary status to either the inclusion or the exclusion of specific persons within and across various functional spheres an ultimately hopeless endeavour. It is in that sense that 'the second-order observation changes everything'.[54] It 'transforms latency into contingency'.[55] It even 'transforms what is observed by first-order observations. Thus, it modalises everything that seems to be given and gives it the form of contingency, of being-possible-in-another way' – at least in terms of a potential horizon of alternatives.[56] It is this structural contingency-awareness which ultimately motivates opposition to relegation to the excluded side of the distinction. Hence, this structural 'release of possibilities' in functionally differentiated communications prevents the observation of specific political orders as given and allows social systems to observe how orders are upheld through specific – yet contingent – distinctions, which could always be otherwise.[57] While such second-order observations are a structural characteristic of all social systems, they do not usually amount to an antagonistic transformation of specific functional spheres as long as functional operations are able to reflect and to experiment with 'more possibilities than those which have been designated',[58] *inter alia*, by resorting to the possibilities offered by the full inclusion postulate. This, however, changes in a setting of frozen crossings. Being based on the structural expectation of the inclusion of specific persons and the systematic exclusion of other (specified) persons, Middle East politics are overburdened by upholding frozen crossings against the functional prerequisites of politics as a globally debordered functional system which is able to observe the contingency of its own distinctions.

It is for this reason that inclusion/exclusion cannot be understood as an overarching super-code of (some regions of) world society, as occasionally implied by Luhmann. It rather has a specific purpose within a functionally differentiated world society, namely to visibilize the contingency of frozen crossings and to warn of distortions in the regular operation of code-specific communications. Moreover, since these crossings are often upheld, the thematization of inclusion/exclusion does not merely evaporate but nurtures an antagonistic transformation of Middle East politics. The arguments in this section should not be seen as downplaying the societal relevance and discriminatory practices of the ways in which the inclusion/exclusion distinction permeates Middle East politics. As Stichweh has argued, a communication-theoretical perspective 'does not relativize the (empirical) sincerity of this distinction. But it emphasizes the reversibility of situations', even in situations of frozen crossings.[59] It is in this sense that the essentialization of inclusion/exclusion in the Middle East, that is, the relegation of specific persons to either side of the border, shapes the 'identity' of regional politics. Thus, both the contingency of frozen crossings upheld in political communications and the ways in which these frozen crossings contradict the basic features of globally debordered functional communications are re-inscribed into Middle East politics by means of the inclusion/exclusion distinction. Inclusion/exclusion might, therefore, not be an overarching meta-code in the Middle East but it nevertheless engenders the antagonistic 'identity' of regional politics by remembering the contingency of this distinction.[60]

Another Middle East mosaic: extended frozen crossings and chain exclusions

On the basis of these theoretical clarifications on the relationship between frozen crossings, functional differentiation and the inclusion/exclusion paradigm, this section addresses in greater empirical detail the ways in which patterns of inclusion/exclusion affect the Middle East. The key argument unfolded here is that the pervasiveness of inclusion/exclusion as a central mode of (second-order) observations within and across various functional spheres nurtures the centrality of identity-related and conflictive forms of political (and other functional) communications in and on the Middle East, understood here as the creeping antagonization of Middle East politics. Thus, the form of inclusion/exclusion provides the mechanism through which society is able systematically to observe the contingency of frozen crossings within and across various functional spheres, without, however, having the ability simply to change these dynamics. This reach of frozen crossings across a variety of societal spheres is referred to here as 'extended frozen crossings'. While Chapter 5 addresses in greater detail the relationship between this antagonization of Middle East politics stemming from the crisis of politics and other societal spheres as identified here and in the previous chapter and the centrality of 'identity' and 'conflict' in regional (political) communications, the remainder of this chapter focuses on how the communication-theoretical prerequisites of such an antagonization play out in regional politics. Briefly, it argues that the centrality of inclusion/exclusion as a key form through which functional systems observe themselves in system-specific communications in and on the Middle East, 'perturbate' – rather than reify – the regional distortion of political and other code-oriented communications. What can be identified is an 'ironic twist' of the inclusion/exclusion paradigm, insofar as what appears at first sight as an awkward primacy of various forms of social stratification in the region along inclusionary/exclusionary identity-lines (for example, religion, culture, ethnicity, gender, nation, family, tribe and so on) at closer inspection firmly underlines the pervasiveness of functional differentiation as the prime form of differentiation in the Middle East – and world society at large.

The analysis of this 'ironic twist' proceeds in three steps. First, by addressing the often referred to 'crisis of science/knowledge' in the region, the following paragraphs focus on the extension of frozen crossings beyond the sphere of political communications. Second, by drawing from the discussion on gender inequalities in the Middle East, the subsequent part looks at how these *extended* frozen crossings are accompanied by the relegation of specific groups of persons to either side of system-specific distinctions, thereby overburdening political (and other functional) communications with the constant upholding of frozen crossings and the subsequent chain inclusions/exclusions of specific groups of persons across various functional spheres. The third step concludes the chapter, with an examination of the relationship between these dynamics of inclusion/exclusion, on the one hand, and the polycontextuality of a functionally differentiated (world) society, on the other. It argues that the observation of extended frozen crossings through the prism of inclusion/exclusion constantly challenges the regional distortions in code-oriented communications, thereby undermining all attempts to reify the unequal distribution of power, knowledge and other 'resources' in the Middle East along seemingly stable identity-lines. By doing so, the form of inclusion/exclusion as the second-order observation of (extended) frozen crossings provides the basis for the creeping antagonization of Middle East politics. More precisely, the overall context of a functionally differentiated world society ensures that region-specific exclusions within and across different functional spheres must be processed on the basis of the full inclusion postulate, thereby constantly undermining the reification of chain inclusions/ exclusions within these spheres. As a word of caution it should be emphasized here that what might appear as a naive empowerment of the powerless (and a disempowerment of the powerful) must not be mistaken for an (apolitical) relativism with regard to the concrete manifestations of frozen crossings and unequal power (wealth, knowledge and so on) distributions in the region. On the contrary, as will be further outlined in Chapter 5, the confrontation between frozen crossings and the inclusion/exclusion paradigm does not lead to a gradual abolition of frozen crossings, but rather shapes the subtle transformation and replacement of politics by antagonistic, relatively stable and highly integrative conflict dynamics.

Reference to 'crises' in the Middle East, in general, and Middle East politics, in particular, is common in countless policy documents and academic writings on the region. While the previous chapter has already alluded to the crisis of Middle East politics, this and the following paragraphs take a closer look at the noteworthy centrality in perceptions of the region of 'crises' across a variety of (functional) contexts. To take a few examples, scholars and policymakers have identified, *inter alia*, 'crises' of law, science, education, media, knowledge, politics, security, citizenship, identity, human rights, economy and, more generally, human development in the Middle East.[61] This is not the place to embark on the nuances – and the individual accuracy – of each of these manifold perceptions of crisis, nor critically to deconstruct the political interests and (hegemonic) discourses which might occasionally shape such diagnoses. Rather, what is of interest here is that when observed from a comparative and communication-theoretical perspective many of these crisis-perceptions centre on key features which have been highlighted in this and the previous chapter with regard to the dynamics of inclusion/exclusion, in general, and region-specific forms of political communications, in particular. More precisely, such crisis perceptions address, in one way or the other, specific dynamics of (functional) communications, particularly those dynamics which impede the quasi-technical crossing between the two sides of code-specific distinctions. For example, scholars focusing on the role of *shari'a* law in many Arab countries have addressed the fundamentally static character of *contemporary* mainstream understandings of Islamic law. What was once a tradition of interpretation of Islamic law has given way to a practice which, in its present mainstream outlook, regards *shari'a* law as a monolithic 'existing body of holy law' which must directly and without any further interpretation 'be applied to contemporary society and contemporary politics',[62] thereby severely hampering the ability of legal communications to oscillate between both sides of the distinction legal/not-legal.[63] This 'distortion'[64] in legal communications, which could be enriched by accounts of similar distortions from various other functional spheres, is accompanied by the notorious tendency of various functional communications to relegate specific persons to either side of the distinction.[65] To draw once more from the example of law, the debate on citizenship rights and the status of human rights in the Middle East has persuasively shown that notwithstanding the fundamental differences between legal systems in the region – which run the whole spectrum from rule-of-law states such as Israel to highly autocratic legal orders such as Syria – legal systems throughout the region tend massively to favour specific groups of persons (for example, dominant ethnic/religious groups, men) at the expense of others (secondary ethnic/religious groups, women).[66]

Despite the significant differences between political, legal and economic orders in the region and notwithstanding the obvious importance of acknowledging heterogeneity and pluralism in the Middle East, there is indeed some indication that the perception of 'crises' across various societal spheres in the region has more to it than merely an alarmist or conspiratorial appeal. When related to what has been said above on the main dynamics of inclusion/exclusion in a functionally differentiated world society, it is noticeable that such perceptions of 'crisis' centre, first, on distortions in code-oriented communications and, second, on the relegation (and essentialization) of specific groups of persons to either side of the distinction of the borders demarcated by these codes. In other words, (functional) communications are hampered by the lack or weakness of programmes which facilitate the quasi-technical crossing between codes and ensure the pervasiveness of the full inclusion postulate. Ultimately, these dynamics prevent a more successful (temporary) invisibilization of the founding paradoxes of (political, legal, religious, economic and so on) orders in the Middle East. As a result, the frozen crossings identified in the previous chapter with regard to political communications reach out to other societal spheres and the perception of 'crisis' becomes the semantic form through which functional systems observe these *extended* frozen crossings. To reiterate what has been said above, this argument does not mean that there are no successful strategies of deparadoxification or attempts to facilitate crossing and ensure the potentiality of inclusion across various functional spheres in the region.[67] However, the intensity with which distortions in code-oriented communications, on the one hand, and the relegation of specific groups of persons to either side of the distinction, on the other, are addressed with regard to various societal contexts, underline the significance of frozen crossings in the Middle East beyond the sphere of politics.

Seen from that perspective, the invocation of 'crises' is not necessarily a sinister conspiracy aimed at de-legitimizing 'Islam', 'Arabness' or

'Zionism' and the specific political, legal and societal projects (for example, a Muslim or Jewish state) associated with these labels by a hegemonic Western agenda from either leftist or rightist, democratic or neo-liberal outlooks. From the perspective of the theoretical arguments unfolded above, the ingredients of 'crisis' (distortion/relegation) do indeed closely correspond with the main theoretical features of inclusion/exclusion. They point to a shared system(at)ic underpinning of these various regional phenomena, and 'crisis' then just becomes another word for the ability of functional systems to observe problems in both code-oriented communications and in the application of the full inclusion postulate. By doing so, the inclusion/exclusion paradigm, as highlighted above, operates as a second-order observation which constantly visibilizes and problematizes frozen crossings across various societal spheres. It is precisely by constantly drawing attention to the contingent status of frozen crossings that the inclusion/exclusion paradigm – or semantic forms such as 'crisis' which derive from this distinction – undermines the static (political, legal, religious and so on) orders emanating from (extended) frozen crossings. Consequently, notwithstanding the seeming solidity of (extended) frozen crossings in many societal spheres in the region, the world societal horizon of all communications in and on the Middle East structurally ensures that these orders clash with rather than replace functional differentiation as the prime form of differentiation in world society – and it is precisely on this dimension that the antagonization of Middle East politics gains shape. It would, of course, be tempting to elaborate on this argument in great empirical detail across a variety of (functional) contexts. However, for the narrower purpose of this study, it suffices to illustrate the ramifications of these dynamics with some more illustrations from the widespread arguments on a scientific/educational 'crisis' in the Middle East. Such a communication-theoretical perspective then allows us to address the role of 'crises' as part of the overall antagonization of Middle East politics without resorting to untenable culturalist assumptions on Middle Eastern (Muslim, Arab, Jewish and so on) exceptionalism.

Re-reading the 'crisis' of education in the Middle East

The observation of a 'crisis' of education, knowledge and science in the Middle East has enjoyed particular currency since the publication of the 2003 Arab Human Development Report on 'Building a Knowledge Society' under the auspices of the United Nations Development Programme (UNDP) and the Arab Fund for Economic and Social

Development.[68] The report argues that in Arab countries the educational system, in general, and science, in particular, suffers from a 'dual crisis', namely 'restrictions emanating from its social context'; these are, on the one hand, 'rooted constructs, concepts and precepts [which] may hinder human development', and a dispersion of chances for education/knowledge 'in various individual and non-formal forms', on the other.[69] The 'restrictions' relate to structural problems in knowledge generation, such as, *inter alia*, traditional practices of education which focus on the memorization of 'books containing undisputable texts in which knowledge is objectified so as to hold incontestable facts' or other forms of minimizing any critical engagement with existing knowledge in classrooms and seminars.[70] 'Restrictions' further comprise a dramatic scarcity of access to information media, and the report refers, for example, to the remarkably low number of newspapers/computers in the region in comparison to other world regions, to the overall 'narrative and descriptive' approach to news in television reporting, which does not 'place events in the general social, economic and cultural context',[71] and to the stunning negligence towards book printing (linked to low readership, problems of infrastructure and censorship) and translation – with the total number of books translated into Arabic since the Al-Ma'moun era of the ninth century until today amounting to 10,000 books, 'equivalent to what Spain translates in one year'.[72] As a result of these inward-looking and self-referential dynamics, the report maintains that Arab countries suffer from an overall uncritical engagement with knowledge. In sum, the report concludes, these dynamics affect the ability critically to address and contextualize Arab history and society by emphasizing an alleged ' "specificity" of Arab societies', while fostering the 'neglect of everything that is not "related to our reality"'.[73]

Without further embarking on an exegesis of this widely cited report,[74] what is interesting to note is that this analysis – with different terminology – closely resembles the features of distortions and relegation dynamics of code-oriented (scientific) communications which were addressed in the first part of this chapter. Thus, what the report refers to as 'restrictions', closely resembles the problem of 'distortion' of code-oriented communications insofar as the overall effect of such restrictions – whether in the form of a politicization or ideologization of knowledge, in which a specific political, religious or cultural project is regarded as undisputable 'truth'[75] – is to impede the quasi-technical crossing in scientific and other knowledge-related communications between the two sides of the distinction true/false. To avoid misunderstandings, it should be briefly noted that this distinction between true/false is not a back-door re-introduction of ontological (and hegemonic) notions of specific truths (and non-truths). It merely refers to the process of connectivity between those communications which observe themselves as scientific communications, thereby enabling the differentiation of science as a distinct social system. It is, hence, not about a 'pre-scientific understanding of truth'; Luhmann subsequently emphasizes that 'the (autopoietically reproduced) *unity* of the [science] system is located in the difference between true and not-true (and not simply in [specific] knowledge)'.[76] Thus, truth as a generalized medium of communication is an ' "institutionalized label" ' for the processing of scientific communications, in the same way as 'power' operates as the generalized medium of communication in politics.[77] What matters is not to fall victim to a mystification of knowledge by merely focusing on the positive side of the distinction. While it is true [sic] that the positive side (truth) is required for both the differentiation of science as a functional system in world society and for the subsequent connectivity of those communications which observe themselves on the basis of the distinction true/false, the negative side of the distinction (non-truth) maintains its paramount importance by ensuring contingency reflection and environmental openness of the system. This relationship between the two sides of the distinction (and specific scientific programmes, that is, theories and methodologies that facilitate – or at least do not severely hamper – the oscillation between both sides) not only serves the purpose of continuously creating 'new, unfamiliar, surprising knowledge'[78] but also nurtures the constant 'change of existing knowledge structures' inherent in the evolution of scientific communications.[79] Of course, as is the case with regard to all code-oriented communications, the relationship between both sides of the distinction is asymmetric insofar as connectivity (and, therefore, the evolution of specific social systems such as politics and science) is ensured by the positive side of the code – and that is 'why science is not searching for and producing new and surprising knowledge for its own sake, but in order to suppress it immediately by transforming it into expectable knowledge'.[80] In sum, from the perspective of the code it does not matter whether a specific knowledge is (is observed as) true or not-true, but rather that 'in order to gain a world [sic] with the help of the code, truth and non-truth must initially be treated as strictly equal so that order becomes possible and even expectable' – and contingency reflection remains simultaneously possible.[81]

It is precisely on this level of powerful impediments to the crossing between both sides of the distinction that the 'crisis' of science/knowledge in the Middle East gains its basic contours. These distortions in code-oriented communications relate to two main dimensions. First, as an editorial in *as-sharq al-awsat* has argued, the 'educational crisis in the Arab world' relates to those 'diseases of memorization and repetition, as well as the abolition of skills of critical thinking' which were highlighted by the AHDR.[82] The effect of this celebration of tradition is 'intolerance and the culture of fanaticism, which causes one to view that he is the righteous one and that everybody else is wrong. Such a culture does not establish the concept of cultural pluralism and does not spread the idea of diversity in the faces of truth.'[83] In other words, powerful concepts such as 'culture', 'nation' or 'religion' serve as severe impediments to the ability of scientific communications to oscillate between both sides of the distinction in order to generate knowledge. Second, many authors have pointed to an overt ideologization and politicization of scientific and other knowledge-related communications in and on the Middle East. Salah Al-Mahadin has consequently argued that notwithstanding the partial liberalization and spread of information technology in Jordan, the frozen crossings in scientific communications remain solid due to ' "normative practices" in the field of education [which] have failed to recommend proper courses of actions due to their failure to address causes and uncover context-based political praxis'.[84] In other words, deeply entrenched programmes serve as a 'hidden context' which severely hampers the easy crossing between both sides of the distinction by equating a specific (for example, political) project with truth, such as in this case the Hashemitization of history, politics, religion and culture in Jordan. It is on the basis of such observations of frozen crossings in scientific communications in and on the Middle East that Mamoun Fandy has argued that 'the crisis of education in the Muslim world is not primarily one of infrastructure – a hardware problem – but lies in "software": what is being taught, how it is being taught and the people who are teaching it'.[85] Notwithstanding the political objectives which might at times accompany such general analyses, detailed empirical investigations tend to converge with this overall assessment. To pick again the case of Jordan, the work by Yitzhak Reiter on affirmative action policies, by Betty S. Anderson on school textbooks and by Salah Al-Mahadin on gender-related issues in pedagogy all point to the impact of this Hashemitization of scientific narratives and about what is able to serve as 'truth' – and how (alternative) perspectives which challenge this narrative are severely hampered by these practices even in a relatively liberal state in the region.[86]

Such impediments with regard to scientific communications in and on the Middle East do not, of course, only occur in Jordan or even in the more monolithic states in the region. Frozen crossings relate more generally to all those instances in which scientific communications are based on 'unquestionable' truths, thereby preventing or inhibiting the 'discovery' of new and surprising knowledge. Edward Said's underlying notions of 'Orientalism' form the unquestioned subtext of many analyses of Middle East politics and society; the effect of such assumptions of 'the "specificity" of Arab societies'[87] informs (and limits) not only many 'internal' but also many 'external' perspectives on the region. It is beyond the scope of this chapter to discuss the degree to which Said's deconstruction of Western 'images' of the Middle East falls into the trap of depending on the reification of 'Orient' and 'Occident' in the first place. What matters here, however, is the observation that the distortion of code-oriented communications relates in particular to (overt and covert) ontologies of truth which hamper the oscillation between both sides of the distinctions. Consequently, frozen crossings in scientific communications in and on the Middle East are not restricted to autocratic states but affect 'Western' academia as well. It is on this basis that the vigorous debate in Israel surrounding the research by the so-called New Historians and Critical Sociologists provides another insightful example. In a nutshell, this debate centres around the attempts by some (mainly Israeli) historians and sociologists to challenge allegedly unquestioned 'truths' in Israeli social science and humanities, in particular those relating to the more problematic aspects in the history of the Zionist movement, the Yishuv administration and the State of Israel. In the wake of this debate, scholars have questioned the traditional Zionist narratives surrounding, *inter alia*, the war of 1948 and the reasons for the expulsion of the Palestinian population from the territories of what later became Israel (in particular the question of whether large parts of the Palestinian population were forcefully expelled by the Jewish forces, including the occurrence of massacres against civilians); the overall assessment of the settlement of Jews in Palestine in the late nineteenth and early twentieth centuries (and whether it can be described as colonialism); or the reasons behind the lasting confrontation between Israel and her Arab neighbours since 1948 (whether the reasons lie in the Arab states' unwillingness to recognize Israel or in Israel's strategically, ideologically or psychologically motivated recourse to force).[88]

As Chaim Waxmann points out with a view to the work of the New Historians, it is not only the accuracy of their respective claims (and the many counter-claims) which deserves attention, since 'for anyone other than a historian, that need not be an issue of major significance'.[89] What is equally interesting is the 'vehement acrimony' with which supporters and opponents have engaged in the debate.[90] As Eliezer Ben Rafael has observed, this controversy has from the outset been accompanied by an 'ideological-political crusade' based on a 'personalized strategy of stigmatization' which 'contradicts any notion of science ethics'.[91] What could have been a refreshing academic debate has developed into 'acrimony and aggressivity between participants [who] have made their argumentation a genuine contention that could not be confined *within the limits* of academic debate'.[92] From the perspective of this chapter it is interesting to note that such references to transgressions from regular scientific communications in the debate on the work of the New Historians and the Critical Sociologists centre around the accusation (and the counter-accusation) that the other side is not primarily interested in the discovery of a (new) scientific truth but rather in the conservation (or the propagation) of a specific ideological programme, namely the conservation of Zionist academia or the propagation of post-Zionist science.[93] Moshe Lissak, a critic of Critical Sociology, has summarized the agenda of the so-called post-Zionists thus: 'according to their claim, the "establishment" sociologists are captive to the "Zionist dream" woven by the founding fathers' and the Zionist programme has nurtured research on Jewish/Israeli history and politics to the extent that scientific truths had to correspond with the ideological fundaments of this political project, for example by claiming a unique specificity of Israeli/Jewish history and politics.[94] Tania Forte confirms in an analysis of Israeli academia that notions of state security indeed 'inform the production of social scientific research and researchers'.[95] This claim has been highlighted in the context of the trial of Teddy Katz, a postgraduate student of Haifa University who wrote his master's thesis on the expulsion of Palestinians in the city of Tantura in the Southern Mount Carmel region in the war of 1948. Katz based his main argument, namely that there was a systematic massacre by the Jewish Alexandroni brigade of 200 unarmed Palestinian villagers in Tantura, on oral testimonies by both former members of the Alexandroni brigade and Palestinians present in Tantura in 1948. After the 'news' of the massacre was reported by the daily *Ma'ariv* in January 2000,[96] Katz was sued for libel by veterans of the brigade. At the subsequent trial some inconsistencies in six individual references – out of a total of 230 – held by Katz were discovered and, as Ilan Pappé claims, as a result of grave health problems and pressure from his family and lawyers, Katz repudiated the results of his research.

Although Katz wanted to retract this repudiation the day after its announcement, the case was made (and transferred to the Israeli Supreme Court in order to assess whether Katz's second retraction was lawful or not – the Court decided that the initial retraction was indeed binding[97]) with media presenting the results of the research as 'fabricated' and Haifa university opening a formal procedure to strip Katz of his title – while according to Pappé the scientific errors in the thesis related only to minor inconsistencies which neither affected the academic quality nor the overall argument.[98] Pappé consequently identified two main consequences of this trial which serve to underline the reach (and perception) of distortions in code-oriented communications operating within comparably ideologized research programmes. First, the trial 'indirectly preempted future research on 1948 that does not subscribe to Zionist ideology by giving future scholars reason to worry about the legal consequences of taking on the struggle over the past'; and second, based on the arguments brought against Katz in academic debates, 'one can assume that the Jewish academic establishment will continue to prevent the legitimization of oral history for 1948', thereby favouring the study of official army documents (which tend not to contain references to massacres) at the expense of testimonies by eye witnesses (which often do so).[99]

Of course, the post-Zionist narratives met with fierce criticism as soon as they emerged.[100] Lissak continued his statement above: 'perhaps there are such researchers who are captive to this [Zionist] dream, but there are also those who are captive to the dream of those who are *alien* to Israeli society', and many scholars have referred to the ideological underpinnings which inform the post-Zionist narratives of colonialism, ethnic cleansing and apartheid structures in Israel.[101] From a similar perspective, Neill Lochery has criticized the fact that in their quest for establishing new counter-narratives, many of the New Historians' works 'fall into the category of not being pure scholarship, but neither pure pieces of propaganda. However, in terms of balance many of them veer towards being works in which propaganda for a particular side or point of view appears to be the central focus.'[102] Regular calls for a boycott against Israeli scholars, as they have for example re-emerged in the United Kingdom in recent years, further underline the extent to which scientific communications in and on the Middle East are subject to the dynamics of frozen crossings in which the distributions of specific 'truths' or people to either side of the distinction impedes the quasi-technical crossing (and experimentation) with code-oriented communications.[103] To reiterate, this argument is not about the empirical or theoretical accuracy of specific claims in this debate but rather concerns the observation that labels such as Zionist/post-Zionist, left/right, critical/traditional or pro-Israeli/anti-Semitic (or Western/Muslim, Oriental/Occidental, Palestinian/Israeli for that matter) are regularly referred to in debates on Israeli (and Middle East) history and politics in the social sciences and humanities in order to de-legitimize (rather than opposing) specific empirical or theoretical results, thereby severely impeding the quasi-technical crossing in scientific and other knowledge-related communications in and on the Middle East.[104] In this case the difference between these labels does not only relate to their opposing claims but to the unity of these distinction, that is, the dependence of the one side of the distinction on the (marked or unmarked) presence of the excluded other. Herein lies the relationship between the entrapment in such discursive frames, on the one hand, and frozen crossings in scientific communications, on the other. While it might be somewhat exaggerated to see these developments amounting to a 'threat to academic freedom in Israel/Palestine'[105] or being 'part of the broader political war against Israel's legitimacy as a sovereign Jewish state',[106] the occurrence of such distortions in scientific communications in Israel (as well as other democratic countries) nevertheless underlines the world societal context of frozen crossings in various code-oriented communications beyond the case of autocratic Arab countries.

Women, men and the Middle East

Any analysis of 'crises' across various societal spheres would be incomplete if it were only to focus on such distortions in code-oriented communications. In accordance with the two parameters of the inclusion/exclusion paradigm identified above, these distortions are accompanied by the relegation of *specific* groups of persons to either side of the distinctions established by frozen crossings across a variety of functional contexts. Such *chain exclusions* have been well documented in the literature. To take a couple of examples – again from science and education – Yitzhak Reiter has elaborated in detail on how state policies in Jordan geared for an 'academization' of the tribal/Transjordanian population in the kingdom, 'contributed to the exclusion of Jordanians from a Palestinian origin from various public sectors and services including education'.[107] Other examples include the way in which state policies in the educational sector in Israel contribute to the demarcation between specific identity groups (such as Jews versus Arabs, but also Ashkenazi Jews versus Mizrahim) and how these demarcations affect and consolidate the inclusion and exclusion of these identity-groups across a wide range of societal spheres, be it academia itself, the labour market, the legal system or national politics.[108] Such relegations are also widely addressed with regard to the chain exclusions (and inclusions) of other identity-groups in the region, whether with regard to the role of women, the status of the Palestinian population in many Middle East countries, the traditional standing of the Shi'i population in Lebanon, parts of the rural population in Jordan or Syria and many other examples. Against this background of massive relegation dynamics in the region it hardly comes as a surprise that not only the AHDR and international reports but also human development plans from Middle East governments regularly stress the need to overcome these massive forms of 'inequality' which fit uneasily with the full inclusion postulate of (functional) communications.

In more theoretical terms, the effect of such relegation dynamics is that communications across various societal spheres not only demarcate specific groups of people but also privilege one side at the expense of the other, thereby firmly introducing a status quo-oriented asymmetry on the identity-dimension which contradicts the full inclusion postulate.[109] The crucial point here, however, is that these extended frozen crossings do not lead to a re-differentiation of society along these identity lines. Thus, in contrast to many studies on Middle East politics which base their analysis of Middle East exceptionalism on an alleged primacy of identity-related features in the region, a more systematic focus on the communicative underpinnings of the inclusion/exclusion paradigm shows that rather than undermining functional differentiation as the prime form of differentiation in world society, these regional patterns of inclusion/exclusion allow us to observe extended frozen crossings as a problem in ensuring the full inclusion postulate, thereby firmly re-inscribing functional differentiation into all regional communications. It is only due to these linkages between inclusion/exclusion, identity politics and functional differentiation that 'inequalities' on the identity-dimension can actually be understood as a 'problem' rather than a given (and more or less unchangeable) form of distinction in the Middle East.

This line of argument can well be exemplified on the basis of a discussion of the massive gender inequalities in the Middle East. The (extended) frozen crossings that affect the status of men and women in the Middle East reveal how inclusion/exclusion dynamics on the gender-dimension engender this distinction while simultaneously contextualizing the female/male dichotomy within the overriding context of functional differentiation.[110] Thus, despite the pervasiveness of gender distinctions (and other identity-related distinctions) across a variety of societal contexts in the Middle East and notwithstanding the impact these (and other) distinctions have in sustaining the continuous antagonization of Middle East politics, they lack systemic properties. In systems-theoretical parlance, while extended frozen crossings in the Middle East do consolidate the relegation of specific groups of people to either side of the distinction across a variety of societal spheres, the two sides of identity-related distinctions (for example, female/male, Jewish/Arab and so on) do not possess the properties of systemic (binary) distinctions in which there would be an inherent (communicational) asymmetry between both sides (with one side constituting the positive side, the other one the negative side) and in which connectivity between communications would occur on the positive side only while crossing between both sides would always be conceivable. Or, to put it in less abstract terms, distinctions such as male/female, outsider/insider, Israeli/Palestinian, Arab/Western and so on do indeed possess considerable societal leverage, but do not lead to the establishment of 'male', 'female', 'Israeli' or 'Arab' communicative systems. All these categories gain their societal relevance not from their alleged primordial status, but rather from the very fact that they remain firmly embedded in political (and other functional) discursive contexts.

Turning to the societal relevance of the gender distinction in the Middle East, this observation closely relates to Salah Al-Mahadin's critique of 'disciplined gender politics' on the basis of which both international developmental agencies and the Jordanian government aim to tackle the inequality between women and men in the Jordanian educational system. She argues that the impact of such programmes cannot be measured only by increasing numbers of women participating in the educational system so long as the subtle linkages between gender politics and political praxis remain the blind spot of these programmes.[111] As Deniz Kandiyoti has argued in a related context, women 'can work and inhabit the public arena, as long as it does not conflict with the social concepts of masculinity or femininity'.[112] It is on this basis, that Al-Mahadin criticizes the apolitical approach of the 2005 AHDR on 'Towards the Rise of Women in the Arab World'. Thus,

> traditional indices of gender in education as manifested by this report mask the importance of context and the dynamics of political and social practices that are sometimes obscured by figures, over-simplifications and unquestioned notions pertaining to the semiotics of what is generally referred to as 'freedom', 'knowledge', 'equality' and 'good governance.'[113]

While such reports acknowledge (and observe) the relegation of men and women to either side of the distinction, they often fail to overcome the problem of (extended) frozen crossings in regional politics, since 'they do not necessarily reflect any shift in the underlying balance of power which has vested interest[s] in marginalizing women' (and other groups of persons).[114] Even seemingly 'enlightened' outcries against massive dynamics of inclusion/exclusion operate within the discursive confines of frozen crossings in political (and other functional communications) in and on the Middle East and even sustain these crossings, in this case through the creation of the 'universal Jordanian "woman" vying for absolute "space" in a patriarchal-driven text'.[115] In sum, and in somewhat activist parlance, by failing 'to account for such discursive/power practices' both human development reports and the wider literature on gender biases in education and beyond are 'perpetuating traditional discursive practices, roles and stereotypes instead of acting as an emancipatory power'.[116]

One of the fields in which this discrepancy between problematizations of inclusion/exclusion dynamics and the prolongation of the confines of frozen crossings is most obvious is the level of the legal status of women in many Arab countries. While international declarations as well as national constitutions in the region all formally adhere in one way or the other to the principles of equality between citizens, customary law, penal codes, civil law and tribal law ensure the perpetuation of strong demarcations of specific identity-groups along the inclusion/exclusion divide. As far as the role of women is concerned, this relates, for example, to the case of Jordan where 'all citizens are equal before the civil code, but women become inferior as part of the organizing principle of the personal status law'.[117] Similar practices have been observed in other countries in the regions where notwithstanding the fact that 'governments had made important headway in legislation ensuring equal employment as well as increased educational opportunities for women, this in no way solved or effectively tackled crucial issues pertaining to women's rights in the domestic realm. Issues like divorce, polygamy, inheritance and domestic violence remained hidden in the private sphere, where religious law still ruled',[118] thereby constraining the role of women in many other societal spheres as well. Fadia Faqir has elaborated on the dramatic consequences of these frozen crossings in the legal domain in her study on the killing of women by family members in defence of (male) honour in Jordan. While article 6 of the Jordanian constitution formally ensures equality between men and women, article 340 of the penal code ensures the prevalence of massive differences by indirectly legitimizing such acts, a practice which firmly upholds the borders between men and women far beyond the legal realm.[119] Similar observations have been made with regard to the status of married women in Lebanon. Thus, while the Lebanese constitution formally ensures equality between the sexes, the fifteen personal-law stipulations of the recognized religious groups in the country ensure the extension of frozen crossings, thereby negatively affecting the status of women across a variety of societal spheres. As soon as a woman marries, she becomes in legal terms largely the property of her husband and her right to act as a witness in court or to renew her own passport is constrained.[120] This not only affects, as is often observed, the role of Muslim women in the region but also relates to the status of women from other religious groups, as is evident, for example, in Lamia Shehaded's study on the way in which Christian personal status law in Lebanon is based on the law of coverture (that is, the loss of the women's own legal personality after marriage in which her personality merges with and is submerged by the (dominant) legal status of her husband), and which 'flagrantly discriminates against women on different levels'.[121]

From a related angle, Cassandra Balchin has studied the way in which enactments of identity-related differences by (Western) donor institutions within the overall communicative environment of frozen crossings might actually reinforce the antagonistic dynamics associated with systematic inclusion/exclusion dynamics on the gender-dimension on a global level.[122] She argues that the discursive context within which donor agencies deal with the question of 'what does it mean for women to live in Muslim society?' is shaped by the underlying framing of Islam as traditional and pre-modern. However, this culturalization of the Middle East has the effect of perpetuating – rather than transcending – the overall discursive context of frozen crossings as demonstrated above. Hence, 'while diversity in Muslim countries and communities is often acknowledged' such approaches assume that 'there are sufficient similarities to speak of "Muslim women" as a group and that this group is distinct from "other" groups of women'.[123] To repeat what has been said above, this statement is not intended to belittle the obvious and massive forms of chain exclusion of women (and other identity-groups) in the Middle East, which are well documented in the literature. It wants, however, to draw attention to the way in which even political (and other functional) communications that address these inequalities critically risk reifying the underlying discursive practices which foster the pervasiveness of frozen crossings in the Middle East in the first place.

This is also the background of Serge D. Elie's critique of the tendency in many fields of area studies to 'defend' the role of women in the Middle

East against 'Western' interpretations and cultural patterns. According to Elie, this tendency to engage with and understand the 'local' often results in 'the pursuit of ethnography as aimless conviviality with the natives and dedicated solely to the "recounting of petits recits of localizable collectivities"'.[124] While it is indeed necessary to correct simplistic 'external' stereotypes about the status of women in the Middle East, in general, and Islam, in particular – for example, by studying the diversity of political, religious, economic, family-related or artistic roles performed by women in the region – the 'discursive colonialization of gender in the Middle East'[125] nevertheless tends to pay too little attention to the historical trajectories which inform gender discourses in the region and which structurally 'ensure women's relative exclusion from the public sphere and seclusion in the more modest abodes of present-day Muslim societies'.[126] Elie has polemically referred to such culturalist approaches which ultimately empower notions of the Middle East as 'homosocial societies characterized by a corporate orientation and the prevalence of familism',[127] as the 'harem syndrome'. This 'harem syndrome' unites otherwise uneasy companions such as 'critical' researchers, on the one hand, and traditional segments in the region, on the other, in their quest for 'local' specificities and the 'real' understanding of an 'authentic' Middle East. Thus, for different reasons, both sides are 'the intellectual progeny of the anti-Orientalist debate'.[128] Intentionally or not, such cultural embeddings not only provide a welcome basis for opposition by many Middle East states to global human rights regimes,[129] but also favour a 'cult of domesticity of women'.[130] In line with what has been said above, it is, *inter alia*, this 'cult of domesticity' which ensures the prolongation of extended frozen crossings with regard to the role of women in the region in spite of the obvious differences between different women's status in the Middle East, the manifold state-led and societal changes and 'reform programmes', and even the diverse approaches on the role of women amongst traditional and/or Islamist circles. In a nutshell, the 'discursive colonialization of gender in the Middle East' facilitates the continuous relegation of men and women to distinct sides in code-oriented communications. As Elie argues fervently, the persistence of such chain exclusions across a variety of societal spheres remains possible since in many societal settings 'the Arab Middle East is essentialized into an Islam that is emblematic of reactive antimodernizers, purveyors of the social blight afflicting women in the forms of seclusion, veiling, and polygyny, not to mention the cult of virginity, the practice of clitoridectomy, and the availability to men of instantaneous divorce by mere repudiation.'[131]

To conclude, the observation of a 'crisis' in scientific communications in and on the Middle East as well as the debate on gender inequalities in the region underline the pervasiveness of extended frozen crossings – understood as serious 'distortions' to quasi-technical crossings and contingency reflections – inherent in many scientific, political and other (functional) communications in and on the region. Moreover, these extended frozen crossings are accompanied by the 'relegation' of specific groups of persons across a variety of societal spheres. By addressing these two dynamics, this chapter has argued that the 'frozen crossings' identified in the previous chapter with regard to the 'crisis' of politics in the region, also affect societal communications in and on the Middle East more generally. However, rather than consolidating the emergent orders of extended frozen crossings, the form of inclusion/exclusion allows (functional) communications continuously to observe the contingency (and relative stability) of these orders, thereby nurturing the creeping antagonization of regional politics. It is on this basis that this chapter maintains that notwithstanding the linkage of (functional) communications with *specific* programmes and *specific* groups of persons, the widespread understanding of inclusion/exclusion as a kind of super-code in many (non-Western) parts of the world is imprecise. Thus, the massive status quo orientation of such frozen crossings, which indeed hampers the quasi-technical crossing between the two sides of code-oriented communications (for example, power/powerlessness in politics, true/false in science), does not lead to an overall stabilization of the unequal distribution of power and knowledge (or wealth, faith and so on) in the Middle East. Theoretically speaking, social systems observe the centrality of such extended frozen crossings in their (first-order) operations through the simultaneous second-order observation of patterns of inclusion/exclusion, thereby firmly re-inscribing functional differentiation into these contexts. This ability of functional communications to observe 'crises' in code-oriented operations ensures that both distortions in code-oriented communications and the relegation of specific groups of persons to either side of the inclusion/exclusion divide are constantly challenged within these systemic discourses – 'crisis' then is one semantic form which underlines the antagonistic features of these extended frozen crossings.

World society and the polycontextuality of inclusion/exclusion

As observed at the beginning of this chapter, the antagonistic status of (extended) frozen crossings does not only relate to the ability of different (functional) systems to observe how code-related operations ensure the differentiation of various societal spheres, *inter alia*, through the form of inclusion/exclusion. Moreover, the polycontextual features of world society, that is, the differentiation of world society in manifold (functional) spheres that have no in-built hierarchy between them, equips the inclusion/exclusion paradigm with additional salience in fostering the creeping antagonization of Middle East politics. Corresponding with Žižek's dictum 'include me out!/exclude me in!', extended frozen crossings in the Middle East have continuously to struggle with what could be called – following George Spencer Brown – a re-entry of the form (inclusion/exclusion) within the form.[132] As the previous chapter analysed at length, frozen crossings in Middle East politics do not only result in a reification of specific programmes/persons which become associated with either side of the distinction powerful/powerless (or truth/non-truth for that matter). At the same time, the features of politics as a functional system that processes those communications which recognize themselves on the basis of the distinction powerful/powerless ensure that these distinctions do not result in an unquestioned, quasi-stratified essentialization of these power distributions. Thus, as outlined in Chapter 3, the inherent ability of crossing is 'remembered' in political communications in and on the Middle East to the extent that references to powerlessness often become a powerful resource in Middle East politics (for example, portraying a specific side in Middle East conflicts as less powerful, thereby legitimizing extraordinary measures in the defence of the allegedly powerless[133] – 'exclude me in!'), while massive displays of power are often no more than a colourful façade veiling the fragility of political orders ('include me out'!).

On the other hand, it is also the polycontextuality in the relationship between different functional spheres in world society which ensures the constant observation of the contingent, yet nevertheless stable presence of (extended) frozen crossings and dynamics of inclusion/exclusion in the region. In other words, massive exclusions (and inclusions) of specific groups of persons in the Middle East, in general, and unequal power distributions in the region, in particular, are regularly observed and scandalized not only in opposing political narratives (for example, by domestic opposition groups, donors, international organizations and the like) but through the inclusion of the (politically) excluded in various other (functional) communications, such as the scandalization of political exclusions in religious, academic, media-related or artistic communications. Without embarking on this argument in greater detail, the literature on 'fundamentalist' religious movements in the Middle East has regularly stressed the pervasiveness of such dynamics. As Quintan Wictorowicz and Suha Taji Farouki have emphasized in their study of the Al-Afaf charitable society in Jordan, which sustains a network of welfare institutions and engages in facilitating (financially, organizationally) the marriage of Muslim youth at an early age, 'seemingly apolitical activities, such as education and health care provision become political when they challenge other cultural codes and institutions', for example, by challenging the Hashemite claim to a monopoly with regard to the interpretation of (Muslim) values.[134] The role of seemingly apolitical welfare institutions in sustaining (and creating) the political power of groups that claim to represent the 'excluded' is also well documented with regard to the role of the Hezbollah movement in Lebanon or the Hamas movement in Palestine and the wide network of hospitals, infirmaries, dental clinics, pharmacies, and services for the unemployed and the poor provided by these organizations – alongside the recruitment of new personnel for their less peaceful activities.[135] Moreover, other authors have addressed the way in which pious religious movements in the region, in particular the Salafi movement in Jordan and Syria, affect the balance of power in the region (specifically the debate on what constitutes Muslim politics), precisely by withdrawing from any direct political interference as do, for example, activist Muslim groups such as Hamas or Hezbollah. By basing their activities almost exclusively on 'fluid networks of personalities' the Salafis 'fulfil the same functions as formal organizations, but are more effective in evading repression and limitation by the regime because of the fluidity and multiplicity of such informal institutions'.[136] Finally, a similar function of religious groups has also been studied in Israel, where the Shas party has successfully managed to turn the 'synagogue into civil society' by ensuring that its social activities not only equip their constituency with a 'Sephardi-religious' identity but also by scandalizing the perceived exclusion of and discrimination against Mizrahim in Israeli politics more generally.[137] At risk of repetition, it is not convincing to frame this 'new religio-politics'[138] as the competition between tradition (religion) and modernity (state, nation, market economy and so on) since, on closer inspection, both (and many other) discourses occupy the same 'functional space'. Thus, an observation by Jeremy Stolow on the Ashkenazi-Haredi Agudat Israel movement can equally be reformulated with a view to the role of many other (isolationist or activist) religious groups in Middle East politics:

transnational religious movements become trapped by the very logic they appear to oppose. Indeed, however much movements like Agudat Israel decry the legitimacy of the national imaginaries and state institutions with which they come into contact, it is also striking how their 'merely tactical' involvements draw them ever-deeper into the social logic of modern, state-centric governmentality, and its panoply of mechanisms for securing territory, producing subjects and ruling over populations.[139]

The various practices of empowerment of the excluded (and disempowerment of the powerful) in the Middle East, of which 'religio-politics' are only one dimension,[140] not only serve the function of ensuring the full inclusion postulate within distinct functional settings, but also provide a constant 'perturbation' and challenge to frozen crossings in the Middle East, more generally, and regional politics, in particular. Notwithstanding the authenticity and seeming solidity of massively unequal distributions of power, knowledge and wealth in the Middle East, the form of inclusion/exclusion constantly reminds functional systems both of the 'emptiness' of code-oriented operations and the pervasiveness of functional differentiation in world society. Ultimately, these antagonistic features render the reification of concrete (political) orders in the region unviable – the price being the centrality of (antagonistic) identities and conflicts. It is these conflictive dynamics – as well as the place of peace in Middle East politics – which will be discussed in greater detail in the final part of the book.

Part III

Rethinking Conflicts and Peace in the Middle East

5
Identities and Conflicts: the 'Deep Perturbation' of Middle East Politics

באַרבע בבוקר חושדים אוהבים משוררים ומשוגעים. כי חי המראה הם שבלונת לנפש / *At four in the morning poets, lovers and madmen suspect – that the life of the mirror is the mold of the soul*
שרון אס / Sharron Hass[1]

Constructions and all that: identities and conflicts in the Middle East

As Raymond Hinnebusch once claimed, 'Middle East area specialists have always acknowledged the importance of identities for an understanding of the region.'[2] And indeed, the indisputable centrality of identity-related norms and values (such as, *inter alia*, Arabism, Shi'ism, Zionism and Islam) in shaping both the interests of key political actors and the wider structures of conflict and cooperation in the region has even been able to bridge the often deep divide between 'rational' and 'constructivist' approaches to regional politics in IR. In particular it has been the dual focus on the ways in which powerful state elites engineer, use and manipulate such identities in order to secure their political survival on the national and regional levels and how autonomous state behaviour is at the same time constrained by equally powerful sub-state and trans-state identities (for example, clans, tribes, Arab nationalism, Shi'ism, Islam, national-orthodox Judaism and so on), that has informed key perspectives on this topic.[3] Ultimately, this approach is based on the assumption that somehow both (primordial or inter-subjective) identities and (objective) interests matter. Another reason for the relative ease with which notions of identity have been incorporated into various research agendas on Middle East politics arguably relates to the intensity of conflict dynamics in the region. Thus, the usually diametrically opposed perspectives of different conflict parties within the same conflict setting calls for an explanation of how such *multiplications* of an allegedly objective reality become possible.[4] And again, the answer is found in assuming that, somehow, both identities and interests have to be considered in order to account for the main dynamics of regional politics and the opposing interests of conflict parties. The balance between the factors becomes a matter of preference. While middle-ground social constructivists[5] emphasize the constraining impact of identities on interests, positivist approaches argue that 'the partial key to understanding the international politics of the Middle East provided by constructivism must be *deepened* by attention to identity's interrelationship with the materialist structures analysed by utilitarian approaches'.[6]

Seen from the perspective of this division of labour, powerful ethnoreligious identities that have an impact on regional politics – such as, Arab, Muslim, Palestinian, Druze, Jewish, Israeli, Maronite or Shi'i identities – are the result of historical processes, which shape communities by establishing a sense of shared primordial belonging within the respective group (but also heated divisions about the precise meaning of identity within these groups), often in opposition to a specific opponent.[7] In contrast, interests comprise a realm which, at least partially, remains detached from such a mix of primordial and inter-subjective constellations, and which is, consequently, shaped by autonomous calculations of more or less rational subjects, thereby preceding interaction. Apart from broader theoretical considerations on the fallacies of treating 'ideational' and 'material' factors as two separate phenomena – thereby ignoring the fact that both depend on their communicative construction in the first place – such an approach is also problematic from a more empirical perspective. Focusing on the ways in which the interrelationship between identities and interests 'makes the Middle East unique',[8] risks downplaying the structurally global (communicative) context within which the Middle East (and territories, interests and identities therein) emerge as meaningful social categories. In other words, the risk is an explicit or implicit reification of the Middle East as a civilizational universe of its own characterized by particularistic and idiosyncratic identities and cultures. When pitched against an allegedly universal logic of rationality, these identities almost automatically become the main factor of explanation for the key dynamics of regional politics, and in particular are seen as providing the answer to the ardent question of 'why is there so much conflict in the Middle East?'[9]

In spite of constructivists' delight in being seen as non-mainstream and located at the fringes of their disciplines, the study of identities and their impact on the structures of conflict and cooperation have been in the heartland of Middle East studies for a long time. Yet, arguably, the main focus of analysis is still primarily laid on either identifying the conflictive nature of different identity groups (by focusing on opposing interests which result from different identities) or, in the more critical tradition, on unmasking the constructedness of identities as well as the hegemonic practices shaping the relations between different identity groups. This chapter does not contest the viability of either strategy. Rather it argues that only when merging the focus on the necessary reality assumptions that stabilize conflictive identities in the Middle East with a simultaneous perspective on their structural contingency can a theoretically and empirically compelling perspective on the question of how the creeping antagonization of Middle East politics affects identities and conflicts in the region be attained. Consequently, by addressing both the need to operate under the reality assumption of frozen crossings on the first-order level and the structural knowledge about the contingency and arbitrariness of frozen crossings on a second-order level (inclusion/exclusion), this chapter approaches this crucial question by focusing on 'communications all the way down'.[10] Thus, the creeping antagonization of Middle East politics renders the explicit thematization of (antagonistic) identities a cornerstone of political communications in and on the region, because knowledge about 'identity' carries too much informational meaning to be ignored. It is this constant thematization of contradictory identities which facilitates lock-in effects of social conflicts by nurturing the general societal expectation that communication offers are likely to be rejected because they originate from an antagonistic (and threatening) Other – and, in turn that communication offers by the Other need to be rejected because they either threaten to perpetuate existing asymmetric power constellations or to alter this asymmetry. Such a research vista on the 'deep perturbation' of Middle East politics by conflict dynamics allows us to shift the focus from an alleged disintegration by conflicts to the question of how conflicts, understood as social orders in their own right, constantly attempt to solve the problem of their own continuation. This focus on how conflicts in fact integrate (antagonistic) identities also underlines the argument that the centrality of identities and conflicts in Middle East politics is not a feature specific to the region but already part of the operations of structurally debordered world societal communications.[11] This not only helps to account for the (world) wide societal reach of antagonistic moments in political communications in and on the Middle East and how they even encroach into seemingly benevolent practices of conflict resolution – both by regional and extra-regional actors – but also allows us to address the main function of social conflicts in Middle East politics, namely constantly to translate this creeping antagonization into tangible societal structures, thereby preventing the reification of concrete orders of frozen crossings, as totalizing as they might appear.

In order to elaborate on this argument, this chapter is divided into five further sections. The following section provides some more general theoretical clarifications on the status of 'identity' and 'conflict' in world society theory as far as these are relevant here. The subsequent sections then address, first, the role of the explicit thematization of (antagonistic) identities in nurturing manifold contradictory moments in Middle East politics; second, the way in which this centrality of identities in political communications refigures in formal and informal institutionalization practices in the Middle East – with a special focus on such practices in Lebanon and Israel – thereby firmly embedding antagonistic expectations in regional politics beyond the obvious case of violent conflict constellations; and third, the dynamics through which conflicts, understood as distinct social systems, use this plausibility of antagonistic identity distinctions in order to ensure their (fragile) continuation by rendering the logic of frozen crossings and hot contestations the hegemonic and taken-for-granted idea-system of regional politics. The chapter concludes with some final considerations on the status of peace in regional politics.

Antagonized identities, 'deep perturbations' and conflict systems

What are the societal effects of the creeping antagonization of Middle East politics, which has been analysed in the previous chapters and which results from the simultaneous manifestation of (extended) frozen crossings in countless (first-order) operations in Middle East politics, on the one hand, and inclusion/exclusion as the form which allows the observation – but not the fundamental alteration – of the contingency of frozen crossings, on the other? Why are frozen crossings in the Middle East upheld across a variety of functional spheres although they are continuously addressed (and scandalized) as highly problematic and antagonistic orders? As this chapter elaborates from both theoretical and empirical perspectives, accounting for the relative stability of (extended) frozen crossings in the Middle East necessitates linking the dynamics of political (and other functional) communications, which have been analysed in chapters 3 and 4, with insights from adequately complex theories of social conflict. What then comes to the fore are two main dynamics. First, the centrality of frozen crossings in Middle East politics (that is, distortions in code-oriented distinctions which foster the systematic and relatively time-consistent inclusion or exclusion of specific groups of persons within and across various functional spheres) renders the constant thematization of (antagonistic) identities a crucial and indispensable element in the actual processing of political (and other functional) communications *independently* of the obvious constructedness of all these identities. The noteworthy centrality of (antagonistic) identities in Middle East politics is, therefore, not an argument in favour of a primacy of region-specific cultural, identity-related or civilizational patterns but, at closer inspection, offers a specific and highly relevant mode of operation within the overall context of a structurally debordered (world) political system.

Second, the constant 'remembrance' of the contingency of these frozen crossings – ensured by the pervasiveness of the inclusion/exclusion distinction – prevents all stable reifications of such systematic relegation practices. As outlined in the previous chapters, these dynamics ultimately blur even the borders between power and powerlessness in the Middle East since, notwithstanding the significance of massive power inequalities in the region, the in-built opposition to frozen crossings within all political communications constantly nurtures the antagonistic transformation of Middle East politics. By structurally facilitating contestations to frozen crossings rather than the acquiescence with such (temporal) manifestations of power, Middle East politics become shaped by a myriad of antagonistic and conflictive moments. However, since such forms of opposition themselves often operate – as actual (first-order) operations – within the overall confines of the overarching structural context of frozen crossings and hot contestations, opposition tends to stabilize rather than undermine the pervasiveness of antagonistic identities in political communications in and on the Middle East. This encounter between many overlapping and cross-cutting antagonistic contestations within the overall context of frozen crossings then results in what can be described as a 'deep perturbation' of Middle East politics by conflict dynamics.

Focusing on this 'deep perturbation' of societal communications in and on the Middle East by conflict dynamics allows us to overcome somewhat simplistic sender-receiver models of social conflicts, which treat these conflicts as concrete 'objects' (for example, conflict issues, security) exchanged between two conflict parties and which, therefore, often tend to attribute responsibility for conflict maintenance either to these (and, alternatively, external) actors or to the intractable nature of those conflictive issues or structures which allegedly cause such binary oppositions. In contrast, the communication-theoretical framework deployed throughout this book turns the spotlight on the self-referential and subtle practices through which conflicts – understood as social systems in their own right – not only create conflict actors and conflict themes in the first place but, more importantly for the discussion here, constantly have to solve the problem of ensuring their own continuation as a distinct social system. It is on this basis that this chapter argues that the creeping antagonization of Middle East politics resulting from (extended) frozen crossings, on the one hand, and the simultaneous opposition to frozen crossings on the basis of the inclusion/exclusion paradigm, on the other, allows conflicts to use the placeless attractor 'Middle East' (and territories, identities and interest related to this attractor, see in detail Chapter 2) in order to ensure the emergence and consolidation of intense forms of conflict in wide parts of Middle East politics. These lock-in effects must, therefore, not be mistaken for any deterministic understanding of these conflict dynamics, but rather as the way in which conflicts attempt to solve the problem of their own (fragile) stabilization.

This chapter argues that shifting the focus away from both the obviously (divergent) interests of conflict actors and the multifaceted details of specific conflict themes, while instead addressing the processes which lead to the emergence and stabilization of conflicts as distinct social systems with their own systemic functions, is a more promising strategy in order to account for the pervasiveness of conflicts in the region.[12] This focus on the reproduction and function of conflicts as communicatively-generated systems is, of course, not meant to belittle the dramatic consequences of conflicts in the region either for individuals who suffer from violence, injustice, oppression and trauma or for wider regional instability.[13] However, it does caution against regarding conflicts primarily through implicitly normative lenses which too quickly problematize the allegedly disintegrative effects of conflicts for the relationship between conflict parties and which, consequently, propose mainly actor-centred strategies of conflict transformation – since by so doing they take insufficient regard of the structural features of conflicts as social systems in their own right. In contrast, this chapter argues that there is a significant value-added in regarding conflicts as *social* and highly integrated structures, which serve a specific function for society. In a nutshell, this societal role of conflicts primarily lies in their function as a (parasitic) immune-system for society, in general, and for specific societal spheres, such as politics, more particularly. As far as Middle East politics are concerned, these systemic properties become clearly visible insofar as conflict systems allow for the translation of the creeping antagonization of political communications in and on the Middle East, which has been identified in Part II, into concrete societal *structures* rather than merely constituting a (politically relatively meaningless) environmental noise of regional politics. By transforming the latency of this antagonization into (communicatively processed) conflict structures, opposition to (extended) frozen crossings in the Middle East becomes part of society's (and politics') first-order operations (that is, world society's communicatively generated reality) rather than remaining a lofty feature of mere self-observation.

Moreover, such a change of perspective has tremendous consequences for the study of conflicts in the Middle East (and beyond) since it provides a theoretically and empirically compelling substantiation of the argument that the centrality of (antagonistic) interests and identities as well as the intensity of conflicts in the Middle East are not evidence of any *sui generis* character of the region. And neither can the intensity of conflicts in the region be attributed to a clash between 'tradition' and 'modernity' in the wake of an alleged gradual penetration of Middle East localities by the forces of a supposedly external globalization.[14] As has already been discussed at length in Chapter 2, such imaginaries of regions as somewhat separate spatial containers and of globalization as something 'external' do not conform with the communicative dynamics which create these regions against the background of a structurally debordered world societal horizon. At closer inspection the centrality of (antagonized) identities in Middle East politics as well as the notorious ubiquity of conflicts in the region need to be understood as operations of a primarily functionally differentiated world society into which the Middle East is already firmly embedded. And, it is on this basis that the Middle East also serves a particular role in world political (and media-related, scientific and other functional) communications by acting as one of world society's main – and most popular – conflict regions.[15] As a welcome side effect, this argument is not only of relevance to all those approaches which, directly or indirectly, proclaim a quasi-ontological specificity of the Middle East. It also touches upon a problematic aspect of world society theory, which has occasionally argued that functional differentiation might be the dominant form of differentiation within the OECD context but only partially covers regions beyond this Western-liberal core where identity-related forms of distinction prevail.[16] This suspicion is nourished by the assumption that the inclusion/exclusion paradigm – or, alternatively, conflict systems or identity-distinctions – overarch functional differentiation in, say, the Middle East, Africa and Latin America. On closer inspection, however, this argument is not really compelling since it builds upon the notions of, first, communication as an object exchanged between different ontologically given spaces and, second, of 'full' versus 'partial' forms of functional differentiation in world society. As outlined in Chapter 2, both perspectives are ultimately untenable from a communication-theoretical perspective. Moreover, such a conceptualization of functional differentiation as a form of differentiation in the (peaceful) West, which consequently needs to be exported to semi-traditional (conflictive) corners of the world, is also problematic since it risks advancing a homogeneous and politicized understanding of peace. By implicitly equating polycontextuality with specific societal programmes such as democracy, rule of law and market economy it reduces functional differentiation into not much more than yet another hegemonic political project. Moreover, such a (mis)understanding of functional differentiation as a specific mode of operation in the West downplays the many conflictive features of this kind of societal differentiation. Functional differentiation is not a recipe for peace. The arguments in this chapter thus propose an understanding of functional differentiation as a highly heterogeneous and particularistic process, which is indeed often characterized by diverse antagonistic features. As a result, functional differentiation can and always will spur the emergence and consolidation of conflicts within distinct societal spheres (such as politics) as well as within world society as the encompassing social system. And that is also the reason why functional differentiation has no in-built peaceful equilibria or end-states towards which this form of differentiation is bound to drift.[17]

Consequently, conflicts – and even intense forms of social conflict which shape the regional and global image of specific territories, such as the Middle East – do not overarch the logics of the operation of politics and other functional spheres as structurally debordered (world) societal systems. They rather need host systems within which they can emerge and stabilize. As such 'parasitic' social systems conflicts also fulfil a specific function for society, namely to create (rather than being the result of) identity-related incompatibilities between conflict parties and conflict themes. By doing so, conflicts, *inter alia*, prevent the stagnation and reification of concrete social orders since the structural 'availability' of opposition ensures that concrete (political) orders cannot become equated with the (functional) system of politics at large – the code always remains an empty signifier. More precisely, while social systems (for example, politics) build on the expectational structure that communication offers are accepted (that is, in this case, impositions by the powerful), conflicts as social systems are based on the counter-expectation that communication offers will be rejected. As Luhmann elaborates, conflicts are, therefore, ubiquitous and ordinary phenomena and relate to 'all those cases in which there is a disaccord to a communication. One could also say: if a disaccord is communicated.'[18] Thus, 'social processes are usually based on the expectation that the continuation of communication is ensured by the acceptance of prior communication (accord). This is not the case with conflicts. Being based on the communication of disaccord, conflicts not only point to the constant possibility of a "no" inherent in all communications but through their specific discursive framework they facilitate the actual, repeated communication of the "no".'[19] It is as a result of these features that conflicts have also been referred to as the 'immune system' of society.[20] Hence, by directing attention towards the functional features of conflicts, 'one can see clearly how the contradiction fulfils its original warning and alarming function. It destroys, for one moment, the totality representation of the system: to be ordered, reduced complexity. For one moment then undefined complexity is re-established.'[21] Disaccord has been voiced – and understood.

This argument underlines the observation that society, in general, and individual social settings, in particular, need conflicts in order to ensure their evolution. Indeed, 'the differentiation of a political system can only happen if within that system conflicts are permitted'.[22] Consequently, by testing 'rejection potentials'[23] within and across various societal spheres, social conflicts ensure that these settings do not transform into monadic, machine-like containers but remain cognitively open towards environmental stimuli and change. This necessitates, however, that a conflict – if only for a moment – challenges the totality assumption of prevailing discourses and societal structures, that is, the assumption that familiar communication offers will always be accepted. 'The contradiction signals, therefore, and that is its function, that the contact could be disconnected.'[24] By translating the creeping antagonization of Middle East politics into concrete conflict structures, social conflicts in the region indeed fulfil such a (world) societal warning and alarming function insofar as they continuously warn against the totalizing reifications of existing power relations in the region which result from the logic of frozen crossings.

However, there is no immediate emancipatory logic to this argument which would allow us to celebrate acts of 'opposition', 'defence' and 'resistance' in the Middle East. Referring to the function of social conflicts does not mean that all forms of opposition are necessarily positive. On the contrary, the relative stability of frozen crossings in the region prevents an easy 'evaporation' of conflicts, for example by thawing power constellations and by replacing discriminatory ideologies and discourses through the institutionalization, on many levels, of effective mechanisms which facilitate crossing between (and de-personalization of) power and powerlessness. Hence, while conflicts in the Middle East do indeed warn against distortions in code-oriented communications, the (relative) pervasiveness of frozen crossings in regional politics stabilizes conflict dynamics to the extent that many forms of opposition to frozen crossings come to replicate – rather than replace – the totalizing logic of these frozen crossings.[25] It is precisely this tendency of conflicts to subvert the logic of operation of their 'host systems' and to transform into solid social systems in their own right, which underlines their more problematic features. Thus, 'conflicts get easily out of control',[26] and become 'over-integrated systems, which tend to concentrate all resources with a view to victory or defeat in a conflict'.[27] As can be observed in Middle East politics, opposition and counter-opposition wind each other up to the degree that the borders between the powerful and the powerless become blurred, with each side considering its own identity and, indeed, physical existence fundamentally threatened by the other. This is also the background of Heinz Messmer's observation that 'whatever else happens inside a conflict, it does create social distances between individual domains'.[28] Seen from that perspective, the widespread equation of conflict with disintegration, a lack of communication and misperceptions seems somewhat naive. Rather, 'the problem of conflict is the too strong integration of its subsystems, which have to mobilise ever more resources for the dispute and have to withdraw it from alternative disposal, and the problem of a complex society then is to care for sufficient disintegration'.[29] Without sufficient opportunities for conflicts to evaporate, 'an "integration-maelstrom" emerges which uses almost all communicative events, in order to build up the antagonistic system and to let it continue'[30] – up to the degree that 'a system with conflictive communications "reorganizes itself as *conflict* to save autopoiesis"'.[31]

The stability of frozen crossings in Middle East politics, on the one hand, and the simultaneous subversion of such reifications of existing power relations by means of the inclusion/exclusion distinction, on the other, therefore, fosters lock-in effects of social conflicts within the overall (world societal) context of political communications in and on the region. This antagonization transforms the question of who is actually relegated to either side of the distinction between powerful/powerless into the undecidable nucleus of Middle East politics – thus ensuring the stabilization of conflicts in the region. As long as frozen crossings endure, opposition can and often needs to be perceived as a menacing threat which, consequently, has to be opposed. To reiterate, this argument does not reintroduce notions of regional specificity through the back-door. Conflicts do not overarch their host system, since this would require that politics as a debordered and global system would in its totality be affected by the structural expectation that communication offers are rejected (that is, an instance in which the code of power would ultimately lose its function). The metaphor that conflicts have a tendency 'to dine their host system',[32] is thus a catchy but theoretically imprecise description of the operative logic of social conflicts since it fails to reflect upon the double world societal horizon which underpins all conflict communications. The problem of the creeping antagonization of Middle East politics is not that politics in its entirety would be affected by conflict dynamics – a notion which could only be upheld if the Middle East were to be conceived of as an autonomous entity comprising its own political system or, alternatively, if all political communications in world society were to be replaced by conflict dynamics. The crucial argument here is not that conflicts overarch the logic of operation within distinct specific societal spheres – thereby replacing functional differentiation by conflict patterns – but rather that social conflicts use the (antagonized) placeless attractor 'Middle East' in order to ensure their stabilization within the overall context of a structurally debordered political system.

By rendering opposition to menacing forms of opposition – which, if successful threatens to replicate rather than overcome the cruel relegation dynamics inherent in the context of frozen crossings – a key feature of Middle East politics, the confrontation between antagonistic identities becomes the prime mechanism through which conflicts in Middle East politics ensure their stabilization. Therefore, and notwithstanding the obvious constructedness of identities, a systematic analysis of Middle East politics needs to consider why these antagonistic relations between different identity groups have to be taken for granted in many political communications in and on the region. This chapter does not aim to repeat the well-known and convincing arguments on the constructedness of *all* social identities, independently of whether one refers to imagined communities such as the nation, the religion, the state, gender or specific ethnicities which all need to constitute themselves vis-à-vis a (benevolent or radical) Other.[33] Based on the understanding that 'collective identity is produced by the social construction of boundaries',[34] the crucial point rather is that such deconstructions of identities cannot be reflected upon in actual political (and other functional) operations because they also operate in the (first-order) context of frozen crossings. Thus, notwithstanding the obvious fact that conflicts are always a 'co-produced pattern',[35] (antagonistic) identities need to be taken for granted because 'identity' carries too much relevant meaning to be ignored, that is, the crucial information as to which side of code-oriented communications (for example, powerful/powerless) a specific person belongs. In other words, while the form of inclusion/exclusion enables the observation of the contingency of existing power relations and identities in Middle East politics, first-order operations nevertheless have constantly to reproduce these antagonisms since in the most fundamental way they 'guarantee reality'.[36] As Luhmann notes, 'only the second-order observer sees that the first-order observer "reduces complexity"; and this then means that it makes no sense to demand from him to reduce complexity'.[37] As a result, the constant and explicit thematization of identities in political and other functional communications ensures the lasting and 'deep perturbation' of Middle East politics by conflict dynamics because it fundamentally matters – often in the most existential sense of the word – on which side of the border a specific person is located.

The observation by Shmuel Eisenstadt and Bernhard Giesen that an identity 'fulfils its "function" only if the social processes constructing it are kept latent'[38] and that the crucial task then is to 'reconstruct the process by which latency is achieved and by which the fragile social order is considered to be the self-evident order of things',[39] strongly underlines the 'deep perturbation' of Middle East politics by conflict dynamics. The overall function of antagonistic identities is to make frozen crossings and hot contestations appear as the self-evident order of things which, consequently, has to be continuously re-inscribed into all political communications – thereby rendering the continuation of conflict communications likely. Seen from that perspective it also becomes clear that the occasionally raised objection that there is a certain incompatibility between functional differentiation, on the one hand, and the centrality of identities in some world region, on the other, is not really convincing.[40] As this chapter shows, particularistic identities are neither the cause nor the result of an allegedly alternative (identity-related) form of differentiation in the Middle East but have to be analysed against the backdrop of self-referential modes of operations in the context of politics and conflicts as two structurally debordered (and communicatively generated) social systems of world society.[41]

Moreover, this 'deep perturbation' of Middle East politics by conflict dynamics ensures the continuous reproduction of antagonistic identities since the 'differentiation of conflict reasons and conflict themes' – which is the prime mechanism of preventing conflicts from dominating wider parts of their host systems – is hampered in Middle East politics. Thus, the difficulties in pursuing various peace processes in the region, whether in Israel/Palestine or in Lebanon, only underline Luhmann's critique of those conflict resolution approaches which are based on the 'illusion that all conflicts can politically be reduced to conflicts of interests'.[42] Thus, issue-conflicts and 'conflicts of interests are in the end trivial conflicts',[43] because the predominant focus on specific conflict themes – rather than identities – 'prevents the societal "pillarization" of conflicts [which would have] the consequence that distinct social groups recognize themselves as identical opponents in all conflicts'.[44] This is, however, precisely what happens in the context of the creeping antagonization of Middle East politics in which such a societal pillarization of conflicts along relatively stable identity-lines constantly makes plausible the re-erection of frozen crossings and the pursuit of hot contestations.

To summarize, this chapter advances the argument that conflicts in the Middle East represent neither a pathological state-of-nature nor a breakdown of social relations. On the contrary, conflicts are specific types of social system which adhere to the same dynamics regarding their inception and maintenance as all other social orders – with the small but crucial difference that in contrast to other societal spheres, which are based on the structural expectation that communication offers are accepted, social conflicts ensure their stabilization by anticipating opposition to communication offers. Consequently, the social distances – but also the communicative integration – between the very identities created within such conflict settings increase and it is then the result of the creeping antagonization of Middle East politics that the shift from 'identities' to 'issues' as well as the overall societal containment of conflicts is severely hampered. Obviously, such an understanding of conflicts differs markedly from the widespread equation of conflicts with disintegration, misunderstandings and lack of communication.[45] In such conceptualizations, conflict resolution is, consequently, often portrayed as a demanding but nevertheless technocratic exercise in addressing at the right time the right interlocutors in conflict societies, deciphering the underlying conflict themes and designing possible compromise solutions (either by force, by stealth or by establishing a reasoned consensus) – in other words by establishing integration and ensuring (effective) communication.[46] However, such an understanding – as widespread as it is in the media, amongst policy-makers and many academic analyses – fails to address the specific features of conflicts-as-social-systems. It not only systematically ignores the fact that integration rather than disintegration is the prime 'problem' of conflict settings but also nurtures the illusion that themes and actors constitute conflicts rather than being a (crucial) side product in the self-referential consolidation of conflicts as distinct social systems in their own right.

The focus in this chapter on the stabilization and centrality of conflicts and antagonized identities in the Middle East does in no way mean that *all* political communications in and on the region are necessarily subject to conflict dynamics. This not only seems untenable from a theoretical perspective but would also contradict proper empirical evaluation. As will be discussed in the concluding chapter, there is indeed widespread cooperation and even instances of amity in regional politics. And indeed, these cooperative dynamics are often the blind spot of scientific, political or media-related discourses which – unintentionally or for strategic reasons – 'forget' about the less conflictive aspects of Middle East politics. But before turning to these more hopeful dynamics, a proper analysis of Middle East politics needs to take seriously the centrality of identities and the pervasiveness of conflict dynamics in the region. The crucial task then is to account for the constant fortification of frozen crossings in regional politics without taking recourse to the fallacious construction of the Middle East as an inherently conflictive universe.

Revisiting identities and conflicts in Middle East politics

As we have already noted, it is precisely the widespread focus on cultures and identities (or other allegedly 'unique' features of the region) and the impact these factors are assumed to have on the pervasiveness of conflicts and other problematic features in regional politics (such as the notorious lack of freedom, the centrality of autocracies and so on) which has rightfully been criticized as the underlying Orientalist tradition in Middle East studies.[47] Based on the 'the Orient/Occident divide'[48] – with the 'Orient' being characterized by the irrationality, emotionality and aggressiveness of semi-modern cultures while the 'Occident' represents universalist rationality and reason – a twofold hegemonic project can easily be projected onto the Middle East, both in the scientific and the policy-oriented tradition. Thus, by contrasting a 'Kantian' West with a 'Hobbesian'[49] Middle East, both 'external' and 'internal' securitization practices can easily be legitimized. In this context, the 'West' transforms into an 'imagined community'[50] in which individuals, 'civil'[51] societies, nations and states have learned to live peacefully with each other and to engage in the sharing of sovereignty and even supranational integration – while the Middle East appears as an area of deeply entrenched (conflictive) cultures and identities where actors still need to resort to violence and other ruthless means in order to secure their survival. The reasons for the pervasiveness of conflicts and instability become projected upon an allegedly violent predisposition of antagonistic identities/interests in the region. While this predisposition might or might not change in the future, in the meantime, external interventions against this 'new barbarism'[52] emanating from the Middle East are required in order to safeguard regional and, indeed, global security. This move justifies diverse surveillance practices and stigmatizations of Middle Easterners in many Western countries, particularly of Muslims and Arabs – but also, on another level, of Jews and Israelis as the measures of protection and surveillance of synagogues and Israeli embassies in many countries amply illustrates.[53] It also includes the 'need' to secure peace in an unstable region by projecting 'rational' and mainly Western political, military, economic and cultural power to the region, be it in the form of EU security advisers for the Palestinian police force or the deployment of UN troops in order to secure a fragile peace in the aftermath of the 2006 Lebanon war. With regard to the 'internal' dimension, this construction of the Middle East as an inherently Hobbesian space, *inter alia*, serves as a powerful legitimation for stabilizing – or violently attacking – the existing power relations in the region. This relates, in particular, to those practices by (autocratic and democratic) state elites in the region which frame concepts such as opposition, democracy, compromise-seeking and human rights as 'Western' or 'idealist' and (temporarily or permanently) unsuitable to a region where, unfortunately, power can only be secured by regular assertions of violence – and similar justifications are often sought for various forms of hot contestations such as, for example, the alleged need for violent resistance or collective punishment.

As these examples document, practices of Orientalism are not restricted to Western scholars and policymakers. They also structure the dynamics of regional and 'domestic Orientalism'[54] and characterize all those discourses which frame a distinct group (usually the Other) as inherently violent and aggressive and which, therefore, often pave the way for an intervention (usually by the Self) in order to protect and secure overall (national, ethnic or regional) safety and stability. Take, for example, the popular regional (and global) constructions of Israel as inherently violent, for example, the notion of Israelis/Jews as colonial settlers erecting an apartheid state because they somehow *want* to rule over others. Yet, it also relates to the aforementioned 'new barbarism thesis',[55] that is, the portraying of Muslims, Palestinians or Arabs as backward and vengeful people subject to an almost natural cultural *socialization* with violence, intolerance and terrorism.[56] It is almost needless to say that both discourses, widespread as they are, serve as powerful justifications for heavy securitization practices (for example, for protecting Palestine as a place threatened by ethnic cleansing or the notion of Israel as a state struggling for its survival) and violent interventions in order to protect the securitized Self. With reference again to the Palestine-Israel conflict, such necessary interventions then refer, for example, to assertions of a right of resistance by almost *all* means against foreign occupation, in general, and Israeli 'troublemakers',[57] in particular. They also figure prominently in the legitimization practices for erecting checkpoints and settlement outposts as well as fences and walls, which severely curtail the movement of *all* Palestinians since, at least potentially, each one of them could be a terrorist. Such mutual Orientalization can also relate to more benevolent practices and can, for example, be well studied in the context of the popular trend to establish 'cultural dialogue' between the West and Islam. What such notions of 'cultural dialogue' fail to address is not only that they need to create a fundamental difference (which then needs to be bridged) between these 'cultures' in the first place but also that they often subtly re-inscribe a hierarchy into this relationship, since it is, most of the time, primarily Islam which should learn to adopt (Western) 'civilized' practices of achieving a reasoned consensus within the overall (institutionalized) framework of a more or less ideal speech situation.[58]

What these various examples illustrate is less any unique conflictive disposition of Middle Eastern cultures and identities and more the fact that political communications in and on the Middle East are often heavily securitized on a global scale. More precisely, the pervasiveness of culture and (antagonistic) identities in regional politics is not the result of region-specific dynamics linked to specific actors or (conflict) issues but is rather the effect of the overall creeping antagonization of Middle East politics – that is, (political) communications in and on the region which are embedded into a (structurally debordered) world societal context.

Recall that a central effect of these antagonization dynamics are severe relegation dynamics (in particular the systematic relegation of specific groups of people to either side of code-oriented distinctions across a variety of societal spheres) which are scandalized, but most of the time not fundamentally altered, on the basis of the inclusion/exclusion paradigm. What matters in particular is the observation that in the overall context of frozen crossings and hot contestations the explicit thematization of 'identity' needs to become a central feature of political and other functional communications. Thus, 'identity' carries too much informational meaning to be ignored since it simply matters – often in the most existential way – on which side of the distinction (for example, powerful/powerless) a specific person is located. As long as frozen crossings in political and other functional communications on the Middle East endure, the continuation of this constant thematization of (antagonistic) identities becomes likely.

The institutionalization of antagonisms in Middle East politics

The various Middle East conflicts provide plenty of illustration of the ways in which antagonistic identities remain constant and explicit features of political communications. Yet, the contradictory logic of frozen crossings and hot contestations does not only relate to the obvious case of violent confrontations in the region, whether with regard to the more or less violent suppression of Islamist movements in Syria or Jordan, skirmishes between the Lebanese army and militants in the Palestinian refugee camp Nahr Al-Barid, torture practices and killings between the militias of Fatah and Hamas in Palestine or, to refer to the most popular candidate, the never-ending succession of strikes and counter-strikes in the Israeli-Palestinian conflict. Owing to the broad societal reach of the creeping antagonization of Middle East politics contradictions do not simply dissolve but are 'institutionalized' as *routine* practices in various contexts, thereby in turn stabilizing the logic of frozen crossings and hot contestations as the unquestioned idea-system of political communications in and on the Middle East.[59] A good example of these dynamics is the degree to which identity distinctions have become, formally or informally, integrated into Middle East constitutional politics, thereby affecting the chances of political inclusion and exclusion in different nation-states, for example, in the context of the confessionalized institutional set-up of Lebanon's consociational democracy. Thus, and notwithstanding the certainly accurate observation that the major Lebanese communities in fact occasionally hold surprisingly similar views on key political issues, such as the relationship between Lebanon and Syria, the status of Palestinian refugees and the issue of formal rights of representation for the major ethno-religious groups,[60] confessional status (being Maronite, Sunni, Shi'i, Druze, Catholic or Orthodox, to mention six of the eighteen formally recognized sects) nevertheless has a tremendous impact on national politics. Still based on the Lebanese census of 1932, political representation in Lebanon is strongly linked with identity ascriptions. This extends beyond the well-known exclusivity in the entitlement of specific groups for leading positions in the state (that is, the president being a Maronite, the prime minister a Sunni and the speaker of parliament a Shi'i), the prearranged distribution of parliamentary seats since the Ta'if Agreement of 1989 among Christians (50 per cent) and Muslims (50 per cent) and the tremendous bias of the Lebanese electoral system in favour of perpetuating the centrality of these ethno-religious identities at the expense of a greater representation of weaker social groups and issue-oriented political parties.[61]

What matters, therefore, is the fact that the centrality of identities in Lebanese politics, enshrined in its constitution, electoral laws and informal practices, not only renders the explicit thematization of identities a cornerstone of political communications but also continues to nurture manifold antagonistic moments between these identities. As Rania Maktabi observes, notwithstanding the fragile (re)consolidation of Lebanese democracy following the Ta'if agreement, the 'heavy politicization'[62] of identity in the daily operations of Lebanese politics continuously nurtures a high level of securitization with regard to confessional status. Thus, 'as long as representation [and power] continues to run along ethnic lines in Lebanon debates over numbers and the presumed or alleged size of groups will continue',[63] thereby keeping in motion the cycle of suspicions and counter-suspicions about the (sinister) plans of other groups in changing the delicate balance of power to their advantage. Moreover, 'Lebanon's malaise'[64] of politicized *and* antagonized inter-confessional relations is exacerbated by the 'vertical' securitization of ethno-religious identities, thereby underlining the societal reach of the creeping antagonization of Middle East politics, which is not limited to relations between major identity groups. As Nizar Hamzeh has argued, the pillarized sectarianism in Lebanon goes hand-in-hand with quasi-authoritarian patron-client relations *within* the various sects, that is, the relations between political (and military) leaders, on the one hand, and their 'natural' constituencies, on the other. Hence, 'like confessionalism, this vulgar clientelism [sic] has been institutionalized into Lebanon's political system, thus making the Lebanese state an association of a variety of patrons'.[65] While not downplaying the cooperative and welfare-oriented policies which developed within and between these networks of clientelism, perceived or real changes in power relations tend to foster securitization practices which, in turn, fortify the symbolic borders between the various confessional groups but also serve as a legitimization for internal authoritarian policies. In sum, 'once threatened ... by political and economic modernization which was supposed to alter the bargaining relationship between traditional patrons and their clients, [clientelism] responded by giving birth to sectarian political parties or militias using cruder forms of coercion and repression'[66] both with regard to inter- and intra-group policies.

Similar examples of how the constant and explicit thematization of (antagonistic) identities in political communications has been engrained into institutional structures of political arenas throughout the Middle East are well-documented in the literature, both with regard to democracies (for example, the securitization of Israel's Jewish identity and the precarious status of national minorities, in particular Israeli Palestinians) and autocratic countries (for example, the status of Palestinians in Jordan), to cite but two central cases.[67] Exceptions to such dynamics – as for example the appointment in January 2007 of Israeli Palestinian Raleb Majadele as Israel's first-ever Arab minister (of science, culture and sports) or the first-ever appointment of an Israeli Palestinian as Head of Department at an Israeli university, as happened in 2006 when Amal Jamal was elected to this post at the Department of Political Science at Tel Aviv University[68] – might be celebrated by many as a sign of the strength of Israel's democratic culture but equally attracts 'angry criticism' by others framing such steps as yet another 'lethal blow to Zionism'.[69] This is not to downplay the significance of such events, which, if they were to gain momentum, might even contribute to a broader desecuritization of identities in Middle East politics. However, in the current constellation these and other examples serve to document the virtual necessity explicitly to address the identity of persons in political communications (either praising or condemning such developments) because, at least for the time being, these identities carry too much political information to be ignored. This does not preclude the possibility that society could experiment with a cautious opening of symbolic 'border check-points', yet the widespread perception of such events as noteworthy 'exceptions' underlines that this is still a far cry from a more systematic abrogation from the overall antagonization of identities in regional politics. Again to take the example of national minorities in Israel, this argument is sustained by the ongoing taboo of referring to 'Israeli Palestinians' and instead referring to this group as Arabs (or even an Arab 'sector') or, alternatively, as Muslims, Christians, Bedouins, Druze and Circassians, thereby embedding such alternative identity-ascriptions within the overall confines of antagonized politics.[70] As has already been observed in the case of Lebanon, it is no surprise that the dynamics of securitization of identity in Israel are not confined to 'horizontal' relations between different ethno-religious groups, as if these were given, closed-off units. As manifold studies and policy reports show, the creeping antagonization of political communications filters through in a 'vertical' manner, as scenarios of a potential 'civil war' between the secular and religious 'sectors' in Israel[71] or in the widespread perception of a deeply entrenched opposition and structural violence between (allegedly) elitist Ashkenazim and (allegedly) second-class Mizrahim illustrates.[72] At closer inspection, these securitization practices do thus not pitch primordially given identities against each other but rather constantly create and recreate cross-cut antagonistic identities for the very purpose of guaranteeing the reality of orders of frozen crossings and hot contestations in Middle East politics.

As these cases illustrate, the pervasiveness of such orders does not only relate to the many violent outbursts in regional politics but also affects political communications on the region both within and outside the Middle East on a much wider scale. Instances of this antagonization are, for example, deeply embedded in many political communications which construct the Middle East as a conflictive space pervaded by mutually exclusive interests and identities, and which, thereby, justify (external or internal) interventions in order to 'protect' a threatened security and assure 'peace' – and this not only relates to prejudices in scientific disguise which construct the Middle East (and Islam) as historically or naturally aggressive and bloodthirsty. While not questioning the fact that overcoming violent conflicts in the Middle East would have a positive impact from a human needs perspective,[73] the focus on the creeping antagonization of Middle East politics nevertheless reveals that many benevolent practices of conflict resolution also ultimately risk operating within the confines of frozen crossings and hot contestations by framing their own solutions as external, enlightened and rational prescriptions which need to be imposed on all-too emotional, stubborn and shortsighted decision-makers and publics in the Middle East. By doing so, however, such 'external' interventions overlook the fact that they are often already part of the overall conflict constellation insofar as they base their interventions on the distinction between the identity of the reasoned and rational (external) Self, which knows about both the real contours of 'peace' as well as the content of a reasoned compromise, and the intransigent identity of the violent and threatening (local) Other(s), that is, one or several conflict parties, which, for whatever reason, resist the reasoned and universal logic of conflict resolution. This underlines Oliver Richmond's observation that many 'external' perspectives and notions of 'external' peace, which only wait to be exported into zones of conflict, are based on a slim balance between 'consent and coercion' insofar as they not only reify powerful images of specific places as conflict zones but 'effectively nominate omniscient third parties to be placed in a position to transfer external notions of peace into conflict societies and environments', which are regarded as being unable to do so on their own.[74]

More precisely, such seemingly innocent 'external' interventions are already often part of the overall antagonization of Middle East politics because, as a side-product, they perpetuate the explicit thematization of antagonistic identities in many political communications on the region – in this case the hierarchical distinction between an 'external' identity of peace and an 'internal' identity of intractable conflict constellations and violence. In this context, a report by the German Institute of Global and Area Studies has cautioned against the hegemonic role of NGOs professionalized in the field of conflict resolution – specifically, the International Crisis Group – and the way in which reports by these organizations actually shape the international agenda of how conflicts, *inter alia*, in the Middle East, ought to be understood (that is, who are the relevant conflict actors? What are the relevant conflict themes? What should a compromise solution look like?)[75] This is not to deny that reports by the Crisis Group on the Middle East are well-informed, carefully worded and more or less balanced analyses of the complex conflict constellations in Lebanon, Syria or Israel-Palestine.[76] However, and notwithstanding the contribution of Crisis Group and many other NGOs in informing a global public about the general consequences of conflicts in different world regions as well as about the position of various conflict parties which might be less well-known to a wider (Western) public, it is notable that Crisis Group reports advance a generally technocratic image of conflicts which risks re-inscribing antagonistic identity constructions into conflict resolution approaches. Thus, these reports usually close with 'policy recommendations', directed *solely* towards local and global political actors. Consequently, conflict resolution (or the lack thereof) becomes constructed as mainly a matter of these actors' political will. However, by failing to tackle the 'deeper world societal [sic] embedding of the wars and violent conflicts studied [in these reports]',[77] they always risk sustaining notions of a rational external peace which ought to be projected on stubborn conflict parties unwilling or unable to achieve the common good. To reiterate, rather than rejecting these reports, this argument adds, from the perspective of conflict theory, another 'good reason for a critical approach'[78] towards these and other seemingly pragmatic and reasonable solutions to Middle Eastern conflicts by tracing the pervasiveness of the creeping antagonization of Middle East politics and the ways in which it affects even seemingly pragmatic and objective conflict stories. This argument highlights the immense difficulties – or even the impossibility – of resisting being drawn, in some way or other, into the logic of explicitly thematizing antagonistic identities when talking about (and acting in) these conflicts, in the form of re-inscribing an antagonistic identity distinction between a reasoned (and, therefore, superior) third-party perspective on conflicts and (inferior) conflict behaviour into political communications on the region.[79]

Of course, the explicit thematization of identities in political communications need not necessarily be conducted in an antagonistic manner. (Negative) Othering processes are not the only way in which identities are topical in political and other functional communications. Different identities can be and indeed often are framed in terms of amity, trust, friendship, admiration, partnership and attraction, both in the political and other societal realms[80] – and this is certainly also the objective of many benevolent external interventions, such as the aforementioned conflict resolution approaches. While critical approaches in IR and the social sciences have, rightly, cautioned against taking such instances of positive identity relations at face value and have instead suggested deconstruction of the more or less visible structures of inequality and hegemony which often accompany such seemingly generous practices, there is, both from a theoretical and an empirical perspective, no reason to assume that all identity relations (or society at large) are characterized by underlying contradictions. For example, reports from the early Oslo period show that many Israelis and Palestinians were, if only for a short period of time, genuinely attracted by the prospect of peace and, at least in many personal encounters,[81] were able to establish a symmetry and trusting curiosity – and even friendship – with the Other. Yet, the rapid collapse of the Oslo peace process underlines once more the pervasiveness of the creeping antagonization of Middle East politics and not only because some observers claimed always to have known that the institutional structures of Oslo were defective from the beginning.[82]

Thus, the problem of Oslo was not primarily that 'radicals' on both sides held hostage a generally peace-willing wider public, but rather that negative identity ascriptions and fear of the other side are still considered plausible amongst large parts of the population both in Palestine and Israel – and, indeed, amongst a world societal public too. This idea-system was, therefore, easily re-inscribed onto the matrix of Oslo once the first setbacks occurred. Rather than addressing the failure of Oslo in a prophetical or cynical manner – that is, by arguing that Oslo was deficient from the outset or by assuming that the Other never really had the intention to engage in genuine peace – or by simply attributing this failure to the allegedly intractable nature of conflict themes, it might be empirically and theoretically more compelling to take the subtle effects of the creeping antagonization of Middle East politics seriously and to explicitly address the communicative dynamics which render the continuation of conflicts within the overall context of frozen crossings and hot contestations likely.

Identity as the ideological battleground of Middle East conflicts

The arguments in this chapter resonate to a degree with Immanuel Wallerstein's noteworthy concept of culture as the main 'ideological battleground' of world society. Wallerstein maintains that culture is a subtle practice through which the modern world-system ensures that 'the contradictory tensions of the world-systems [are] contained', thereby subtly invigorating the stability of this (contradictory) setting.[83] This containment relates to two different dimensions of culture. First, culture as a comprehensive *idea-system* of (contradictory) social settings is the 'assertion of unchanging realities amidst a world that is, in fact, ceaselessly changing',[84] that is, the overarching context of distinct (contradictory) societal constellations which are taken for granted in communications. Second, however, culture is not merely such a structural embedding of communications, but also relates to notions of culture as *identity*. The main function of identities is to make sense of the manifold differences between people which emerge in the context of the everyday (contradictory) operations of the overarching idea-system (for example, different levels of development, rights and so on). However, in order to avoid an immediate collapse of the (contradictory) idea-system, which produces these inequalities in the first place, the various contradictions do not become directly attributed to the hegemonic 'cultural frame'[85] – which after all 'guarantees reality'.[86] It is on this basis that Wallerstein has argued that identities can be understood as the reification and 'justification of the inequities of the system, as the attempt to keep them unchanging in a world that is ceaselessly threatening to change', thereby conditioning the (relative) stability of the contradictory idea-system.[87] What matters is the observation that the explicit thematization *and* reification of (naturally or socially generated) identities in societal communications is often the by-product of those (un-thematized) contradictory social settings that had initially produced these cultures and identities. In this way, contradictory social settings ensure their stability since inequalities produced within the overall context of the overarching 'cultural frame' are not attributed directly to the system but to particularistic cultures and identities.[88] Seen from that perspective, 'culture is nothing else but the memory of society, thus the filter of forgetting/remembering', in this case the remembering of antagonisms and the forgetting of the many cooperative, peaceful and amicable 'histories' of the Middle East, in general, and of regional identity relations, in particular.[89]

While this book neither shares Wallerstein's assumption that the world-system primarily is a capitalist world-system (that is, dominated by one functional system) nor subscribes to the view that world society in its entirety is structured by underlying contradictions and antagonisms, there is nevertheless a huge value to this classification when accounting for the role of identity and conflicts in Middle East politics. First, Wallerstein rightfully points to the necessarily global context within which 'cultures' and identities are constantly created and re-created. Second, and this is more central to the discussion in this section, Wallerstein's approach is interesting insofar as it provides a fruitful basis for accounting for the ways in which those societal settings, which are indeed characterized by significant contradictions and inequalities – such as the orders of 'frozen crossings' and 'hot contestations' in Middle East politics – tend to resort to notions of culture and identity in order to make sense of – and thereby to stabilize – the reality of these very settings. Hence, the significance of the creeping antagonization of Middle East politics lies in its encouragement constantly to thematize antagonistic identities in political and other functional discourses, thereby translating the logic of frozen crossings and hot contestations into the taken-for-granted order of Middle East politics. Such dynamics enable the stabilization of these settings because the massive inequalities produced by this overarching idea-system can easily be attributed to seemingly pervasive and diametrically opposed identities and interests – thereby legitimating equally ruthless opposition to impositions by the Other. It is in that sense that the logic of frozen crossings can indeed be understood as the underlying 'culture' of world societal communications in and on the Middle East, thereby underlining Luhmann's observation that culture is the '*re-description* of descriptions which orient daily life'.[90] It is precisely on this basis that the ubiquitous thematization of (antagonistic) identities in Middle East politics becomes the key vehicle in accounting for inequalities (for example, powerful/powerless) without questioning the taken-for-granted context of the contradictory orders of frozen crossings which produces these identities in the first place. It is in this sense that culture, understood as the idea-system of contradictory social orders 'formulates a problem of "identity" which it cannot solve by itself – and precisely for that reason problematizes'.[91]

Such lock-in effects of communications, which centre on the thematization of antagonistic identities, are a well-studied phenomenon in conflict studies. As Heinz Messmer has shown on the basis of detailed empirical studies, in such identity and subordination conflicts 'each side experiences the action of the other as the causal reason for ongoing disappointment and on that basis infers back to the specific attributes of the other's character'.[92] Such intense forms of social conflict are, therefore, characterized by radically opposed perspectives of how conflict and violence are experienced. Such opposed perspectives relate in particular to assumptions about the responsibility for the emergence and continuity of the conflict, on the one hand, and to radically divergent perceptions about the real power distributions therein, on the other. More precisely, each side attributes responsibility for the continuity of the conflict to an-Other (blaming),[93] consequently demanding that the other conflict party give in first. This is underlined by the notable use of game-metaphors in Middle East politics, such as the regular reference within the context of the Israeli-Palestinian conflict to the idea 'that the ball is in the Palestinian/Israeli court' – of course for some miraculous reason the ball never is within the Self's court. As a result of these dynamics, each side feels threatened by the Other and, consequently, opposition tends to be perceived as a sign of the intransigent features of the Other (identity conflict) or even as a menacing threat (subordination conflict).

It is precisely this tendency – that within fully differentiated conflict systems, opposition tends to be interpreted as a dangerous threat – which further substantiates the key argument referred to above, namely that the creeping antagonization of Middle East politics ultimately blurs the border between power and powerlessness – and is doing so in order to ensure the continuation of conflict communications. This is not to argue that in terms of military capacity or the control of the state apparatus some actors would not be more 'powerful' than others. Rather, it highlights the insight that due to the aforementioned multiplication of diametrically opposed perspectives in identity and subordination conflicts each side feels *genuinely* threatened by an-Other – for examples, Palestinians in the West Bank and Gaza Strip feel threatened by the Israeli army and Jewish settlers, Israelis in turn are threatened by Palestinian suicide bombers, Iran's nuclear ambitions and anti-Semitic rhetoric as well as an Arab state system which has so far failed to ensure Israel's regional integration, Arabs in turn feel threatened by Western and Israeli military and economic power and supremacy as well as Israel's lacklustre efforts to seek regional integration, the West by Islamic fundamentalism and population growth rates in Arab countries, Islamists by the Western cultural models (and the attractions of consumerism), and so on. This is not meant to further elaborate on all these complex conflict settings, yet it strongly underlines the observation that 'fully differentiated conflict constellations of this type [identity/subordination conflict] are characterized by a structure which fosters paradoxical forms of anomalous relationships which, sometimes, reproduce the conflict in a permanent and seemingly intractable manner', since such orders are always based on the assumption that the (adversarial) Other holds considerable and threatening power resources.[94] This is precisely what happens if frozen crossings are regarded as the taken-for-granted idea-system, such as in Middle East politics where the constant thematization of (antagonistic) identities ensures that such lock-in effects are indeed likely. Thus, with thematizations of identity operating under the reality-assumption of frozen crossings and hot contestations, opposition can easily be regarded as a (menacing) threat. As a result, contradictions do not simply evaporate but, in the name of protecting the securitized Self, stabilize the antagonistic order in the form of solid conflict systems. It is on this basis that it can indeed be argued 'that the problem of conflict can be restated not as a problem of a disruption of communication but as a problem of continuing conflict communication'.[95] The creeping antagonization of Middle East politics is the means through which conflicts solve the ardent problem of their (self-referential) continuation. To avoid any misunderstandings, it must clearly be emphasized that 'despite their tendency to become locked-in, [identity and subordination] conflicts are not structurally given, and there is no historical determinacy'.[96] In fact, conflicts always have to solve the problem of how to ensure the 'continuous communication of incompatibilities, which are themselves no ontological givens but depend on discursive "processes of constructing a shared understanding of what is to be considered and collectively responded to" as a social phenomenon'.[97] It is on this basis that this chapter has argued that the constant thematization of antagonistic identities in political and other functional communications in and on the Middle East ensures that frozen crossings and hot contestations are indeed the widely shared understanding of what needs to be considered and collectively responded to as the social reality of Middle East politics. Otherwise, to refer yet again to the Palestinian-Israeli conflict, one of the parties could simply try to give in first and to trust that the other side will follow suit – the more so because opinion polls on both sides document consistently that a huge majority both in Israel and Palestine (and many Arab countries) support peace *and* the need to compromise.

To summarize, it can be argued that social conflicts in Middle East politics indeed fulfil an alarming function for society insofar as they transform the creeping antagonization of Middle East politics into concrete and pervasive (conflict) structures.[98] Consequently, opposition to frozen crossings does not remain a lofty feature of desperate contestations by the disempowered or of mere (academic) second-order observations reflecting on the contingency of the systematic patterns of inclusion/exclusion in the region. Ultimately, the reality of intense forms of social conflicts in the Middle East prevents any permanent consolidation of *concrete* orders of frozen crossings. However, at the same time, these conflicts use antagonistic identities in order to solve the problem of how to ensure the continuation of conflict communications – thereby turning the overall *idea-system* of frozen crossings and hot contestations into the blind-spot of conflict communications. Moreover, as the above examples of various peace processes and conflict resolution dynamics demonstrate, the power of conflict systems relates not only to the more obvious cases of the manifold violent conflicts in the region. It can also be traced in the subtle encroachment of seemingly benevolent practices through these conflict dynamics. Such benign dynamics are often also entrapped within the overall confines of an explicit thematization of antagonistic identities, thereby, unintentionally, perpetuating the conflictive moments in political communications in and on the Middle East. It is in that sense, that one can indeed speak of a deep perturbation of Middle East politics by conflict dynamics without attributing this pervasiveness of conflicts to any specificity of regional identities, interests and cultures but rather by underlining the structural world societal context within which this antagonization evolves and constantly reproduces itself.

World society and Middle East conflicts

Notwithstanding the pervasiveness of the creeping antagonization of Middle East politics and the centrality of (violent) conflicts in the region, it is essential to highlight once again the structurally relational, dynamic and always changeable character of (antagonistic) identities and conflicts. On that basis and by shifting the spotlight onto communications as the basic unit of society, this chapter has proposed an alternative reading of what are often referred to as the 'root causes' of conflicts and the status of the Middle East as one of world society's most popular conflict regions. However, rather than merely claiming that identities and conflicts are what actors make of it (to paraphrase Alexander Wendt's iconic phrase),[99] thereby highlighting the undisputable social constructedness of all conflicts and identities, this chapter has elaborated on the communicative dynamics which render likely the communication of antagonistic identities and conflicts within the overall context of frozen crossings and hot contestations as their overarching idea-system. These dynamics relate, on the one hand, to the necessity of an explicit thematization of antagonistic identities in Middle East politics, which facilitates the lock-in effects of social conflict and dis-privileges the general expectation that communication offers are accepted. A communication-theoretical perspective then allows us to see that the resultant centrality of antagonistic identities and conflicts is not a feature unique to Middle East politics (and culture) but unfolds against the background of a structurally de-bordered world societal horizon. And, this not only relates to interest-driven 'external' interventions by hegemonic political and economic actors but also to the subtle ways through which notions of antagonistic identities encroach into seemingly innocent practices, for example, with regard to 'reasoned' proposals for conflict resolution and notions of 'cultural dialogue' which both often tend to re-inscribe an antagonistic hierarchy between a rational outside and an irrational inside into political communications on the region. On that basis this chapter also maintains that too quick a normative condemnation of violence and conflicts in the region often hinders a clear perspective on either the function of the explicit thematization of antagonistic identities in Middle East politics or the structures of conflict in the region. Thus, by translating the creeping antagonization of political communications in and on the region into concrete societal structures, social conflicts in the region constantly direct attention towards the contingency both of frozen crossings and, ironically, of the antagonistic identities which result from the regular operations of this overarching idea-system. By encouraging opposition to the blunt relegation dynamics inherent in that context, any reification of such orders is prevented. In that sense social conflicts in relation to the Middle East indeed fulfil their alarming function for (world) society.

However, this chapter has also elaborated on the problematic aspects of these conflicts, in particular the severe lock-in effects which accompany the heavy securitization of the Middle East (and identities in the region). Thus, by blurring the border between the powerful and the powerless (with identities feeling constantly fundamentally threatened by an-Other), social conflicts in the Middle East solve the problem of their (fragile) continuation in a broadly effective manner. In that sense the Middle East (and territories, identities and interest therein) is indeed a placeless attractor for conflict communications, since such lock-in effects shape political communications on the region on a world societal scale – in turn legitimizing all possible intervention practices (either from inside or outside the region) in order to secure 'peace'. Yet, these lock-in effects, as solid and durable as they might appear, ultimately always have a fragile status. Thus, Middle East politics are not a distinct system but are part of a structurally debordered world societal context and it is this horizon which ensures that Middle East conflicts always retain a tenuous status.

In other words, the world societal horizon of all communications ultimately prevents any reification of antagonistic identities and conflict constellations. This relates, for example, to the manifold practices of 'remembering' peace and cooperation in the region, such as in those studies and popular narratives which highlight and remember the many instances of peaceful or at least conciliatory relations between different identity groups in the Ottoman empire, between Jews and Palestinians both in the Yishuv period and the early Oslo period or, as Kirsten E. Schulze has demonstrated, between Jews and other confessional groups in Lebanon even after the establishment of the state of Israel and the Six Days War of 1967.[100] What all these invocations of history have in common is that they make a convincing claim for the idea that identities and interest in the region are in fact highly dynamic and historically generated social artefacts, always subject to change and open to reinterpretation. Of course, such a focus on the, intentionally or unintentionally, often neglected mosaic of peace and cooperation in the Middle East – both in the (constantly re-written) past as well as an unwritten future – should not motivate an escapist logic which simply ignores the pervasiveness of the 'deep perturbation' of Middle East politics (and identities) by severe conflict dynamics. Yet, it corroborates the argument that the communicative dynamics which constantly create and recreate these identities and conflicts against the background of a world societal horizon at the same time prevent any permanent reification of antagonistic political orders. This echoes Ernesto Laclau's claim that identities are 'vulnerable to any new system of relations'[101] and that, therefore, the polycontextual, and dynamic features of a constantly changing world society, integrated by communications as their basic unit, ensure that identities always remain incomplete. Thus, since identities are dependent on (constantly changing) relational patterns, the *actual* operations of a myriad of societal communications might always, incidentally, trigger changes in identity constructions (even of 'radicals' and 'fundamentalists'), independently of their menacing self-descriptions. Moreover, by always keeping available the mere *possibility* of communicating (and, thereby, remembering) about how antagonistic identities would look like in the Middle East 'in an environment of peace',[102] any permanent closure of identities and conflicts is structurally impossible – the 'yes' always remains on the horizon. Looking to this horizon, the following chapter concludes this study with some final reflections on the place of peace in regional politics.

6
Beyond Orientalization and Civilization: Concluding Remarks

Tutto nel mondo è burla. L'uom è nato burlone / All the world's a
prank, and man is born a clown
Guiseppe Verdi – Falstaff (atto terzo, seconda parte)[1]

Whither peace in the Middle East?

This book has two main points of departure. First, the limited success of various liberalization and democratization efforts as well as the collapse of several peace processes throughout the Middle East in the 1990s and early 2000s requires an explanation that transcends theoretically and empirically unconvincing notions of regional specificity. The creeping antagonization of Middle East politics as well as the deep perturbation of regional politics by conflict dynamics cannot sufficiently be understood on the basis of allegedly unique characteristics of the regional political 'system' or specificities of regional cultures, interests and identities. Indeed, the focus of this book on the centrality of frozen crossings and hot contestations, severe dynamics of inclusion/exclusion as well as Othering processes in Middle East politics has provided ample evidence that the undoubtedly heavy securitization dynamics in the region need to be studied from a communication-theoretical perspective which focuses on the world societal embedding of *all* political and conflict-related communications in and on this region. Second, and following on this argument, a central observation has been that any study on Middle East politics must be aware of its own embedding within this overall context of the creeping antagonization of political, scientific and other functional communications in and on the region. More precisely, when accounting for the obvious centrality of antagonistic identities and conflicts in the Middle East, the implicit or explicit reification of these identities and conflicts in the traditions of either Orientalization (that is, the creation of an image of a 'real' Middle East which is, however, largely inaccessible to Westerners, thereby attributing responsibility for conflicts to the allegedly hegemonic Other) or Civilization (that is, the creation of an image of Middle Eastern cultures and identities as, on some level, fundamentally different, thereby attributing responsibility for conflicts to this allegedly cultural Other) has to be avoided.

The significant impact which both the 'critical' and 'realist' traditions have on the study of Middle East politics only demonstrates the difficulties of writing about identity and conflict in the region without simultaneously re-inscribing objectivist notions of conflict and identity into political or scientific discourses. Avoiding this dilemma is more difficult than might initially be suspected since both discourses are not simply wrong but, in particular in their nuanced versions, address issues of crucial relevance. Yet, on a more conceptual level they are both problematic insofar as they advance notions of an underlying ontologically given contradiction which allegedly shapes Middle East politics, either by focusing on a structurally violent and hegemonic global system or on conflict-oriented local cultures. While this is not to downplay the pervasiveness of Middle East conflicts, any 'empirical theory'[2] must however *systematically* take into consideration that communications are neither entirely contradictory nor affirmative – the 'no' but also the 'yes' are always at society's disposal. In other words, contradictions might be the result of concrete societal processes but they cannot be regarded as in some way preceding communication, as notions of a 'real' yet inaccessible Middle East as well as of the 'reality' of conflictive cultures in a Hobbesian Middle East imply. In other words, what is also necessary is to account for the centrality of antagonistic identities and conflicts in the Middle East without – intentionally or unintentionally – ignoring or downplaying the many dynamics of cooperation, coexistence and even peace in the region.

Of course, these concluding remarks are not meant to provide a wholesale, theoretically and empirically ambitious overview on cooperation and peace in the region – which would deserve, and indeed should have, another book-length study. And certainly such a study would have to engage in detail with crucial insights from the area of peace studies. To mention a few central insights from this research tradition, peace comprises more than the mere absence of war or the fragile stabilization of a cold peace, which is the widest form of peace in the contemporary Middle East, at least as far as inter-state relations and fragile social contracts within many Middle Eastern nation-states are concerned.

As the Arab Human Development Reports have argued, thereby echoing a central claim in peace research from Galtung to Burton,[3] wider notions of security, empathy, reconciliation, justice and human needs have also to be taken into consideration in order to establish a 'positive peace'.[4] Moreover, peace not only requires the participation of decision-makers and political (and other) societal elites but also comprises a systematic involvement of 'civil society' and wider parts of the population, thereby ensuring a vertical sedimentation of cross-border cooperation and, ultimately, integration.[5] Finally, most commentators agree that the aim of conflict resolution is not to get rid of conflicts altogether but rather to reconcile 'conflict' cultures with the much wider project of a 'civilization of conflicts' along the lines of 'constructive pacifism' as has been emphasised by Dieter Senghaas.[6] Such a process-oriented perspective on the manifold dynamics of de-securitization seems not only reasonable from a more general theoretical perspective – thus, it is simply not possible to conceive of a conflict-free society – but is also underlined by the necessary focus on the function of social conflicts, namely their role in rendering societal evolution possible. A total absence of conflicts, seen from that perspective, would indeed appear as a broadly totalizing project advancing either a victor's peace[7] (in the aftermath of a subordination conflict) or a hegemonic peace (as the outcome of an identity conflict). Indeed, the way in which various discourses of peace, liberation and security from within and outside the region constantly create and recreate the Middle East (and territories therein) as zones of intervention underlines the importance of this observation. In this sense Lothar Brock's statement that under any circumstances 'peace politics remain ... incomplete'[8] has both a strong empirical and normative validity. In sum, as Oliver Richmond has argued, the challenge of establishing 'peace' – in the Middle East and beyond – needs to be,

> constructed in terms of the creation of a positivist epistemology of peace, and one which attempts to avoid orientalism and totalism, while still aspiring to the plausibility, if not possibility of universalism. Part of the problem with this approach is its complexity. But this is also where its sophistication lies. The recognition of the sheer complexity both of conflict, and of the peace projects of internationals in relation to threats, disasters, and conflict, is necessary.[9]

As noted above, the purpose of these concluding remarks is not to complement the analysis in this book on the complexities of (antagonistic) identities and conflicts in regional politics with an equally detailed empirical and theoretical focus on peace and cooperation. However, what is needed is to account for the manifold actualized and potential invocations of peace in the region – in the past, the present and un-written futures[10] – in order not to be seduced by the subtle logic of the creeping antagonization of Middle East politics. As Louise Fawcett has reminded us, there is indeed a long history of Middle East politics beyond conflicts in spite of the more widespread image of the Middle East as world society's most popular conflict space.[11] Thus, 'against this vision of disorder, there is a contrasting and compelling vision of order, one long familiar to regional scholars: peoples cohabiting a rela-tively seamless space, of tolerance and diversity – cultural, linguistic and religious'.[12] Of course, such instances of remembering the Middle East (or the Mediterranean) as a shared political, economic and cultural space[13] are inhibited by the experiences of trauma resulting from histor-ical or contemporary conflict constellations as well as a widespread dis-appointment with regard to failures of various (faltering) peace processes and liberalization projects.[14] However, the various practices in the Middle East of overcoming the 'total negation of the otherness of the Other'[15] are well-documented with regard to manifold dynamics in overcoming distrust, blaming and prejudices, for example, on the basis of people-to-people projects, educational projects which raise awareness about the history and traumas of the Other(s) as well as the many joint professional teams and cross-border economic cooperation projects which exist in the region.[16] The fact that many of these experiences of cooperation are based on the understanding that within a strongly secur-itized environment peace-building is a 'protracted process'[17] characterized by many inconsistencies and the constant possibility of setbacks might also be helpful in reassessing the many 'lost opportunities' of Middle East peace-building, for example, in the context of the failed Camp David talks and Syrian-Israeli negotiations.[18] Thus, the (current) failures of reconciliation are not primarily related to an intransigent nature of the Other or to insurmountable structural conditions, which impede on interest convergence, but rather highlight the pervasiveness with which the 'deep perturbation' of Middle East politics by conflict dynamics works to ensure the persistence of antagonisms.[19] And, as has been referred to throughout this book, such practices of securitiza-tion are not a regional prerogative – for this would only replicate the notion of identities and cultures as somewhat stable and separate containers – but relate to many political communications on the Middle East both within and outside the region. They thus also comprise the widespread practices of stereotyping Muslims/Arabs as traditional, conflict-prone and potentially violent, thereby ignoring the immense diversity, heterogeneity and, indeed, modernity of the Middle East.[20] It might seem obvious to say that in the overall context of the creeping antagonization of Middle East politics other groups as well, such as, *inter alia*, Israelis/Jews or Westerners are also subject to such adversarial identity constructions both in the region and outside. Seen from that perspective, a peaceful Middle East must not be mistaken for a conflict-free region but rather relates as a Middle East in which the creeping antagonization of regional politics no longer operates as the overarching cultural frame of (political) communications. In that context, and to refer to an argument by Thomas Diez on the European integration project, the 'self' history of the Middle East as a war-torn region subject to intense forms of securitization might at one point in time even become the region's 'historical Other'.[21]

The often-voiced invocation that (temporarily or permanently) the Middle East is, unfortunately, not suited in becoming a Kantian space is less an argument with impressive empirical persuasive power than it is proof of the more or less subtle ways with which the creeping antagonization of Middle East politics presents itself as the unques-tioned and taken-for-granted order of regional politics – either by advo-cating a natural conflict-proneness of the Middle East or by framing 'cooperation' as generally positive but as currently being dangerous, naive or unsuitable. Yet, as with all identities, this identity of the Middle East as a 'perennial conflict region'[22] is also necessarily incom-plete. Notwithstanding the cultural hegemony of the creeping antago-nization in many political and other functional communications in world society, which continuously make plausible notions of a conflic-tive Middle East, the constant and structurally given memory of peace-ful pasts, presents and futures – both in the form of actualized or potential orders – must wholly undermine the totality assumptions accompanying the understanding of the Middle East as somehow natu-rally conflictive. As this study has demonstrated, the reasons for the remarkable centrality of the antagonistic thematization of identities as well as the intensity of conflicts in the region (but also the relevance and importance of peace and cooperation) do not relate to any substan-tive differences (for example, in terms of interests and identities) which distinguish the Middle East from other places. They are, rather, the result of contingent communications constantly unfolding within a primarily functionally differentiated world society. Studies on the region are well advised to leave the mystification of the region – which is most explicit in both the Orientalized celebration and the 'realist' condemnation of an 'authentic' Middle East – behind, and to demystify the Middle East by focusing on these contingent, dynamic and non-linear processes which shape concrete semantics and structures in world society. As this book has shown by focusing on political communications in and on the Middle East, small nuances in communications rather than substantive discrepancies between regions/cultures constantly produce and reproduce frozen crossings and hot contestations in Middle East politics. The ensuing centrality of conflictive identities as well as the deep perturbation of regional politics by severe conflict dynamics always remains firmly embedded within the context of world society as the encompassing social system of all societal operations – and it is this world societal horizon which subverts any totalizing identity of the creeping antagonization of Middle East politics.

Notes

Preface

1. Interview with Nora Ephron and Susan Edmison, 1965, http://www.
   interferenza.com/bcs/interw/65-aug.htm.

1. Introduction: globalization, world society and the study of the Middle East in international relations

1. From the album 'American III: Solitary Man', Warner Music International,
   2000.
2. M. H. Kerr, *The Arab Cold War: Gamal 'Abd Al-Nasir and His Rivals, 1958–1970*,
   Oxford: Oxford University Press, 1971; A. Bank and M. Valbjørn, 'Signs of a
   New Arab Cold War: the 2006 Lebanon War and the Sunni-Shi'i Divide', *Middle East Report*, Spring, 2007.
3. See below in this chapter.
4. N. Luhmann, *Die Wissenschaft der Gesellschaft*, Frankfurt: Suhrkamp, 1992,
   p. 85. This and all subsequent translations from German texts are made by
   the author.
5. P. Bilgin, 'Is the "Orientalist" Past the Future of Middle East Studies?', *Third World Quarterly*, 25(2), 2004: 431.
6. G. M. Steinberg, 'Postcolonial Theory and the Ideology of Peace Studies',
   Israel Studies, 13(4), 2007: 786–96.
7. Central here of course is E. W. Said, *Orientalism*, Harmondsworth: Penguin,
   1995.
8. N. Luhmann, 'Vorbemerkungen zu einer Theorie sozialer Systeme', in
   Aufsätze und Reden, ed. O. Jahraus, Stuttgart: Philipp Reclam, 2001, p. 7.
9. Ibid., p. 9.
10. Ibid.
11. Luhmann, *Aufsätze und Reden*.
12. Luhmann, *Die Gesellschaft der Gesellschaft*, Frankfurt: Suhrkamp, 1998.
13. This has also affected Middle East politics. See various studies on non-linear,
    chaotic and eclectic processes in conflict settings as well as in cooperation
    projects, for example, S. Steinberg, 'Discourse Categories in Encounters
    between Palestinians and Israelis', *International Journal of Politics, Culture
    and Society*, 17(3), 2004: 471–89; K. Rasler, 'Shocks, Expectancy, and the
    De-Escalation of Protracted Conflicts: the Israeli-Palestinian Case', *Journal
    of Peace Research*, 37(6), 2000: 699–720.
14. This and subsequent chapters will elaborate on both concepts in much
    greater theoretical and empirical detail.
15. N. Luhmann, 'Vorbemerkungen zu einer Theorie sozialer Systeme', in
    Aufsätze und Reden, p. 8.

16. See also Lisa Anderson's plea for transcending and challenging 'apparently universal scientific generalizations' through insights from Middle East studies; L. Anderson, 'Politics in the Middle East: Opportunities and Limits in the Quest for Theory', in M. Tessler et al. (eds), *Area Studies and Social Science: Strategies for Understanding Middle East Politics*, Bloomington and Indianapolis: Indiana University Press, 1999, p. 9. For other powerful accounts on the primacy of local vis-à-vis global dynamics, see P. S. Khoury and J. Kostiner (eds), *Tribes and State Formation in the Middle East*, London and New York: Tauris, 1991, and L. L. Layne, *Home and Homeland: the Dialogics of Tribal and National Identity in Jordan*, Princeton: Princeton University Press, 1994.

17. On this distinction between 'global' and 'universal' approaches see also the second section of this chapter. There is a wide literature, in IR and beyond, which applies 'universal' social sciences theories to the study of specific topics of Middle East politics. See amongst others L. Fawcett (ed.), *International Relations of the Middle East*, Oxford: Oxford University Press, 2005; Y. Sayigh and A. Shlaim, *The Cold War and the Middle East*, Oxford: Clarendon, 1997; L. A. Brand, *Jordan's Inter-Arab Relations: the Political Economy of Alliance Making*, New York: Columbia University Press, 1994; F. Halliday, *The Middle East in International Relations: Power, Politics and Ideology*, Cambridge: Cambridge University Press, 2005; R. Hinnebusch, *The International Politics of the Middle East*, Manchester: Manchester University Press, 2003.

18. D. Jung (ed.), *The Middle East and Palestine: Global Politics and Regional Conflict*, Basingstoke: Palgrave Macmillan, 2004; L. Fawcett, *International Relations*; C. M. Henry and R. Springborg, *Globalisation and the Politics of Development in the Middle East*, Cambridge: Cambridge University Press, 2001; R. Khalidi, 'The Middle East as an Area in an Era of Globalization', in A. Mirsepassi et al. (eds), *Localizing Knowledge in a Globalizing World: Recasting the Area Studies Debate*, Syracuse: Syracuse University Press, 2003. For a critical perspective see Y. Sayigh, 'Globalization Manqué: Regional Fragmentation and Authoritarian-Liberalism in the Middle East', in L. Fawcett and Y. Sayigh (eds), *The Third World Beyond the Cold War: Continuity and Change*, Oxford: Oxford University Press, 1999.

19. See for an overview S. Stetter (ed.), *Territorial Conflicts in World Society: Modern Systems Theory, International Relations and Conflict Studies*, London and New York: Routledge. See also further below in this chapter.

20. On 'perturbation' see in greater detail chapter 5. See also N. Luhmann, *Soziale Systeme: Grundriß einer allgemeinen Theorie*, Frankfurt: Suhrkamp, 1987, pp. 506–9. For an interesting discussion of globalization and IR see B. Buzan, *From International to World Society: English School Theory and the Social Structure of Globalisation*, Cambridge: Cambridge University Press, 2004.

21. J. W. Burton, *World Society*, Cambridge: Cambridge University Press, 1972.

22. Ibid., p. 20.

23. See U. Beck, *Der kosmopolitische Blick oder: Krieg ist Frieden*, Frankfurt: Suhrkamp, 2004.

24. See for critical debates on the reach of culture-oriented and state-centred analyses, M. Valbjørn, 'The Meeting of the Twain: Bridging the Gap between International Relations and Middle East Studies', *Cooperation and Conflict*, 38(2), 2003: 163–73; G. Nonnemann, 'Rentiers and Autocrats, Monarchs and Democrats, State and Society: the Middle East between Globalization, Human "Agency", and Europe', *International Affairs*, 77(1), 2001: 141–62.

25. See F. Halliday, *The Middle East in International Relations*, pp. 25–7; M. Beck, 'Von theoretischen Wüsten, Oasen und Karawanen: Der Vordere Orient in den Internationalen Beziehungen', *Zeitschrift für Internationale Beziehungen*, 9(2), 2002: 305–30.

26. This is particularly true for the literature on Islamism and other religious fundamentalist movements in the Middle East and how these 'traditional' movements relate to and manipulate 'modern' dynamics of technological and scientific globalization. See amongst many others D. Diner, *Versiegelte Zeit: Über den Stillstand in der islamischen Welt*, Berlin: Propyläen, 2005; F. Halliday, *Nation and Religion in the Middle East*, Boulder: Lynne Rienner, 2000; M. R. Neyestani, 'Cultural and Religious Identities in an Era of Information and Communication Globalization', *Alternatives: Turkish Journal of International Relations*, 4(4), 2005: 33–9; S. A. Arjomand, 'Islam, Political Change and Globalization', *Thesis Eleven*, 76(1), 2004: 9–28.

27. See M. Tessler et al., *Area Studies and Social Science*.

28. See from a general IR perspective L. Brock, 'World Society from the Bottom Up', in M. Albert and L. Hilkermeier (eds), *Observing International Relations: Niklas Luhmann and World Politics*, London and New York: Routledge, 2004, p. 89. For a classical critique in Middle East studies see also N. N. Ayubi, *Over-Stating the Arab State: Politics and Society in the Middle East*, London: Tauris, 1995.

29. See in particular N. Luhmann, *Die Gesellschaft der Gesellschaft*, pp. 145–71; R. Stichweh, *Die Weltgesellschaft: Soziologische Analysen*, Frankfurt: Suhrkamp, 2000; B. Heintz et al. (eds), *Weltgesellschaft: Theoretische Zugänge und empirische Problemlagen*, Sonderheft der Zeitschrift für Soziologie, Stuttgart: Lucius & Lucius, 2005. For world society theory and IR see M. Albert and L. Hilkermeier, *Observing International Relations*, S. Stetter, *Territorial Conflicts*.

30. This territorial depiction does not carry any political connotations. It should, however, be noted that in Syrian nationalist discourses the notion of *bilad as-sham* occupies a mystifying, expansionist place. See E. Zisser, 'Who's Afraid of Syrian Nationalism? National and State Identity in Syria', *Middle Eastern Studies*, 42(2), 2006: 179–98.

31. No attempts have been made in this book to exactly transliterate Arabic and Hebrew names and words, for this would only complicate legibility.

32. See R. Stichweh, *Die Weltgesellschaft*, pp.198–200.

33. See L. Guazzone (ed.), *The Middle East in Global Change: the Politics and Economics of Interdependence and Fragmentation*, Basingstoke: Macmillan, 1997.

34. See also M. Albert, 'On Governance, Democracy and European Systems: on Systems Theory and European Integration', *Review of International Studies*, 28(2), 2002: 293–309; S. Stetter, 'Regions of Conflict in World Society: the Place of the Middle East and sub-Saharan Africa', in S. Stetter, *Territorial Conflicts in World Society*, pp. 43–8.

35. S. Guzzini, 'Constructivism and International Relations: an Analysis of Luhmann's Conceptualization of Power', in M. Albert and L. Hilkermeier, *Observing International Relations*, pp. 209–22.

36. E.W. Said, *Orientalism*.

37. See F. Halliday, *Islam and the Myth of Confrontation: Religion and Politics in the Middle East*, London: Tauris, 1996, pp. 195–217.

38. This does not contradict the aforementioned observation on an underlying spectre of Orientalism in Middle East studies. The scheme of Orientalism,

on the one hand, enables an analysis of the impact of globalization on Middle East politics and society while, on the other hand, framing this globalization as an ultimately 'external', mainly Western interference into regional dynamics. See for this A. S. Ahmed, *Islam under Siege: Living Dangerously in a Post-Honor World*, Cambridge: Polity, 2003.

39. See S. Gabriel, 'Is the Jewish Diaspora Unique? Reflections on the Diaspora's Current Situation', *Israel Affairs*, 10(1), 2005: 1–35; S. Morrison, '"Os Turcos", the Syrian-Lebanese Community of Sao Paolo, Brazil', *Journal of Muslim Minority Affairs*, 25(3), 2005: 423–38.

40. G. Luciani, 'Oil and Political Economy in the International Relations of the Middle East', in L. Fawcett, *International Relations*; H. Hakimian and Z. Moshaver (eds), *The State and Global Change: the Political Economy of Transition in the Middle East and North Africa*, Richmond: Curzon, 2001; L. Guazzone, *The Middle East in Global Change*.

41. See B. Tibi, *The Challenge of Fundamentalism*, Berkeley: University of California Press, 1998; J. L. Esposito, *Unholy War: Terror in the Name of Islam*, Oxford: Oxford University Press, 2002; S. J. Al-Azm, 'Islam, Terrorism and the West', *Comparative Studies of South Asia, Africa and the Middle East*, 25(1), 2005: 6–15.

42. That is the central argument in B. Tibi, *Islamischer Fundamentalismus, moderne Wissenschaft und Technologie*, Frankfurt: Suhrkamp, 1992; for a different perspective see K. P. Japp, 'Zur Soziologie des fundamentalistischen Terrorismus', *Soziale Systeme*, 9(1), 2003: 54–87.

43. Y. Sayigh and A. Shlaim, *The Cold War and the Middle East*; P. Sluglett, 'The Cold War and the Middle East', in L. Fawcett, *International Relations*.

44. S. Zubaida, *Law and Power in the Islamic World*, London: Tauris, 2005; H. Frisch, 'Nationalising a Universal Text: the Quran in Arafat's Rhetoric', *Middle Eastern Studies*, 41(3), 2005: 321–36.

45. See B. Buzan and O. Wæver, *Regions and Powers: the Structure of International Security*, Cambridge: Cambridge University Press, 2005. See also S. Stetter, 'Regions of Conflict in World Society'.

46. A. Ehteshami, 'Islam, Muslim Polities, and Democracy', *Democratization*, 11(4), 2004: 90–110; B. Korany et al. (eds), *Political Liberalization and Democratization in the Arab World*, 2 vols, Boulder: Lynne Rienner, 1995 and 1998.

47. S. Stetter, 'Democratisation without Democracy: the Implementation of EU Assistance for Democratisation Processes in Palestine', *Mediterranean Politics*, 8(3), 2003: 153–73.

48. See especially G. Ben Porat, 'A New Middle East? Globalization, Peace and the "Double Movement"', *International Relations*, 19(1), 2005: 39–62; see also A. Shlaim, 'The Rise and Fall of the Oslo Peace Process', in L. Fawcett, *International Relations*.

49. L. A. Brand, 'The Effects of the Peace Process on Political Liberalization in Jordan', *Journal of Palestine Studies*, 28(2), 1999: 52–67; V. Perthes, 'Editorial: Elites in the Orient, or: Why Focus on Middle Eastern Elites?', *Orient*, 44(4), 2003: 531–5; B. E. Sasley, 'The Effects of Political Liberalization on Security', in T. A. Jacoby and B. E. Sasley (eds), *Redefining Security in the Middle East*, Manchester: Manchester University Press, 2002.

50. E. L. Rogan, 'The Emergence of the Middle East into the Modern State System', in L. Fawcett, *International Relations*. See also F. Halliday, *The Middle East in International Relations*, pp. 25–7.

51. M. Beck, 'Von theoretischen Wüsten, Oasen und Karawanen'.
52. F. G. Gause III, 'Systemic Approaches to Middle East International Relations', *International Studies Review*, 1(1), 1999: 11–31; N. N. Ayubi, *Over-Stating the Arab State*.
53. I. A. Karawan, 'Political Parties between State Power and Islamist Opposition', in C. E. Butterworth and I. W. Zartman (eds), *Between the State and Islam*, Cambridge: Cambridge University Press, 2001; E. Lust-Okar, *Structuring Conflict in the Arab World: Incumbents, Opponents, and Institutions*, Cambridge: Cambridge University Press, 2005.
54. M. Barnett, *Dialogues in Arab Politics: Negotiations in Regional Order*, New York, Columbia University Press, 1998; N. Rejwan, *Israel's Place in the Middle East: a Pluralist Perspective*, Gainesville: University of Florida Press, 1998.
55. M. Tessler et al., *Area Studies and Social Science*, p. vii.
56. See also M. Barnett, 'On the Uniqueness of Israel: Multiple Readings', in M. Barnett (ed.), *Israel in Comparative Perspective: Challenging the Conventional Wisdom*, Albany: State University of New York Press, 1998; M. Hafez, *Why Muslims Rebel: Repression and Resistance in the Islamic World*, Boulder: Lynne Rienner, 2003.
57. J. Massad, *Colonial Effects: the Making of National Identity in Jordan*, New York: Columbia University Press, 2001; R. Kook, 'Between Uniqueness and Exclusion: the Politics of Identity in Israel', in M. Barnett, *Israel in Comparative Perspective*; L. L. Layne, *Home and Homeland*.
58. See in greater detail chapter 2.
59. F. Halliday, *The Middle East in International Relations*.
60. It should be emphasized here that such a globalized perspective cannot be separated from a historical perspective. This is based on the observation in many advanced globalization theories that globalization is not a new phenomenon relating to McDonaldization, the spread of neo-liberal economic practices or neo-conservative ideology. In fact, as many scholars working on the Middle East are well aware, globalization – and its impact on the region – is a centuries-old process.
61. R. O. Keohane and J. S. Nye, Jr (eds), *Governance in a Globalizing World*, Washington, DC: Brookings Institution Press, 2000, p. 2.
62. R. Robertson, *Globalization: Social Theory and Global Culture*, London: Sage, 1992, p. 8.
63. H. A. Innis, *Empire and Communications*, Toronto: University of Toronto Press, 1972.
64. J. W. Burton, *World Society*, p. 42.
65. See for an interesting adaptation of this idea http://www.worldmapper.org.
66. J.W. Burton, *World Society*, p. 47.
67. See A. Wimmer, 'Globalization *Avant la Lettre*: a Comparative View of Isomorphization and Heteromorphization in an Inter-Connecting World', *Comparative Studies in Society and History*, 43(3), 2001: 439.
68. There are, of course, other theories which link globalization and communication (technology). See in particular H. A. Innis, *Empire and Communications*.
69. See F. Braudel, *The Mediterranean and the Mediterranean World in the Age of Phillip II*, 2 vols, Berkeley: University of California Press, 1996; B. Lewis, *The Middle East: 2000 Years of History from the Rise of Christianity to the Present Day*, London: Weidenfeld and Nicolson, 1995.

70. This perspective is well summarized by C. M. Henry, 'The Clash of Globalisations in the Middle East', in L. Fawcett, *International Relations*, pp. 110–11, who argues that 'globalisation has been internalised in Arabic as "awlaama", a newly coined word, but it is still more widely perceived as an external threat than an opportunity to join the world economy'. Or as A. S. Ahmed, *Islam under Siege*, p. 47 notes from a more general cultural perspective and with a view to the Middle East: 'over the last decades the pace and scale of political, cultural, and technological changes coming from the West have unsettled people living in traditional societies. There is a widespread feeling among them that too much change is taking place at too great a pace.'

71. See R. Lohlker, 'Cyberjihad: Das Internet als Feld der Agitation', *Orient*, 43(3), 2002: 507–36; M. E. Ayish, 'Arab World Television in Transition: Current Trends and Future Prospects', *Orient*, 41(3), 2000: 415–34.

72. See M. Barnett, *Dialogues in Arab Politics*, p. 10.

73. See in much greater detail Chapter 2.

74. G. Ritzer, *The McDonaldization of Society*, London: Sage, 1995; B. Maiguashca, 'Governance and Resistance in World Politics', *Review of International Studies*, Special Issue, 29, 2003: 3–28.

75. See M. M. Hafez, *Why Muslims Rebel*.

76. See I. Wallerstein, *The Modern World-System: Capitalist Agriculture and the Origins of the European World-System*, New York: Academic Press, 1974; I. Wallerstein, *The Capitalist World-Economy: Essays*, Cambridge: Cambridge University Press, 1980.

77. I. Wallerstein, *Geopolitics and Geoculture: Essays on the Changing World-System*, Cambridge: Cambridge University Press, 1994, p. 163.

78. C. Chase-Dunn 'Globalizations: a World-Systems Perspective', *Journal of World-Systems Research*, 5(2), 1999: p. 189.

79. In that context, C. Chase-Dunn, 'Globalizations', p. 190 refers to the 'relative decline of United States hegemony'; see also I. Wallerstein, *Geopolitics and Geoculture*, p. 178.

80. C. M. Henry and R. Springborg, *Globalisation and the Politics of Development*; L. Guazzone, *The Middle East in Global Change*.

81. G. Luciani, 'Resources, Revenues, and Authoritarianism in the Arab World: Beyond the Rentier State', in B. Korany et al., *Political Liberalization and Democratization*.

82. R. Hinnebusch, 'Syria: the Politics of Economic Liberalisation', *Third World Quarterly*, 18(2), 1997: 249–65; M. Mufti, 'Elite Bargains and the Onset of Political Liberalization in Jordan', *Comparative Political Studies*, 32(1), 1999: 100–29.

83. As a classical account see R. Arad et al., *The Economics of Peacemaking: Focus on the Egyptian-Israeli Situation*, London: Macmillan, 1983; N. Hashai, 'Forecasting Trade Potential between Former Non-Trading Neighbors: the Israeli-Arab Case', *Journal of World Trade*, 38(2), 2004: 267–84.

84. See also P. Bilgin, *Regional Security in the Middle East: a Critical Perspective*, London and New York: Routledge, 2005, p. 9.

85. I. Wallerstein, *Geopolitics and Geoculture*, p. 167

86. See A. Nocke, 'Israel and the Emergence of Mediterranean Identity: Expressions of Locality in Music and Literature', *Israel Studies*, 11(1), 2006: 143–73.

87. See I. Wallerstein, *Geopolitics and Geoculture*.

88. Ibid. See in detail Chapter 5. Note that these discriminatory patterns work in both directions as witnessed by the massive stereotypes against the West in many discourses throughout the Middle East.

89. See J. W. Meyer et al. (eds), *Institutional Structure: Constituting State, Society, and the Individual*, Newbury Park: Sage, 1987; J. W. Meyer et al., 'World Society and the Nation-State', *American Journal of Sociology*, 103(1), 1997: 144–81. See also the journal *International Organization* (60(4), 2006) with several articles on the global 'Diffusion of Liberalism'.

90. J. W. Meyer et al., 'World Society', p. 157.

91. Ibid., p. 147; see also W. W. Powell and P. J. DiMaggio, *The New Institutionalism in Organizational Analysis*, Chicago: University of Chicago Press, 1991.

92. J. W. Meyer et al., 'World Society', p. 148.

93. Ibid., p. 156.

94. Ibid., p. 154.

95. See A. Wimmer, 'Globalization *Avant la Lettre*'.

96. J. Nevo and I. Pappé (eds), *Jordan in the Middle East: the Making of a Pivotal State, 1948–1988*, London: Frank Cass, 1994; T. Charles, 'Syria: a State and its Narratives', *Middle Eastern Studies*, 37(2), 2001: 199–206; J. S. Migdal, 'State Building and the Nation State', *Journal of International Affairs*, 58(1), 1994: 17–46.

97. J. W. Meyer et al., 'World Society', p. 169.

98. J. Jankowski and I. Gershoni (eds), *Rethinking Nationalism in the Arab Middle East*, New York: Columbia University Press, 1997; B. Tibi, *Arab Nationalism: Between Islam and the Nation-State*, Basingstoke: Macmillan, 1997; E. Zisser, 'Who's Afraid of Syrian Nationalism? National and State Identity in Syria', *Middle Eastern Studies*, 42(2), 2006: 179–98; I. S. Lustick, 'Hegemony and the Riddle of Nationalism', in L. Binder (ed.), *Ethnic Conflict and International Politics in the Middle East*, Gainesville: University of Florida Press, 1999.

99. J. W. Meyer et al., 'World Society', p. 160.

100. See also I. Gershoni, 'Rethinking the Formation of Arab Nationalism in the Middle East, 1920–1945: Old and New Narratives', in J. Jankowski and I. Gershoni, *Rethinking Nationalism*.

101. See D. R. Divine, 'Zionism and the Transformation of Jewish Society', *Modern Judaism*, 20(3), 2000: 257–76.

102. M. Barnett, *Dialogues in Arab Politics*.

103. H. Bull, *The Anarchical Society: a Study of Order in World Politics*, London and New York: Columbia University Press, 1977.

104. See also F. Halliday, *The Middle East in International Relations*, pp. 25–30.

105. This has also been emphasized by the four Arab Human Development Reports of the United Nations Development Programme. See also C. M. Henry and R. Sprinborg, *Globalisation and the Politics of Development*.

106. J. W. Meyer et al., 'World Society', p. 164.

107. Ibid.

108. Ibid., see also M. Albert's argument on the emergence of a world public opinion, which in a sense provides the fundamentals for the global perception of such a shared modernity: M. Albert, 'Politik der Weltgesellschaft und Politik der Globalisierung: Überlegungen zur Emergenz von Weltstaatlichkeit', in B. Heintz et al., *Weltgesellschaft*, 232–3.

109. See, for example, J. Arnason and G. Stauth, 'Civilization and State Formation in the Islamic Context: Re-Reading Ibn-Khaldun', *Thesis Eleven*, 76(1), 2004: 29–47.

110. S. N. Eisenstadt, *Comparative Civilizations and Multiple Modernities*, Leiden and Boston: Brill, 2003.

111. J. W. Meyer et al., 'World Society', p. 174.

112. I borrow here from S. Pinker, *The Blank Slate: the Modern Denial of Human Nature*, London: Allen Lane, 2002.

113. S. N. Eisenstadt, 'The Continual Reconstruction of Multiple Modern Civilizations and Collective Identities', in G. Preyer and M. Bös (eds), *Borderlines in a Globalized World*, Dordrecht: Springer, 2002, p. 11.

114. See A. Wimmer, 'Globalization *Avant la Lettre*'.

115. Amongst the leadership literature see E. Zisser, 'Bashar Al-Asad and his Regime: Continuity and Change', *Orient*, 45(2), 2004: 239–55; L. Adoni, 'King Abdallah: in his Father's Footsteps?', *Journal of Palestine Studies*, 29(3), 2000: 77–89.

116. See N. Luhmann, *Die Gesellschaft der Gesellschaft*; R. Stichweh, *Die Weltgesellschaft*; B. Heintz et al., *Weltgesellschaft*. For modern systems theory/ world society theory and IR see Albert and Hilkermeier, *Observing International Relations*; S. Stetter, *Territorial Conflicts in World Society*

117. See also M. Albert et al., 'On Order and Conflict: International Relations and the "Communicative Turn"', *Review of International Studies*, Special Issue, 2008: 1–25.

118. See also Chapter 2.

119. Note that Alter and Ego do not represent persons or actors. The Ego/Alter distinction rather relates to the communicative processing of double contingency and the establishing of order, see M. Albert et al., 'On Order and Conflict'.

120. M. Albert et al., 'Order and Conflict'.

121. P. Bilgin, *Regional Security in the Middle East*.

122. See also U. Stäheli, *Sinnzusammenbrüche: Eine dekonstruktive Lektüre von Niklas Luhmanns Systemtheorie*, Weilerswist: Velbrück, 2000.

123. A. Nassehi, 'Die Theorie funktionaler Differenzierung im Horizont ihrer Kritik', *Zeitschrift für Soziologie*, 33(2), 2004: 98–118. N. Luhmann, *Die Gesellschaft der Gesellschaft*, pp. 707–88; N. Luhmann, *Die Politik der Gesellschaft*, Frankfurt: Suhrkamp, 2000, pp. 69–139.

124. This focus allows us to address the theories of Meyer and Wallerstein not as contradictory but rather as complementary perspectives on world society.

125. See L. Brock, 'World Society from the Bottom Up', and M. Albert, 'Politik der Weltgesellschaft und Politik der Globalisierung'.

126. See also U. Stäheli, *Sinnzusammenbrüche*; N. A. Andersen, *Discursive Analytical Strategies: Understanding Foucault, Koselleck, Laclau, Luhmann*, Bristol: Policy Press, 2003; S. Stetter, 'The Politics of De-Paradoxification in Euro-Mediterranean Relations: Semantics and Structures of "Cultural Dialogue"', *Mediterranean Politics*, 10(3), 2005: 331–48.

127. See O. Richmond, *The Transformation of Peace*, Basingstoke: Palgrave Macmillan, 2005.

128. See H. Messmer, *Der soziale Konflikt: Kommunikative Emergenz und systemische Reproduktion*, Stuttgart: Lucius & Lucius, 2003; T. Diez et al., 'The European Union and Border Conflicts: the Transformative Power of Integration', *International Organization*, 60(3), 2006: 563–93.

129. Insofar as an 'antagonism is the disruption of a system of differences, of a symbolic universe, by an "outside" which negates it – the Real … which

impedes it from fully constituting itself' – and communication then is the means by which to structurally embed this constant oscillation between totalizing effects and incompleteness in society, E. Laclau, *New Reflections on the Revolution of Our Time*, London: Verso, 1990, p. 168.

2. Regionalization and debordering: the Middle East between global interconnectivity and functional differentiation

1. M. Darwish, *Wir haben ein Land aus Worten*, Zürich: Ammann, 2002.
2. This alleged tension between the 'local' and the 'global' has been the wider conceptual context of the so-called area-studies controversy in (North American) Middle East studies. See M. Tessler et al., *Area Studies and Social Science*; A. Mirsepassi et al., *Localizing Knowledge*; M. Valbjørn, 'Toward a "Mesopotamian Turn": Disciplinarity and the Study of the International Relations of the Middle East', *Journal of Mediterranean Studies*, 14(1/2), 2004: 47–75. See also the discussion in Chapter 1. As David Held has put it, referring to Anthony Giddens, 'local transformation is as much an element of globalization as the lateral extension of social relations across space and time', see D. Held, *Democracy and the Global Order*, Cambridge: Polity, 1995, p. 278.
3. See, for example, M. Sedgwick, 'Marginal Muslims in Cyberspace: Traditionalists, New Communities and the Blurring of Distinctions', in B. O. Utvik and K. S. Vikor (eds), *The Middle East in a Globalized World*, Bergen: Nordic Society for Middle Eastern Studies, 2000; N. Lahoud, 'Tradition in Contemporary Arabic Political Discourse', *Critique: Critical Middle Eastern Studies*, 13(3), 2004: 313–33; Z. Beckermann, 'Israeli Traditionalists and Liberals: a Social-Constructivist Perspective', *Israel Studies*, 4(2), 1999: 90–114. For a critique of this distinction between tradition/modernity, see K. P. Japp, 'Zur Soziologie des fundamentalistischen Terrorismus'.
4. See D. Diner, *Versiegelte Zeit*, pp. 227–34.
5. See in particular B. Tibi, *Islamischer Fundamentalismus*. See also R. W. Hefner, 'Introduction: Modernity and the Remaking of Muslim Politics', in R. W. Hefner (ed.), *Remaking Muslim Politics: Pluralism, Contestation, Democratization*, Princeton: Princeton University Press, 2005; E. S. Hurd, 'Appropriating Islam: the Islamic Other in the Consolidation of Western Modernity', *Critique: Critical Middle Eastern Studies*, 12(1), 2003: 25–41; Z. Zohar, 'Oriental Jewry Confronts Modernity: the Case of Rabbi Ovadiah Yosef', *Modern Judaism*, 24(2), 2004: 120–49.
6. See also M. V. Hatem, 'In the Eye of the Storm: Islamic Societies and Muslim Women in Globalization Discourses', *Comparative Studies of South Asia, Africa and the Middle East*, 26(1), 2006: 22–35.
7. A. Hamzawy, 'Vom Primat der Verschwörung: Zeitgenössische arabische Debatten', *Orient*, 43(3), 2002: 345–63.
8. B. Tibi, *Islamischer Fundamentalismus*, p. 33.
9. M. Barnett, *Dialogues in Arab Politics*. S. T. Hunter, 'The Rise of Islamist Movements and the Western Response: Clash of Civilizations or Clash of Interest?', in L. Guazzone (ed.), *The Islamist Dilemma: the Political Role of Islamist Movements in the Contemporary Arab World*, Reading: Ithaca,

1995; I. Kalin, 'Islam and the West: Deconstructing Monolithic Perceptions – a Conversation with Professor Esposito', *Journal of Muslim Minority Affairs*, 21(1), 2001: 155–63.

10. See A. Sagi and Y. Stern, 'Wanted, a Leader of Vision', *Ha-Aretz*, 12 January 2007.

11. See A. H. Sa'di, 'Modernization as an Explanatory Discourse of Zionist-Palestinian Relations', *British Journal of Middle Eastern Studies*, 24(1), 1997: 25–48.

12. On the notion of territorial containers see also H. Patomäki, 'Problems of Democratizing Global Governance: Time, Space and the Emancipatory Process', *European Journal of International Relations*, 9(3), 2003: 347–76.

13. This discursive strategy also shapes the widespread and powerful reference to the 'situation on the ground' in the Middle East which cannot be fully understood by 'outsiders' coming from more peaceful regions of the world. This frame of reference is based on the belief that 'hostility is a permanent situation' in the Middle East and that 'the violent nature of the region does not allow for real peace', M. Benvenisti, 'The Stale Myth of Battlefield Bravado', *Ha-Aretz*, 13 April 2007.

14. In that context the diffusion of global structures and normative cultures, such as the state, nationalism or sovereignty stressed by the Stanford School or the English School (see Chapter 1), provide another reason for the inherent conceptual problems of such approaches.

15. This argument, of course, also relates to the invisibilization of fluidity and dynamism in the construction of other regions, such as, for example, Europe. See T. Diez, 'Europe's Other and the Return of Geopolitics', *Cambridge Review of International Affairs*, 17(2), 2004: 319–55. For the Middle East see in particular P. Bilgin, *Regional Security in the Middle East*.

16. On attractors see also E. Vathakou, 'The Autopoiesis of Conflict Transformation: an Example of a "Butterfly Effect" in Greek-Turkish Relations', in S. Stetter, *Territorial Conflicts in World Society*; For a different, teleological understanding of attractors see A. Wendt, 'Why a World State is Inevitable', *European Journal of International Relations*, 9(4), 2005: 491–542.

17. J. Walter, 'Politik als System? Systembegriffe und Systemmetaphern in der Politikwissenschaft und in den Internationalen Beziehungen', *Zeitschrift für Internationale Beziehungen*, 12(2), 2005: 275–300.

18. This does not, of course, mean that the distinction intra-regional/extra-regional would be superfluous. However, from a systems-theoretical perspective it remains unclear why this distinction (and the units constituted by this distinction) should be systemic in character, that is, operating as self-referential entities.

19. F. Gause III, 'Systemic Approaches to Middle East International Relations'.

20. On the linkage between functional differentiation as the prime form of differentiation in world society and the obvious regional discrepancies in societal evolution see also N. Luhmann, 'Kausalität im Süden', *Soziale Systeme*, 1(1), 1995: 19. Thus, regional differences only acquire recognition 'through modern world society'. Only the comprehensive societal system of world society renders visible the differences in the realization of functional performances across regions.

21. See M. Albert and L. Brock, 'Debordering the World of States: New Spaces in International Relations', in M. Albert et al., *Civilizing World Politics: Society*

and Community Beyond the State, Oxford: Rowman & Littlefield, 2000; S. Stetter, 'Theorising the European Neighbourhood Policy: Debordering and Rebordering in the Mediterranean', EUI Working Papers, RSCAS No. 2005/34, European University Institute, Robert Schuman Centre for Advanced Studies, Mediterranean Programme Series: Florence, 2005.

22. See also H. Patomäki, 'Problems of Democratizing Local Government'.
23. See Chapter 1. Notions of functional differentiation, although a central (if contested) concept in sociology, still occupy a limited role in IR. Thus, within IR and political science the usual working assumption is that there is a primacy of politics as the central functional sphere in world society. However, see K.-U. Hellmann, 'Einleitung', in K.-U. Hellmann and R. Schmalz-Bruns (eds), *Theorie der Politik: Niklas Luhmanns politische Soziologie*, Frankfurt: Suhrkamp, 2002; for a reflection on how systems theory could operate as the 'twelfth camel' of IR (see N. Luhmann, 'Die Rückgabe des zwölften Kamels: Zum Sinn einer soziologischen Anaylse des Rechts', *Zeitschrift für Rechtssoziologie*, 21(1), 2000: 3–60), thereby allowing political science and IR to 'observe' the embedding of the discipline and its research objects into its societal environment.
24. K. Kuhm, 'Raum als Medium gesellschaftlicher Kommunikation', *Soziale Systeme*, 6(2), 2000: 321–48.; R. Stichweh, *Die Weltgesellschaft*, p. 217.
25. On media reporting and the emergence of regional clusters in world society see S. Stetter, 'Regions of Conflict in World Society'.
26. See R. Stichweh, *Die Weltgesellschaft*, pp. 198–200. This chapter does not follow Stichweh in postulating that regionness is primarily the result of region-specific forms of structural coupling between different functional systems. It rather focuses on how world societal communications in and on specific regions render these spaces (placeless) signposts for political and other functional communications.
27. Such re-inscriptions of segmentary/territorial and symbolic borders into political communications are, in fact, a widespread securitization practice in the Middle East. For symbolic re-inscriptions see also Chapter 5.
28. On conflicts, see Chapter 5.
29. For an overview on critical geography see G. Ó Tuathail et al., *The Geopolitics Reader*, London and New York: Routledge, 2006; G. Ó Tuathail, *Critical Geopolitics: the Politics of Writing Global Space*, Minneapolis: University of Minnesota Press, 1996; N. Kliot and D. Newman, *Geopolitics at the End of the Twentieth Century: the Changing World Political Map*, Frank Cass: London, 2000.
30. See T. A. Jacoby and B. E. Sasley, *Redefining Security*; P. Bilgin, 'Whose Middle East? Geopolitical Interventions and Practices of Security', *International Relations*, 18(1), 2004: 25–41.
31. See also the discussion in Chapter 3 on the limits and paradoxes of power in Middle East politics.
32. M. Albert and L. Brock, 'Debordering the World of States', p. 20.
33. They are placeless insofar as communications, understood as the unity of a threefold selection process, cannot be pinned down to a single corresponding place in time. This relates to the notion of empty signifiers in poststructuralism, see T. Bonacker, 'Debordering by Human Rights: the Challenge of Postterritorial Conflicts in World Society', in S. Stetter, *Territorial Conflicts in World Society*, pp. 23–4.

34. P. Pawelka, 'Der Vordere Orient in der Weltpolitik: Sozialwissenschaftliche Modelle und Forschungsperspektiven', *Orient*, 41(1), 2000: 571–91.
35. F. Gause III, 'Systemic Approaches to Middle East International Relations'; Buzan and Wæver, *Regions and Powers*.
36. See also L. Anderson, 'Democracy in the Arab World: a Critique of the Political Culture Approach', in Korany et al., *Political Liberalization and Democratization in the Arab World*.
37. See P. Bilgin, *Regional Security in the Middle East*; M. Barnett, *Dialogues in Arab Politics*.
38. This not only relates to 'current' spatial representations but also affects the constructions of specific readings of history, for example, through archaeology. See R. S. Hallote and A. H. Joffe, 'The Politics of Israeli Archaeology: Between "Nationalism" and "Science" in the Age of the Second Republic', *Israel Studies*, 7(3), 2002: 84–116.
39. See, for example, J. Palmer Harik, 'Democracy (Again) Derailed: Lebanon's Ta'if Paradox', in Korany et al., *Political Liberalization and Democatization*.
40. See, for example, the discursive battlefield in the global framing of Israel between, 'a small state, surrounded by enemies committed to its destruction' (E. A. Cohen et al., 'Israel's Revolution in Security Affairs', *Survival*, 40(1), 1998: 48–67) which for decades 'has focused on a quest for peace in the region in which it is located' (B. Reich, 'Israel's Quest for Peace', *Mediterranean Quarterly*, 13(2), 2002: 67–95) and completely opposing narratives which pitch Israel's regional policies in a colonialist, expansionist context (see the discussion in R. Aaronsohn, 'Settlement in Eretz Israel: a Colonialist Entreprise? "Critical" Scholarship and Historical Geography', *Israel Studies*, 1(2), 1996: 214–29; B. Kimmerling, 'Jurisdiction in an Immigrant-Settler Society: the "Jewish and Democratic" State', *Comparative Political Studies*, 35(10), 2002: 1119–44).
41. J. Peteet, 'Words as Interventions: Naming in the Israeli-Palestinian Conflict', *Third World Quarterly*, 26(1), 2005: 159.
42. The same holds true for other diaspora communities. See S. Morrison, ' "Os Turcos" '; for the Palestinian diaspora see also B. Kampmark, 'Hanan Ashrawi and the Prize Protest: the Value and Limits of Debating Peace in the Australian Diaspora', *Journal of Muslim Minority Affairs*, 25(3), 2005: 348–61.
43. J. Schechla, 'The Invisible People Come to the Light: Israel's "Internally Displaced" and the "Unrecognized Villages" ', *Journal of Palestine Studies*, 31(1), 2001: 20–31.
44. This argument cannot be elaborated here in full detail. Yet, it underscores the importance that academic analyses should not fall into the territorial/cultural trap, thereby using the internal/external distinction as a strategy of (de)legitimizing specific interventions in regional politics. See for example the arguments deployed by the Hamas politician and former Palestinian foreign minister Mahmud Zahhar: M. Zahhar and H. Hijazi, 'Hamas: Waiting for Secular Nationalism to Self-Destruct: an Interview with Mahmud Zahhar', *Journal of Palestine Studies*, 24(3), 1995: 81–8.
45. J. Collins, 'Global Palestine: a Collision for Our Time', *Critique: Critical Middle Eastern Studies*, 16(1), 2007: 3–18.
46. To reiterate, the arguments in this section can equally be extended to case studies on other territories or diaspora communities in/from the Middle East.

47. See also Chapter 3; on legitimacy as the contingency formula of the political system see also N. Luhmann, *Politik der Gesellschaft*, pp. 118–26.

48. See W. Schirmer, 'Addresses in World Societal Conflicts: a Systems Theoretical Contribution to the Theory of the State in International Relations', in S. Stetter, *Territorial Conflicts in World Society*.

49. See also the arguments in Chapter 1 on global diffusion processes outlined by the Stanford School.

50. Securing this global recognition as the 'sole representative of the Palestinian people' was a central element in the political strategy of the PLO. This status was, for example, recognized by the Arab League at its 1974 Rabat Summit and figures in official agreements between the PA and other international actors, such as in the Interim Association Agreement between Palestine and the EU of 1997 (see S. Stetter, *EU Foreign and Interior Policies: Cross-Pillar Politics and the Social Constructions of Sovereignty*, London and New York: Routledge, 2007).

51. See I. S. Lustick, 'The Oslo Agreements as an Obstacle to Peace', *Journal of Palestine Studies*, 27(1), 1997: 61–6; S. Antoon, 'Mahmud Darwish's Allegorical Critique of Oslo', *Journal of Palestine Studies*, 31(2), 2002: 66–77.

52. S. Stetter, 'Of Separate and Joint Universes: National Parliamentary Elections in Israel and Palestine', *Mediterranean Politics*, 11(3), 2006: 425–32.

53. See also the interview with *al-quds al-arabi* editor-in-chief Abdel Bari Atwan on http://www.imra.org.il/story.php3?id=28583.

54. A. Jamal, 'The Palestinian Media: an Obedient Servant or a Vanguard of Democracy?', *Journal of Palestine Studies*, 29(3), 2000: 48.

55. Ibid.

56. Ibid.

57. D. Tschirgi, 'Resolving the Palestinian Refugee Problem: Edward A. Norman's Unintended Contribution to Relevant Lessons in Perspectives, Values, and Consequences', in D. Jung, *The Middle East and Palestine*, p. 199.

59. E. W. Said, *Reflections on Exile, and Other Literary and Cultural Essays*, London: Granta, 2001.

59. D. Tschirgi, 'Resolving the Palestinian Refugee Problem', p. 199; see also the debate between Salman Aub-Sitt and Michael Lerner in *Tikkun*, http://www.counterpunch.org/sitta02122003.html.

60. This does not, of course, relate only to Palestinian refugees but also covers the complex relationship between Palestinian Israelis and Palestine, see S. Lowrance, 'Identity, Grievances, and Political Action: Recent Evidence from the Palestinian Community in Israel', *International Political Science Review*, 27(2), 2006: 167–90.

61. R. Farah, ' "To Veil or Not to Veil is Not the Question": Palestinian Refugee Women Voices on Other Matters', *Development*, 45(1), 2002: 98.

62. See F. Gottheil, 'UNRWA and Moral Hazard', *Middle Eastern Studies*, 42(3), 2006: 409–21.

63. R. Farah, ' "To Veil or Not to Veil" ', p. 98.

64. R. Khalidi, *Palestinian Identity: the Construction of Modern National Consciousness*, New York: Columbia University Press, 1997, pp. 177–209.

65. E. W. Said, *Das Ende des Friedensprozeß*, Berlin: Berlin Verlag, 2000, p. 235.

66. As Article 70 of the Draft Palestinian Constitution states: 'The National Council, composed of 150 representatives of the Palestinian refugees abroad.

It shall be formed to protect the guarantee of justice in representation and share with the Legislative Council in legislating laws connected with general national rights. The members of the National Council shall be chosen according to the election system of the National Council until it is amended.'

67. D. Tschirgi, 'Resolving the Palestinian Refugee Problem', p. 199.
68. See on democratization in Palestine, J. Hilal, 'Problematizing Democracy in Palestine', *Comparative Studies of South Asia, Africa and the Middle East*, 23(1/2), 2003: 163–72.
69. S. Lodo, 'Palestinian Transnational Actors and the Construction of the Homeland', unpublished manuscript, p. 12.
70. See also the discussion in B. Wasserstein, *Israel and Palestine: Why They Fight and Can They Stop?*, London: Profile, 2003.
71. B. Rougier, 'Religious Mobilizations in Palestinian Refugee Camps in Lebanon: the Case of Ain el-Helweh', in D. Jung, *The Middle East and Palestine*, p. 177, my emphasis.
72. Ibid., my emphasis.
73. See T. Diez et al., 'The European Union and Border Conflicts'.
74. R. Bowker, *Palestinian Refugees: Mythology, Identity, and the Search for Peace*, Boulder: Lynne Rienner, 2003, p. 181.
75. Ibid., p. 198.
76. Ibid., p. 201.
77. See on this topic E. Zureik, 'Constructing Palestine through Surveillance Practices', *British Journal of Middle Eastern Studies*, 28(2), 2001: 205–27.
78. F. Gottheil, 'UNRWA and Moral Hazard', p. 418.
79. See in this context also the arguments by Ilan Pappé on the implicit re-inscription of symbolic boundaries in scientific discourses in Middle Eastern 'nationalized' science, I. Pappé, 'Post-Zionist Critique on Israel and Palestinians: Part I: The Academic Debate', *Journal of Palestine Studies*, 26(2), 1997: 29–41.
80. A. Ehteshami, 'Is the Middle East Democratizing', *British Journal of Middle Eastern Studies*, 26(2), 1999: 205.
81. R. Khalidi, *Palestinian Identity*, p. 179.
82. This line of argument is usually based on the assumption that identity groups are specific discourse communities distinguished from the outside through a hypothetically power-free discourse within the confines of the respective in-group.
83. On the role of cities in world society theory see also R. Stichweh, *Die Weltgesellschaft*, pp. 201–3.
84. S. Stetter, 'Entgrenzung von Politikfeldern in der Weltgesellschaft? Eine Bedrohung für die Demokratie?' in A. Brodocz et al. (eds), *Bedrohungen der Demokratie*, Wiesbaden: VS Verlag, forthcoming, 2008.
85. M. Albert, 'Politik der Weltgesellschaft und Politik der Globalisierung', p. 230.
86. M. Albert, 'Einleitung: Weltstaat und Weltstaatlichkeit: Neubestimmungen des Politischen in der Weltgesellschaft', in M. Albert and R. Stichweh (eds), *Weltstaat und Weltstaatlichkeit: Beobachtungen globaler politischer Strukturbildung*, Wiesbaden: VS Verlag, 2007, p. 17.
87. See, for example, A. El-Khatib, 'Jerusalem in the Qur'an', *British Journal of Middle Eastern Studies*, 28(1), 2001: 25–53; K. Armstrong, 'The Holiness of Jerusalem: Asset or Burden?', *Journal of Palestine Studies*, 27(3), 1998: 5–19.

88. On medieval notions of Jerusalem as a world city see S. Sarsar, 'Jerusalem: Between the Local and the Global', *Alternatives: Turkish Journal of International Relations*, 1(4), 2001: 53.

89. K. Armstrong, 'The Holiness of Jerusalem', p. 6.

90. M. Turner, 'The Shared Cultural Significance of Jerusalem', in M. Auga et al. (eds), *Divided Cities in Transition: Challenges Facing Jerusalem and Berlin*, Jerusalem: Al-Manar Press, 2005, p. 126.

91. For example, by addressing the function of unitary semantics in global political communications, see K. P. Japp, 'Zur Soziologie des fundamentalistischen Terrorismus'.

92. R. Khalidi, 'The Centrality of Jerusalem to an End of Conflict Agreement', *Journal of Palestine Studies*, 30(3), 2001: 83.

93. S. Sarsar, 'Jerusalem', p. 65.

94. G. Ben-Porat, 'A State of Holiness: Rethinking Israeli Secularism', *Alternatives*, 25: 223.

95. K. Armstrong, 'The Holiness of Jerusalem', p. 9.

96. See T. Risse, ' "Let's Argue!": Communicative Action in World Politics', *International Organization*, 54(1), 2000: 1–39.

97. UNESCO, 'Report of the Technical Mission to the Old City of Jerusalem (27 February–2 March 2007)', New York: UNESCO, 2007.

98. M. Turner, 'The Shared Cultural Significance of Jerusalem', p. 124.

99. Ibid., p. 133.

100. Ibid., p. 137.

101. Ibid., p. 140.

102. M. Dumper, 'The Christian Churches in Jerusalem in the Post-Oslo Period', *Journal of Palestine Studies*, 31(2), 2002: 60.

103. Ibid.

104. See also an interview with former Israeli Prime Minister Ehud Barak in the *New York Times*, http://www.nybooks.com/articles/15501.

105. I. S. Lustick, 'Yerushalayim and al-Quds: Political Catechism and Political Realities', *Journal of Palestine Studies*, 30(1), 2000: 5.

106. A. Weingrod and A. Manna, 'Living Along the Seam. Israeli Palestinians in Jerusalem', *International Journal of Middle East Studies*, 30(3), 1998: 369.

107. A. Hanieh, 'The Camp David Papers', *Journal of Palestine Studies*, 30(2), 2001: 86. On the linkage between Israel as well as the Palestinian national movement with Christian churches see F. M. Perko, S.J., 'Towards a "Sound and Lasting Basis": Relations between the Holy See, the Zionist Movement, and Israel, 1986–1996', *Israel Studies*, 2(1), 1997: 1–21.

108. E. W. Said, 'Projecting Jerusalem', *Journal of Palestine Studies*, 25(1), 1995: 12.

109. Basic Law, Jerusalem: Capital of Israel, see http://www.jewishvirtuallibrary.org/jsource/Peace/Basic_Law_Jerusalem.html.

110. A. Hanieh, 'The Camp David Papers', p. 96. The Moroccan king chairs the Al-Quds Committee of the Organisation of the Islamic Conference.

111. M. Dumper, 'The Christian Churches in Jerusalem', p. 60.

112. R. Stichweh, *Die Weltgesellschaft*, p. 193.

113. P. Bilgin, *Regional Security in the Middle East*.

114. For example, the link between religious experiences and notions of the beauty of Arabic scripture (see N. Kermani, *Gott ist schön: Das ästhetische Erleben des Koran*, Munich: Beck, 2000), or the role of welfare in traditional Islam.

115. M. Barnett, *Dialogues in Arab Politics*, p. 270.
116. J. Peteet, 'Words as Interventions'.
117. That is also the reason why Stichweh's notion that regions are primarily the result of region-specific forms of structural coupling between different functional spheres is not entirely convincing. This would, *inter alia*, presuppose that there are indeed one or several specific forms of structural coupling unique to distinct regions. However, the point emphasized in this chapter is rather that regions (and other spaces) result from the manifold different and often highly heterogeneous framings of what constitutes a region within and across various functional (and other societal) spheres.
118. See. R. Stichweh, *Die Weltgesellschaft*.
119. J. Peteet, 'Words and Interventions', p. 153.

3.   Power and contestations: crossing the lines between power and powerlessness in the Middle East

1. From the album '. . . And Justice for All', by Vertigo Records, 1988.
2. L. Fawcett, *International Relations*, p. 4.
3. To pick an example, Syria still does not recognize parts of its borders with neighbouring Turkey and holds no diplomatic relations with Lebanon and Israel. See also M. Ma'oz et al. (eds), *Modern Syria: From Ottoman Rule to Pivotal Role in the Middle East*, Brighton: Sussex University Press, 1999.
4. See A. Kaufman, ' "Tell Us Our History": Charles Corm, Mount Lebanon and Lebanese Nationalism', *Middle Eastern Studies*, 40(3), 2004: 1–28; R. Khalidi, *Palestinian Identity*; N. Rejwan, *Israel's Place in the Middle East*.
5. M. Beck, 'Von theoretischen Wüsten, Oasen und Karawanen' p. 315.
6. F. Halliday, *The Middle East in International Relations*, p. 25.
7. Ibid., p. 28; see also R. Hinnebusch and A. Ehteshami (eds), *The Foreign Policies of Middle East States*, Boulder: Lynne Rienner, 2002.
8. See also R. A. Del Sarto, *Contested State Identities and Regional Security in the Euro-Mediterranean Area*, Basingstoke: Palgrave Macmillan, 2006.
9. R. Hinnebusch, 'The Politics of Identity in Middle East International Relations' in L. Fawcett, *International Relations*, p. 152.
10. See R. A. Del Sarto, *Contested State Identities*.
11. See A. H. Al Husban, 'The Place of Local Councils in the Power Network: a Case Study of the North of Jordan (Halid bin el-Walid Municipality)', *Orient*, 46(4), 2005: 565–80; A. N. Hamzeh, 'Lebanon's Islamists and Local Politics: a New Reality', *Third World Quarterly*, 21(5), 2000: 739–59.
12. M. Benvenisti, 'The Stale Myth of Battlefield Bravado', *Ha-Aretz*, 14 April 2006.
13. See in particular E. Lust-Okar, *Structuring Conflict in the Arab World*; M. Barnett, *Dialogues in Arab Politics*.
14. See P. Seale, *Asad of Syria: the Struggle for the Middle East*, Berkeley: University of California Press, 1988; T. Gongora, 'War Making and State Power in the Contemporary Middle East', *International Journal of Middle East Studies*, 29(3), 1997: 323–40; J. Amal, 'Political and Ideological Factors of Conflict in Palestinian Society', in H.-J. Albrecht et al. (eds), *Conflicts and Conflict Resolution in Middle Eastern Societies: Between Tradition and Modernity*,

Berlin: Duncker & Humblot, 2006; T. Scheffler, 'Religious Communalism and Democratization: the Development of Electoral Law in Lebanon', *Orient*, 44(1), 2003: 15–37.
15. See S. Lukes, *Power: a Radical View*, London: Macmillan, 1974; K. Dowding, 'Three-Dimensional Power: a Discussion of Steven Lukes' Power: a Radical View', *Political Studies Review*, 4(2), 2006: 136–45; M. Barnett and R. Duvall, 'Power in International Relations', *International Organization*, 59(1), 2005: 39–75.
16. See M. Albert et al., 'On Order and Conflict'.
17. See F. Halliday, *Islam and the Myth of Confrontation*.
18. See J. P. Arnason and G. Stauth, 'Civilization and State Formation in the Islamic Context'; R. Bahlul, 'Toward an Islamic Conception of Democracy: Islam and the Notion of Public Reason', *Critique: Critical Middle Eastern Studies*, 12(1), 2003: 43–60; N. Ghadbian, *Democratization and the Islamist Challenge in the Arab World*, Boulder: Westview Press, 1997; A. R. Norton, 'Associational Life: Civil Society in Authoritarian Political Systems', in M. Tessler et al., *Area Studies and Social Science*.
19. See N. Luhmann, *Die Politik der Gesellschaft*, p. 29.
20. See B. Buzan and O. Wæver, *Regions and Powers*.
21. See also Chapter 2.
22. See also note 15, this chapter; S. Newman, 'The Place of Power in Political Discourse', *International Political Science Review*, 25(2), 2004: 139–57; the special issue of *Political Studies Review*, 4, 2006 on Steven Lukes' Power: a Radical View; S. Guzzini, 'Structural Power: the Limits of Neorealist Analysis', *International Organization*, 47(3), 1993: 443–78; J. Hart, 'Three Approaches to the Measurement of Power in International Relations', *International Organization*, 30(2), 1976: 289–305.
23. This is not to deny that other theoretical concepts of power would not be helpful for this analysis. Building on the arguments made in Chapter 1, this chapter also draws from other deconstructivist and post-structuralist notions of power which share many similarities (besides all differences) with modern systems theory. See also U. Stäheli, *Sinnzusammenbrüche*.
24. See S. Telhami, 'Power, Legitimacy, and Peace-Making in Arab Coalitions: the New Arabism', in L. Binder, *Ethnic Conflict and International Politics*; M. Kedar, 'In Search of Legitimacy: Assad's Islamic Image in the Syrian Official Press', in M. Ma'oz et al., *Modern Syria*.
25. See Chapter 1.
26. Note that these two sides relate to communications and not to actors; see also Chapter 1 and N. Luhmann, *Soziale Systeme*, pp. 191–241.
27. N. Luhmann, *Die Politik der Gesellschaft*, p. 29.
28. Ibid. p. 47, emphasis in the original.
29. Note that the privileging of one side of the distinction of binary coded communications (and the subsequent distinction between a positive and a negative value) is not a designation of a specific legitimacy for either side of the distinction but rather a statement on the way in which the ongoing connectivity of (unlikely) systemic operations is ensured in communications. See N. Luhmann, *Die Politik der Gesellschaft*, pp. 60–2.
30. N. Luhmann, *Macht*, 3rd edn, Stuttgart: Lucius & Lucius, 2003, p. 22. Note that it is not important here whether Alter and Ego consciously know about these alternatives. What matters instead is that the world societal

horizon of all communications ensures the structural availability of alternatives; see also Chapter 1.

31. N. Luhmann, ibid., p. 50, my emphasis.
32. In particular S. Guzzini, 'Constructivism and International Relations'.
33. Ibid.; see also U. Stäheli, *Sinnzusammenbrüche*.
34. K. Dowding, 'Three-Dimensional Power', p. 137.
35. See Chapter 1, note 119 above.
36. N. Luhmann, *Die Politik der Gesellschaft*, p. 54.
37. See also the next section.
38. See U. Stäheli, *Sinnzusammenbrüche*, p. 235.
39. lllrN. Luhmann, *Macht*, p. 9.
40. Ibid., p. 23.
41. M. Foucault, *Discipline and Punish*, New York: Vintage Books, 1979. See also N. Luhmann, *Macht*, p. 23.
42. To borrow from Derrida, politics appears in all those 'determinations in given situations to be stabilized through a decision of writing', quoted in U. Stäheli, *Sinnzusammenbrüche*, p. 233. Power and politics accordingly operate in situations of undecidability in which this undecidability is resolved by resorting to the underlying threat of force inherent in all power communications. Therefore, a decision is, in a sense, always heterogeneous to a system, since the decision comes from the outside, which lies beyond the logic of undecidability. Power is thus, a paradoxical operation, since on the one hand it constitutes politics as a powerful [sic] system of society, while on the other hand, it remains foreign to the very undecidable decision it confronts by reintroducing a new hegemonic reading. As Kierkegaard thus pointedly argues, 'the instance of the decision is a madness', quoted in ibid., p. 237. It is this communicative understanding which reveals that the 'double inscription' of the political into society, that is, politics as the political system and politics in the sense of radical, hegemonic decisions, is not anathema to modern systems theory. In fact, limiting politics to the institutionalized politics or the state-centred distinction between government/opposition is a much too narrow reading of what modern systems theory has to say about politics.
43. See N. Luhmann, 'Die Paradoxie als Form', in *Aufsätze und Reden*, edited by O. Jahraus, Stuttgart: Philipp Reclam jun., 2001.
44. The code of the political is thus not government/opposition, as U. Stäheli, *Sinnzusammenbrüche*, pp. 255–61 argues.
45. Ibid., p. 261.
46. S. Žižek, *For They Know Not What They Do: Enjoyment as Political Factor*, London: Verso, 1991, p.193.
47. N. Luhmann, *Die Gesellschaft der Gesellschaft*, p. 97.
48. Ibid.
49. D. Krause, *Luhmann-Lexikon: Eine Einführung in das Gesamtwerk von Niklas Luhmann*, 3rd edn, Stuttgart: Lucius & Lucius, 2001, p. 115.
50. U. Stäheli, *Sinnzusammenbrüche*, p. 231.
51. Arguably, democracy, understood as the distinction between government/opposition, is a particularly successful programme insofar as it regulates both deparadoxification (legitimacy by the people) and a quasi-technical crossing between both sides of the code power/powerless, based on the communication of clear time horizons.

52. U. Stäheli, *Sinnzusammenbrüche*, p. 303.
53. N. Luhmann, *Macht*, p. 7.
54. Ibid., p. 14.
55. See Chapter 2.
56. U. Stäheli, *Sinnzusammenbrüche*, pp. 297–308. See also Chapters 4–6 below.
57. That is also the deeper reason why programmes and legitimacy strategies based on clear-cut territorial or cultural inside/outside distinctions are generally unstable invisiblization strategies since they too obviously contradict the world societal embedding of all political communications.
58. This is not a statement on the effectiveness of collectively binding decisions and neither is it about the territorial or functional scope of decisions. What the 'collective' in collectively binding decisions is, is decided self-referentially by (political) communications.
59. See Stetter, 'Regions of Conflict in World Society'.
60. See also B. Korany et al., *Political Liberalization and Democratization*; N. Ghadbian, *Democratization and the Islamist Challenge*; A. Ehteshami, 'Is the Middle East Democratizing?'; R. Hinnebusch, 'Authoritarian Persistence, Democratization Theory and the Middle East: an Overview and Critique', *Democratization*, 13(3), 2006: 373–95. Note that some authors have also pointed to the linkages between (limited) liberalization and the consolidation of authoritarian rule in Middle East 'corporatist states', see A. Ehteshami and E. C. Murphy, 'Transformation of the Corporatist State in the Middle East', *Third World Quarterly*, 17(4), 1996: 753–72.
61. See amongst many others J. Palmer Harik, 'Democracy (Again) Derailed'; A. Shlaim, Avi, 'The Rise and Fall of the Oslo Peace Process', in L. Fawcett, *International Relations*.
62. A. Jamal, 'State-Building, Institutionalization and Democracy: the Palestinian Experience', *Mediterranean Politics*, 6(3), 2001: 1–30; E. Lust-Okar, 'Elections under Authoritarianism: Preliminary Lessons from Jordan', *Democratization*, 13(3), 2006: 456–71; T. Scheffler, 'Religious Communalism and Democratization'.
63. See for an overview of the pros and cons of such a change in trans-regional relations the discussions in L. Guazzone, *The Middle East in Global Change*; V. Perthes (ed.), *Germany and the Middle East: Interest and Options*, Berlin: Heinrich-Böll-Stiftung / Stiftung Wissenschaft und Politik, 2002; G. Nonnemann, 'Rentiers and Autocrats'.
64. On the concept of ethnic democracy see S. Smooha, 'Ethnic Democracy: Israel as an Archetype', *Israel Studies*, 2(2), 1995: 198–241; see also A. Ghanem et al., 'Questioning "Ethnic Democracy": a Response to Sammy Smooha', *Israel Studies*, 3(2), 1997: 253–67; see also R. Cohen-Almagor, 'Cultural Pluralism and the Israeli Nation-Building Ideology', *International Journal of Middle East Studies*, 27(4), 1995: 461–84.
65. R. Nathanson and S. Stetter (eds), *The Middle East Under Fire? EU-Israel Relations in a Region between War and Conflict Resolution*, Berlin and Tel Aviv: Friedrich-Ebert Stiftung, 2007.
66. E. Zisser, 'A False Spring in Damascus', *Orient*, 44(1), 2003: 39–61.
67. G. E. Robinson, 'Defensive Democratization in Jordan', *International Journal of Middle East Studies*, 30(3), 1998: 387–410.
68. Y. Sayigh, 'Globalization Manqué'; R. Hinnebusch, 'Authoritarian Persistence'.

69. I. S. Lustick, 'The Oslo Agreements as an Obstacle to Peace'; A. N. Hamzeh, 'Clientelism, Lebanon: Roots and Trends', *Middle Eastern Studies*, 37(3), 2001: 167–78.
70. This is not to say that powerlessness could not be a powerful resource in political communications. References to alleged asymmetries are a powerful empowering factor in the worldwide (media) struggle between Israelis and Palestinians (used by both sides) and can also be found in many other conflicts. See also R. D. Kuperman, 'Strategies of Asymmetric Warfare and their Implementation in the South Lebanon Conflict', *Foreign Policy Analysis*, 2(1), 2006: 1–20.
71. R. E. Lucas, 'Press Laws as a Survival Strategy in Jordan, 1989–99', *Middle Eastern Studies*, 39(4), 2003: 81.
72. K. Dalacoura, 'Islamist Terrorism and the Middle East Democratic Deficit: Political Exclusion, Repression and the Causes of Terrorism', *Democratization*, 13(3), 2006: 508–25.
73. M. Kamrava, 'Non-Democratic States and Political Liberalisation in the Middle East: a Structural Analysis', *Third World Quarterly*, 19(1), 1998: 63–85.
74. R. Hinnebusch, 'Authoritarian Persistence', p. 391.
75. This includes an overemphasis on the power of the political centre, be it Damascus, Amman or Jerusalem, at the expense of local/peripheral political developments which are equally relevant for understanding Middle East politics. Such an overemphasis on political centres easily reifies first-order narratives of centralization and control, see also A. Bank, 'Re-ORIENTing IR: Innerstaatliche Gewaltkonflikte als Treffpunkt Internationaler Beziehungen und Vergleichender Orientforschung', paper presented at the Offene Sektionstagung der Sektion Internationale Politik der Deutschen Vereinigung für Politische Wissenschaft, Mannheim, September 2006.
76. V. Perthes, 'Editorial: Elites in the Orient, or: Why Focus on Middle Eastern Elites', *Orient*, 44(4), 2003: 533.
77. See also Y. Sayigh, 'Globalization Manqué'.
78. S. Lowrance, 'Deconstructing Democracy: the Arab-Jewish Divide in the Jewish State', *Critique: Critical Middle Eastern Studies*, 13(2), 2004: 175–93.
79. See note 64 above.
80. S. J. Al-Azm, 'Islam, Terrorism and the West'.
81. A. Le More, 'Killing with Kindness: Funding the Demise of a Palestinian State', *International Affairs*, 81(5), 2005: 981–99.
82. N. N. Ayubi, *Over-Stating the Arab State*.
83. This translates, for example, into the inability of politics to be sufficiently irritated by environmental 'perturbations', whether comprised of economic or legal communications or the issue of preventing massive forms of exclusions, as addressed in the Arab Human Development Reports (see also Chapter 4). As Sass and Ghawri argue in a somewhat related context, 'the fundamental break to be faced by Arab societies today may concern the opening of society and the very establishment of a political public able to lead a debate on reform, in the first place, which is not merely academic but politically salient', Y. Ghrawi and P. Sass, 'The Political Reform Debate in the Middle East and North Africa: Arabic Newspapers and Journals June 2004–Feburary 2005', Working Paper FG 6, 2005/01, Berlin: Stiftung Wissenschaft und Politik, 2005, p. 6.

84. M. Kamrava, 'The Politics of Weak Control: State Capacity and Economic Semi-Formality in the Middle East', *Comparative Studies of South Asia, Africa and the Middle East,* 22(1/2), 2002: 43–52.

85. K. Salibi, *The Modern History of Jordan,* London: I.B. Tauris, 1993; M. Ma'oz et al., *Modern Syria.*

86. See P. D. Hoyt, 'Legitimacy, Identity and Political Development in the Arab World: Book Review', *International Studies Review,* 42(1), 1998: 173–6.

87. M. Kamrava, 'The Politics of Weak Control'.

88. Y. Sayigh, 'Globalization Manqué'.

89. This theme was particularly stressed in the Arab Human Development Reports.

90. K. P. Japp and I. Kusche, 'Die Kommunikation des politischen Systems: Zur Differenz von Herstellung und Darstellung im politischen System', *Zeitschrift für Soziologie,* 33(6), 2004: 511–31.

91. See U. Stäheli, *Sinnzusammenbruche.*

92. See K. Salibi, *The Modern History of Jordan*; L. L. Layne, *Home and Homeland.*

93. B. S. Anderson, 'Writing the Nation: Textbooks of the Hashemite Kingdom of Jordan', *Comparative Studies of South Asia, Africa and the Middle East,* 21(1/2), 2001: 13 (emphasis added).

94. N. J. Brown, 'Democracy, History, and the Contest of the Palestinian Curriculum', Washington, DC.: Adam Institute, 2001, p. 15 (emphasis added).

95. For a classic account see M. C. Hudson, *Arab Politics: the Search for Legitimacy,* New Haven: Yale University Press, 1979.

96. See the regular publications on the human rights situation in Syria of the Euro-Mediterranean Human Rights Network on http://euromedrights.net/.

97. E. Zisser, 'Who's Afraid of Syrian Nationalism?'

98. V. Perthes, 'The Political Economy of the Syrian Succession', *Survival,* 43(1), 2001: 152.

99. Ibid.

100. See R. E. Lucas, 'Press Laws as a Survival Strategy'; Q. Wiktorowicz, *The Management of Islamic Activism: Salafis, the Muslim Brotherhood, and State Power in Jordan,* New York: State University of New York Press, 2001.

101. U. Bar-Joseph, 'The Paradox of Israeli Power', *Survival,* 46(4), 2004: 137–55.

102. N. Ben-Yehuda, 'The Masada Mythical Narrative and the Israeli Army', in E. Lomsky-Feder and E. Ben-Ari (eds), *The Military and Militarism in Israeli Society,* Albany: State University of New York Press, 1999; see also M. Azaryahu, 'Mount Herzl: the Creation of Israel's National Cemetery', *Israel Studies,* 1(2), 2005: 46–74.

103. Y. Peled, 'Restoring Ethnic Democracy: the Or Commission and Palestinian Citizenship in Israel', *Citizenship Studies,* 9(1), 2005: 90.

104. Ibid.

105. Y. Sayigh, 'Armed Struggle and State Formation', *Journal of Palestine Studies* 26(4), 1997: 17–32.

106. A. Jamal, 'State-Building, Institutionalization and Democracy'; S. Stetter, 'Democratisation without Democracy'; A. Badawi, 'Policy Failure, Power Relations and the Dynamics of Elite Change in Palestine', *Orient,* 44(4), 2003: 555–77.

107. Y. Sayigh, 'Armed Struggle and State Formation', p. 18.

108. M. Harb and R. Leenders, 'Know the Enemy: Hizbullah, "Terrorism", and the Politics of Perception', *Third World Quarterly,* 26(1), 2005: 173–97.

109. Ibid., my emphasis.
110. D. Tuastad, 'Neo-Orientalism and the New Barbarism Thesis: Aspects of Symbolic Violence in the Middle East Conflict(s)', *Third World Quarterly*, 24(4), 2003: 591–2.
111. J. A. Massad, *Colonial Effects: the Making of Jordanian National Identity*, New York: Columbia University Press, 2001; J. Rynhold, 'Israel's Fence: Can Separation Make Better Neighbours?' *Survival*, 46(1), 2004: 55–76; R. Nasrallah et al., *The Wall: Fragmenting the Palestinian Fabric to Jerusalem*, Jerusalem: International Peace and Cooperation Centre, 2006.
112. See M. Mushlih, 'Hamas: Strategy and Tactics', in L. Binder, *Ethnic Conflict and International Politics*; A. N. Hamzeh, 'Lebanon's Hizbullah: From Islamic Revolution to Parliamentary Accomodation', *Third World Quarterly*, 14(2), 1993: 321–37; M. Harb and R. Leenders, 'Know the Enemy'.
113. S. A. Muscati, 'Reconstructing "Evil": a Critical Assessment of Post-11 September Political Discourses', *Journal of Muslim Minority Affairs*, 23(2), 2003: 249–69.
114. Y. Suleiman, *A War of Words: Language and Conflicts in the Middle East*, Cambridge: Cambridge University Press, 2004.
115. See N. Luhmann, *Macht*, pp. 62–3; N. Luhmann, 'Symbiotische Mechanismen', in *Soziologische Aufklärung 3: Soziales System, Gesellschaft, Organisation*, Opladen: Westdeutscher Verlag, 1981.
116. D. Baecker, 'Gewalt im System', *Soziale Welt*, 47(1), 1996: 92–109.
117 Ibid., p.103.
118 On causality and regionalization dynamics in world society see N. Luhmann, 'Kausalität im Suden'.
119. D. Baecker, 'Gewalt im System', p. 101.
120. Ibid.
121. See N. Luhmann, *Soziale Systeme*, 148–90.
122. D. Baecker, 'Gewalt im System'.
123. K. Dalacoura, 'Islamist Terrorism and the Middle East Democratic Deficit'; T. Gongora, 'War Making and State Power'.
124. G. C. Gambill, 'The Balance of Terror: War by Other Means in the Contemporary Middle East', *Journal of Palestine Studies*, 28(1), 1998: 59.
125. D. Baecker, 'Gewalt im System', p. 101.
126. Note that this is not a statement about 'objective' power but rather about powerful political framings in which either side justifies its violent actions by claims of powerlessness/vulnerability.
127. G. Brücher, 'The Irony of Terror: the Morality-Sensitive Nerve in the Criticism of Violence', in S. Stetter, *Territorial Conflicts in World Society*.
128. T. Bar-On and H. Goldstein, 'Fighting Violence: a Critique of the War on Terrorism', *International Politics*, 42(2), 2005: 240.
129. N. Ghadbian, *Democratization and the Islamist Challenge*; J. Clark, 'Social Movement Theory and Patron Clientelism: Islamic Social Institutions and the Middle Class in Egypt, Jordan and Yemen', *Comparative Political Studies*, 37(8), 2004: 941–68.
130. G. C. Gambill, 'The Balance of Terror', p. 59.
131. See also P. Fuchs, 'Kein Anschluß unter dieser Nummer oder Terror ist wirklich blindwütig', http://www.fen.ch/texte/gast_fuchs_terrorismus.htm.
132. D. Baecker, 'Gewalt im System', pp. 93–100.

133. D. Baecker, 'Die Gewalt des Terrorismus', unpublished paper. Such an approach firmly places violence within a social context. For a radically different concept see A. Açikgenç, 'An Evaluation of Violence from Islam's Perspective', *Alternatives – Turkish Journal of International Relations*, 1(4), 2002: 16–29.

134. G. C. Gambill, 'The Balance of Terror', p. 65.

135. Shaykh Muhammad Husayn Fadlallah and J. Massad, '11 September, Terrorism, Islam, and the Intifada', *Journal of Palestine Studies*, 31(2), 2002: 79.

136. K. P. Japp, 'Zur Soziologie des fundamentalistischen Terrorismus', *Soziale Systeme*, 9(1), 2003: 68.

137. For the vast literature on fundamentalist terrorism and the debate on the role of Islam see H. Khashan. 'Collective Palestinian Frustration and Suicide Bombings', *Third World Quarterly*, 24(6), 2003: 1049–67; J. Alagha, 'Hizbullah and Martydom', *Orient*, 45(1), 2004: 47–74; M. Ferrero, 'Martyrdom Contracts', *Journal of Conflict Resolution*, 50(6), 2006: 855–77. In contrast to communication-theoretical approaches (see K. P. Japp, 'Zur Soziologie des fundamentalistischen Terrorismus'), a huge part of the literature focuses in particular on the individual motivations of 'terrorists', see for this debate D. Gholamasad, 'Zur Sozio- und Psychogenese der Selbstmordattentate der Islamisten', *Orient*, 43(3), 2002: 383–400; L. Andoni, 'Searching for Answers: Gaza's Suicide Bombers', *Journal of Palestine Studies*, 26(4), 1997: 33–45.

138. Quoted in F. S. Hasso, 'Discursive and Political Developments by / of the 2002 Palestinian Women Suicide Bombers / Martyrs', *feminist review*, 81(1), 2005: 44.

139. J. Alagha, 'Hizbullah, Terrorism, and September 11', *Orient*, 44(3), 2003: 409.

140. S. J. Al-Azm, 'Islam, Terrorism and the West', p. 6.

141. A. Hamzawy, 'Vom Primat der Verschwörung'.

142. D. Tuastad, 'Neo-Orientalism and the New Barbarism Thesis'.

143. N. Luhmann, *Macht*, p. 14

144. Note again that this is a statement about communications and not about actors.

145. N. Ghadbian, *Democratization and the Islamist Challenge*; A. Ali, 'Islamism: Emancipation, Protest and Identity', *Journal of Muslim Minority Affairs*, 20(1), 2000: 11–28; B. Korany et al., *Political Liberalization and Democratization*; F. Volpi and F. Cavatorta, 'Forgetting Democratization? Recasting Power and Authority in a Pluralist Muslim World', *Democratization*, 13(3), 2006: 363–72.

146. For the relationship between Islam and democracy see R. Bahlul, 'Toward an Islamic Conception of Democracy'; see also Q. Wiktorowicz and S. T. Farouki, 'Islamic NGOs and Muslim Politics: a Case from Jordan', *Third World Quarterly*, 21(4), 2000: 685–99.

147. It is paramount to note that the existence of armed militias does not only relate to Muslim groups but also shapes the politics of many secular political parties, for example, in Palestine or Lebanon. And, of course, such phenomena are well known with regard to the Jewish settlers' movement.

148. See for a similar discussion H. Baumgarten, 'Die Hamas: Wahlsieg in Palästina: Islamistische Transformation zur Demokratie in einem neopatrimonialen Rentier-System', *Orient*, 47(1), 2006: 26–59.

149. Q. Wiktorowicz, *The Management of Islamic Activism*; S. Fathi, 'Jordanian Survival Strategy: the Election Law as a "Safety Valve" ', *Middle Eastern Studies*, 41(6), 2005: 889–998.

150. That might also be one of the reasons why the introduction of more or less democratic elections has, until today, contributed hardly at all to any reduction in confrontational politics in the region.
151. One might think here of the health and educational services linked to Hezbollah or Hamas. For orthodox Jews see D. C. Jacobson, 'The Ma'ale School: Catalyst for the Entrance of Religious Zionists into the World of Media Production', *Israel Studies*, 9(1), 2004: 31–60.
152. Q. Wiktorowicz, *The Management of Islamic Activism*; P. Mandaville, 'Sufis and Salafis: the Political Discourse of Transnational Islam', in R. W. Hefner (ed.), *Remaking Muslim Politics: Pluralism, Contestation, Democratization*, Princeton: Princeton University Press, 2005.
153. A. R. Norton, 'Associational Life'.
154. C. Houston, 'Islamism, Castoriadis and Autonomy', *Thesis Eleven*, 76(1), 2004: 49–69.

4. Inclusion and exclusion: fragile strategies of deparadoxification in the Middle East

1. From the album 'John Wesley Harding', Columbia Records, 1967.
2. See the classic work by T.H. Marshall, *Class, Citizenship, and Social Development, Essays*, Garden City: Doubleday, 1964; W. R. Brubaker, 'Immigration, Citizenship, and the Nation State in France and Germany: a Comparative Historical Perspective', *Ethnic and Racial Studies*, 18(5), 1990: 379–407. See also R. Stichweh, 'Zur Theorie der politischen Inklusion', in R. Stichweh, *Die Weltgesellschaft*, pp. 67–81.
3. D. Stasiulis and D. Ross, 'Security, Flexible Sovereignty, and the Perils of Multiple Citizenship', *Citizenship Studies*, 10(3), 2006; 329–48; T. Faist et al., 'Dual Citizenship as a Path-Dependent Process', *International Migration Review*, 37(4), 2004: 913–44.
4. M. Koenig, 'Weltgesellschaft, Menschenrechte und der Formwandel des Nationalstaats', in B. Heintz et al., *Weltgesellschaft*, p. 374; see also T. Bonacker, 'Debordering by Human Rights'.
5. See for a detailed discussion on these semantics of national 'societies', H. Tyrell, 'Singular oder Plural: Einleitende Bemerkungen zu Globalisierung und Weltgesellschaft', in B. Heintz et al., *Weltgesellschaft*, pp. 1–50.
6. J. Habermas, *Faktizität und Geltung: Beiträge zur Diskurstheorie des Rechts und des demokratischen Rechtsstaats*, Frankfurt: Suhrkamp, 1992.
7. See D. Archbigu and D. Held (eds), *Cosmopolitan Democracy: an Agenda for a New World Order*, Cambridge: Polity Press, 1995.
8. D. Armstrong (ed.), 'Governance and Resistance in World Politics', *Review of International Studies*, Special Issue, 29, 2003; A. Wimmer, *Nationalist Exclusion and Ethnic Conflict: Shadows of Modernity*, Cambridge: Cambridge University Press, 2002; R. Murphy, *Social Closure: the Theory of Monopolization and Exclusion*, Oxford: Clarendon Press, 1988; F. Parkin, *Marxism and Class Theory: a Bourgeois Critique*, London: Tavistock, 1979.
9. For an overview see R. Maktabi, 'Tune in Religion, Turn on Pluralism, Drop out Citizenship? Membership and Political Participation in Jordan, Kuwait and Lebanon', in B. O. Utvik and T. S. Vikor, *The Middle East in a Globalized*

World; A. F. March, 'The Demands of Citizenship: Translating Political Liberalism into the Language of Islam', *Journal of Muslim Minority Affairs*, 25(3), 2005: 317–45; Y. Peled, 'Ethnic Identity and the Legal Construction of Citizenship: Arab Citizens of the Jewish State', *American Political Science Review*, 86(2), 1992: 432–43; M. K. Al-Sayyid, 'The Concept of Civil Society and the Arab World', in B. Korany et al., *Political Liberalization and Democratization*; E. Boulding, *Building Peace in the Middle East: Challenges for States and Civil Society*, Boulder: Lynne Rienner, 1994; R. Kook, 'Between Uniqueness and Exclusion: the Politics of Identity in Israel', in M. Barnett, *Dialogues in Arab Politics*; K. Dalacoura, 'Islamist Terrorism and the Middle East Democratic Deficit'.

10. M. Barnett, *Dialogues in Arab Politics*; M. Barnett, *Israel in Comparative Perspective*.
11. United Nations Development Programme, Arab Fund for Economic and Social Development and Arab Gulf Programme for United Nations Development Organizations (eds), *Arab Human Development Report 2004: Towards Freedom in the Arab World*, New York: UNDP, 2004, p. 9.
12. See N. Luhmann, *Die Gesellschaft der Gesellschaft*, pp. 678–706.
13. Also from an empirical perspective such an equation between integration and inclusions seems hardly convincing; see A. Bora, ' "Wer gehört dazu?" Überlegungen zur Theorie der Inklusion', in K. U. Hellman and R. Schmalz-Bruns, *Theorie der Politik*. See also on the linkages between the massive forms of integration in exclusionary and conflictive settings Chapter 5.
14. See note 9 above; M. Beck et al. (eds), *Der Nahe Osten im Umbruch: Theoretische Perspektiven auf eine Region zwischen Transformation und Autoritarismus*, Wiesbaden: VS-Verlag, forthcoming, 2008.
15. S. Zubaida, *Law and Power in the Islamic World*; F. Halliday, *Nation and Religion in the Middle East*; M. Barnett, *Dialogues in Arab Politics*.
16. This also comprises the gradualization of citizenship in many Middle East countries. On the notion of membership in (political) organizations see N. Luhmann, *Die Politik des Gesellschaft*, pp. 228–73.
17. R. Stichweh, 'Strangers, Inclusion, and Identities', *Soziale Systeme*, 8(1), 2002: 103.
18. N. Luhmann, *Das Recht der Gesellschaft*, Frankfurt: Suhrkamp, 1995, p. 233.
19. A. Nassehi, 'Exclusion Individuality or Individualization by Inclusion', *Soziale Systeme*, 8(1), 2002: 127.
20. N. Luhmann, 'Inklusion und Exklusion', in *Soziologische Aufklärung 6: Die Soziologie und der Mensch*, Opladen: Westdeutscher Verlag, 1995, pp. 261–2.
21. Such as former Israeli prime minister Ariel Sharon declaring that then-Palestinian President Yassir Arafat 'is no longer relevant'. On the full inclusion principle of functional communications see also R. Stichweh, *Inklusion und Exklusion*, pp. 70–4.
22. A. Nassehi, 'Die Theorie funktionaler Differenzierung im Horizont ihrer Kritik', p. 114.
23. See H. Messmer, *Der soziale Konflikt*; see also Chapter 5 below.
24. This would require that when a person is addressed as a person s/he would be *simultaneously* designated as this person in intimate, economic, legal, religious, art-related and so on communications – an empirically hardly convincing constellation.
25. N. Luhmann, 'Inklusion und Exklusion', p. 263.

26. As a cursory note it should be emphasized that this understanding of integration through exclusion stands in marked contrast to the (empirically problematic) understanding of integration through inclusion in many normative-oriented studies, see A. Bora, ' "Wer gehört dazu?" '

27. In modern systems theory such constellations are discussed with regard to the concept of 'exclusion individuality', see in greater detail N. Luhmann, 'Individuum, Individualität, Individualismus', in *Gesellschaftsstruktur und Semantik: Studien zur Wissenssoziologie der modernen Gesellschaft, Band 3*, Frankfurt: Suhrkamp, 1993.

28. N. Luhmann, *Die Gesellschaft der Gesellschaft*, p. 630.

29. Ibid., p. 631.

30. R. Bowker, *Palestinian Refugees*. As will be further outlined, such exclusions form, in turn, the basis for subsequent inclusions, for example, by radical political parties, global aid organizations, world media or Middle East researchers.

31. A. Nassehi, 'Politik des Staates oder Politik der Gesellschaft: Kollektivität als Problemformel des Politischen', in K.-U. Hellmann and R. Schmalz-Bruns, *Theorie der politik*, p. 47. Of course, this includes negative forms of addressability, too.

32. See, for example, N. Luhmann, 'Inklusion und Exklusion'.

33. N. Luhmann, 'Jenseits von Barbarei', in *Gesellschaftsstruktur und Semantik: Studien zur Wissenssoziologie der modernen Gesellschaft, Band 4*, Frankfurt: Suhrkamp, 1999, p. 147.

34. N. Luhmann, *Die Gesellschaft der Gesellschaft*.

35. Ibid.

36. Chain exclusion can be understood as 'far-reaching exclusion from a functional system ... leading to exclusion from other systems', N. Luhmann, *Die Politik der Gesellschaft*, p. 427.

37. R. Stichweh, *Inklusion und Exklusion*, p. 61.

38. Ibid.

39. Quoted in O. Marchart, 'On Drawing a Line: Politics and the Significatory Logics of Inclusion/Exclusion', *Soziale Systeme*, 8(1), 2002: 79.

40. C. Bohn and A. Hahn, 'Patterns of Inclusion and Exclusion: Property, Nation and Religion', *Soziale Systeme*, 8(1), 2002: 23.

41. N. Luhmann, *Die Gesellschaft der Gesellschaft*, p. 169.

42. See also R. Stichweh, 'Der 11. September und seine Folgen für die Entwicklung der Weltgesellschaft: Zur Genese des terroristischen Weltereignisses', in T. Bonacker and C. Weller (eds), *Konflikte in der Weltgesellschaft: Akteure, Strukturen, Dynamiken*, Frankfurt and New York: Campus, 2006, p. 280.

43. To reiterate, the designation of a positive and a negative side of code-oriented communications does not contain any normative connotations. It rather refers to the observation that connectivity between those communications, which observe themselves on the basis of distinct codes (thereby ensuring system maintenance), is ensured on the positive side, whereas the negative side has the (equally important) function of ensuring environmental openness, irritability, contingency reflection and crossing of code-oriented communications.

44. This relates, for example, to the role of 'intermediaries', that is, local elites in developing countries, who possess privileged access to the (global)

performance functions of various functional systems, see K. Schlichte, *Der Staat in der Weltgesellschaft: Politische Herrschaft in Asien, Afrika und Lateinamerika*, Frankfurt and New York: Campus, 2005.

45. It needs to be strongly emphasized here that this does not imply that there could be any 'perfect' functioning of social systems uninhibited by programmes which structure (that is, limit) presuppositionless crossing. Strategies of deparadoxification, which veil the founding paradox of every order, are always required. But some are more successful in (temporarily) invisibilizing these founding paradoxes.

46. On second-order observations see N. Luhmann, *Die Kunst der Gesellschaft*, Frankfurt: Suhrkamp, 1997, p. 104; N. Luhmann, *Die Religion der Gesellschaft*, p. 308. To paraphrase from the latter source, politics is what can be observed as politics; and this happens on the level of second-order observations.

47. R. Stichweh, 'Strangers, Inclusion, and Identities', p. 106. Note that there is no hierarchy between the two modes of observation and that is what distinguishes modern systems theory's approach to second-order observations from seemingly similar arguments in 'critical' research traditions. Thus, 'only the second-order observer sees that the first-order observer "reduces complexity"; and this then means that it makes no sense to demand from him to reduce complexity' – while first-order observations 'guarantee reality', N. Luhmann, *Die Kunst der Gesellschaft*, p. 104. But also second-order observations (for example, by 'critical' researchers) remain 'uncritical towards their own references … insofar there is no reflexive hierarchy', N. Luhmann, *Die Wissenschaft der Gesellschaft*, p. 85. See also Chapter 5.

48. N. Luhmann, *Die Politik der Gesellschaft*, p. 232.

49. N. Luhmann, *Die Gesellschaft der Gesellschaft*, p. 765.

50. U. Stäheli, 'Fatal Attraction? Popular Modes of Inclusion in the Economic System', *Soziale Systeme*, 8(1), 2002: 113.

51. N. Luhmann, *Die Wissenschaft der Gesellschaft*, p. 346.

52. N. Luhmann, 'Jenseits von Barbarei', pp.142–3.

53. This argument already shows that frozen crossings are not a feature specific to the Middle East but rather a problem which relates to all possible regions (and programmes) in world society.

54. N. Luhmann, *Die Kunst der Gesellschaft*, p. 112.

55. Ibid., p. 147.

56. Ibid., p. 112. For the Middle East and the alternative time-horizons of eschatological religious-political movements, which might be helpful in that regard, see S. Damir-Geilsdorf, 'Das Ende – eine politische Wende? Gegenwärtige muslimische Erinnerungen an die Zukunft', *Orient*, 44(2), 2003: 257–79.

57. N. Luhmann, *Die Kunst der Gesellschaft*, p. 116.

58. N. Luhmann, *Die Wissenschaft der Gesellschaft*, p. 81.

59. R. Stichweh, *Inklusion und Exklusion*, p. 63.

60. See D. Baecker, 'Lenin's Twist, or the R-Factor of Communication', *Soziale Systeme*, 8(1), 2002: 88–100.

61. See the previous chapter and further below in this chapter on more literature on the 'crisis' of politics, law and science/education. This notion of 'crisis' across various societal spheres has also been central to the various Arab Human Development Reports.

62. F. Halliday, *The Middle East in International Relations*, p. 212. See also S. A. Arjomand, 'Islam, Political Change and Globalization'; C. Houston, 'Islamism, Castoriadis and Autonomy'.

63. See from a historical perspective, J. P. Arnason and G. Stauth, 'Civilization and State Formation in the Islamic Context'.

64. F. Halliday, *The Middle East in International Relations*, p. 212.

65. See also M. A. Muhibbu-Din, 'Ahl al-Kitab and Religious Minorities in the Islamic State: Historical Context and Contemporary Challenges', *Journal of Muslim Minority Affairs*, 20(1), 2000: 111–27.

66. T. Scheffler, 'Religious Communalism and Democratization'; M. Galchinsky, 'The Jewish Settlements in the West Bank: International Law and Israeli Jurisprudence', *Israel Studies* 9(3), 2005: 115–36; E. Goldberg et al. (eds), *Rules and Rights in the Middle East: Democracy, Law, and Society*, Seattle: University of Washington Press, 1993.

67. See for example the concept of *zakat* in Islamic law which ensures the inclusion of the poor in economics. E. El-Shagi, 'Islam und wirtschaftliche Entwicklung', *Orient*, 44(3), 2003: 437–49.

68. United Nations Development Programme and Arab Fund for Economic and Social Development (eds), *The Arab Human Development Report 2005: Building a Knowledge Society*, New York: UNDP, 2005.

69. Ibid., p. 38.

70. Ibid., p. 54.

71. Ibid., p. 61.

72. Ibid., p. 67. As the report continues, in the whole Arab region the number of books translated from foreign languages into Arabic currently stands at approximately 330. This is roughly one-fifth of the number of foreign language books translated each year into Greek, a country with approximately 3 per cent of the population of all Arab countries combined.

73. Ibid., p. 75. It might be seen as the self-fulfilling irony of the AHDR that the usual justification that the results of the report are 'true' are garnished by the comment that the 'report has been written by Arabs' as if this would mystically increase the 'truths' contained in this report.

74. See also D. Weiss, 'Wege zu einer arabischen Wissensgesellschaft', *Orient*, 45(1), 2004: 75–90.

75. See also the concept of 'sakrale Zeit' and its impact on knowledge-generation in Muslim history in D. Diner, *Versiegelte Zeit*.

76. N. Luhmann, *Die Wissenschaft der Gesellschaft*, p. 172, my emphasis.

77. Ibid., p. 175.

78. Ibid., p. 216.

79. Ibid., p. 217.

80. Ibid., p. 218.

81. Ibid., p. 206.

82. M. Al-Zaydi, 'Education and Hope', Asharq Alawsat English, http://www.asharqalawsat.com/english/news.asp?section=2&id=8160.

83. Ibid.

84. S. Al-Mahadin, 'Jordanian Women in Education: Politics, Pedagogy and Gender Discourses', *feminist review*, 78(1), 2004: 35.

85. M. Fandy, 'Enriched Islam: the Muslim Crisis of Education', *Survival*, 49(2), 2007: 93.

86. Y. Reiter, 'Higher Education and Sociopolitical Transformation in Jordan', *British Journal of Middle Eastern Studies,* 29(2), 2002: 137–64; B. S. Anderson, 'Writing the Nation'; see also R. Lohlker, 'Cyberjihad'.
87. United Nations Development Programme and Arab Fund for Economic and Social Development (2003), p. 75.
88. See, for example, B. Morris, *The Birth of the Palestinian Refugee Problem, 1947–1949*, Cambridge: Cambridge University Press, 1987; J. Heller, 'Alternative Narratives and Collective Memories: Israel's New Historians and the Use of Historical Context', *Middle Eastern Studies,* 42(4), 2006: 571–86; G. Shafir, 'Israeli Decolonization and Critical Sociology', *Journal of Palestine Studies,* 25(3), 1996: 23–35; S. Aronson, 'The Post-Zionist Discourse and Critique of Israel: a Traditional Zionist Perspective', *Israel Studies,* 8(1), 2003: 105–29. See also R. Wildangel, *Zwischen Achse und Mittelmacht: Palästina und der Nationalsozialismus*, Berlin: Klaus Schwarz, 2007.
89. C. I. Waxman, 'Critical Sociology and the End of Ideology in Israel', *Israel Studies,* 2(1), 2005: 194.
90. Ibid.
91. E. Ben Rafael, 'Critical Versus Non-Critical Sociology: an Evaluation', *Israel Studies,* 2(1), 2005: 175.
92. Ibid., p. 174, my emphasis.
93. Comparable to the sacralization referred to above, D. Diner, *Versiegelte Zeit.* See also Ben Porat, 'A State of Holiness'.
94. M. Lissak, ' "Critical" Sociology and "Establishment" Sociology in the Israeli Academic Community: Ideological Struggles or Academic Discourse?', *Israel Studies,* 1(1), 2005: 289. Thus, a dynamic comparable to the sacralization referred to above; D. Diner, *Versiegelte Zeit.*
95. T. Forte, 'Sifting People, Sorting Papers: Academic Practice and the Notion of State Security in Israel', *Comparative Studies of South Asia, Africa and the Middle East,* 23(1/2), 2003: 215.
96. I. Pappé, 'The Tantura Case in Israel: the Katz Research and Trial', *Journal of Palestine Studies,* 30(3), 2001: 19–39. See also I. Pappé, 'Post-Zionist Critique on Israel and the Palestinians Part II: the Media', *Journal of Palestine Studies,* 26(3), 1997: 37–43.
97. On the further development see http://faculty.biu.ac.il/~steing/conflict/oped/boycott.html.
98. I. Pappé, 'The Tantura Case in Israel', p. 27.
99. Ibid., p. 30.
100. And a general argument here is that the self-description as 'critical' and 'post-Zionist' is in itself a heavily ideologized and hegemonic programme.
101. M. Lissak, ' "Critical" Sociology and "Establishment" Sociology', p. 289, my emphasis.
102. N. Lochery, 'Scholarship or Propaganda: Works on Israel and the Arab-Israeli Conflict, 2001', *Middle Eastern Studies,* 37(4), 2002: 234.
103. This again underscores the world societal and functional embedding. It is not about scientific communications in the Middle East, but about scientific communications in and on the Middle East, more generally. On the boycott see D. Newman, 'The Threat to Academic Freedom in Israel-Palestine', *Tikkun,* 19(4), 2003: 56–66.

104. See also the somewhat related argument in L. A. Brand, 'Academic Freedom: the "Danger" of Critical Thinking', *International Studies Perspective*, 8(4), 2007: 384–95.
105. Ibid.
106. G. Steinberg, 'Boycotting the Jews (*Wall Street Journal* European Edition)', available on http://faculty.biu.ac.il/~steing/conflict/oped/boycott.html.
107. Y. Reiter, 'Higher Education and Sociopolitical Transformation in Jordan', p. 28.
108. W. I. Ackerman, 'Making Jews: an Enduring Challenge in Israeli Education', *Israel Studies*, 2(2), 2005: 1–20; G. Levy, 'From Subjects to Citizens: on Educational Reforms and the Demarcation of the "Israeli Arabs"', *Citizenship Studies*, 9(3), 2005: 271–91.
109. This chapter does not focus on chain inclusions, but this is also a topic. See the focus on elites and intermediaries in the Middle East literature.
110. N. Luhmann, 'Frauen, Männer und George Spencer Brown', *Zeitschrift für Soziologie*, 17(1), 1988: 47–71.
111. S. Al-Mahadin, 'Jordanian Women in Education'. See for the same argument, this time in relation to the status of Palestinians in Jordanian academia, Y. Reiter, 'Higher Education and Sociopolitical Transformation in Jordan'.
112. Quoted in A. Treacher and H. Shukrallah, 'Editorial: the Realm of the Possible: Middle Eastern Women in Political and Social Spaces', *feminist review*, 80(1), 2005: 155.
113. S. Al-Mahadin, 'Jordanian Women in Education', p. 23.
114. Ibid., p. 35.
115. Ibid., p. 32. As Elie notes, in such contexts, the state operates as 'a significant nexus and main theatre for the acting out of gender politics', however, mostly on the symbolic level only; S. D. Elie, 'The Harem Syndrome: Moving beyond Anthropology's Discursive Colonialization of Gender in the Middle East', *Alternatives*, 29(2), 2004: 157.
116. S. Al-Mahadin, 'Jordanian Women in Education', p. 22.
117. Ibid., p. 27.
118. A. Treacher and H. Sukrallah, 'Editorial: the Realm of the Possible', p. 157. See also N. Abdo, 'Gender and Politics under the Palestinian Authority', *Journal of Palestine Studies*, 28(2), 1999: 38–51; H. Herzog, 'Homefront and Battlefront: the Status of Jewish and Palestinian Women in Israel', *Israel Studies*, 3(1), 2005: 61–84.
119. F. Faqir, 'Intrafamily Famicide in Defence of Honour: the Case of Jordan', *Third World Quarterly*, 22(1), 2001: 65–82. This also relates to the formal reservations and declarations by Arab countries in the implementation of the Convention on the Elimination of All Forms of Discrimination Against Women (CEDAW) by the UN General Assembly, see Euro-Mediterranean Human Rights Network, '2006 Change is Possible and Necessary: Achieving Gender Equality in the Euro-Mediterranean Region', Copenhagen: EMHRN, 2006.
120. L. R. Shehaded, 'The Legal Status of Married Women in Lebanon', *International Journal of Middle East Studies*, 30(4), 1998: 501–19.
121. L. R. Shehaded, 'Coverture in Lebanon', *feminist review*, 76(1), 2004: 85.
122. C. Balchin, 'With Her Feet on the Ground: Women, Religion and Development in Muslim Communities', *Development*, 46(4), 2003: 39–49.
123. Ibid., p. 42.
124. S. D. Elie, 'The Harem Syndrome', p. 151.
125. Ibid.

126. Ibid., p. 139.
127. Ibid., p. 149.
128. Ibid., pp. 143–4.
129. A. Duncker, 'Ungleiches Recht für alle? Zur Rechtsgleichheit in islamischen Menschenrechtserklärungen', *Orient*, 45(4), 2004: 565–81.
130. S. D. Elie, 'The Harem Syndrome', p.139.
131. Ibid., p. 140.
132. N. Luhmann, 'Die Paradoxie der Form', in N. Luhmann, *Aufsätze und Reden*, pp. 243–61.
133. See for examples some framings of Israel and Palestine in the context of the Israeli-Palestinian conflict. Both sides are, occasionally, presented by supporters as 'threatened nations' whose enemies strive for their complete destruction. This legitimizes extraordinary measures in exerting power over the other side.
134. Q. Wiktorowicz and S. T. Farouki, 'Islamic NGOs and Muslim Politics', p. 686.
135. See H. Baumgarten, 'Die Hamas'; A. N. Hamzeh, 'Lebanon's Islamists and Local Politics'.
136. Q. Wiktorowicz, 'The Salafi Movement in Jordan', *International Journal of Middle East Studies*, 32(2), 2000: 220.
137. O. Kamil, 'The Synagogue as Civil Society, or How Can We Understand the Shas Party', *Mediterranean Quarterly*, 12(3), 2001: 128–43.
138. J. Stolow, 'Transnationalism and the New Religio-Politics: Reflections on a Jewish Orthodox Case', *Theory, Culture & Society*, 21(2), 2004: 109–37.
139. Ibid., pp. 118–19.
140. 'Democracy' and 'liberalization' would, for example, be other programmes.

5.   Identities and conflicts: the 'deep perturbation' of Middle East politics

1. From the poem 'Four o'Clock in the Morning' (בערבה בבוקר) published in S. Hass, *Natiney Ha-Shemesh* (נתיני השמש), Tel Aviv: Ha-Kibbutz Ha-Meuchad, 2005.
2. R. Hinnebusch, 'The Politics of Identity in Middle East International Relations', p. 150.
3. See M. Barnett, *Dialogues in Arab Politics*; J. Jankowski and I. Gershoni, *Rethinking Nationalism*; S. Telhami and M. Barnett (eds), *Identity and Foreign Policy in the Middle East*, Ithaca: Cornell University Press, 2002; M. Lynch, *State Interests and Public Spheres: the International Politics of Jordan's Identity*, New York: Columbia University Press, 1999; R. Khalidi, *Palestinian Identity*; R. M Nasser, *Palestinian Identity in Jordan and Israel: the Necessary 'Other' in the Making of a Nation*, London: Routledge, 2005.
4. A common strategy is to refer to these diametrically opposed perspectives as different 'perceptions', thereby however often implying that there would be an objective 'third' perspective on such conflicts. Also such a strategy is based on the untenable differentiation between 'ideational' and 'material/objective' factors. See also below in this chapter on how this seemingly innocent differentiation affects hegemonic political communications on Middle East conflicts.

5. E. Adler, 'Seizing the Middle Ground: Constructivism in World Politics', *European Journal of International Relations*, 3(3), 1997: 319–63.
6. R. Hinnebusch, 'The Politics of Identity in Middle East International Relations', p. 170, my emphasis.
7. R. Wasserstein, *Israel and Palestine*. Wasserstein also shows convincingly how conflict parties (in this case Israel and Palestine) observe, copy and mutually adjust their respective conflict discourses.
8. R. Hinnebusch, 'The Politics of Identity in Middle East International Relations', p. 151.
9. M. E. Sørli et al., 'Why is there so much Conflict in the Middle East?', *Journal of Conflict Resolution*, 49(1), 2005: 141–65. This is not to question the empirical results in this study in which the authors argue that different levels of economic development and economic growth, a lack of longer periods of peace, as well as patterns of ethnic dominance and regime types are main factors in accounting for the pervasiveness of conflicts in the region and that there are no grounds for assuming a Middle Eastern exceptionalism when accounting for these conflicts. While this certainly is correct, the authors fail to place their analysis in the framework of an explicit theory of conflicts and rather focus on the social environment of Middle Eastern conflicts. This is, in fact, a widespread problem in much writing on conflicts, see H. Messmer, *Der soziale Konflikt*.
10. M. Albert et al., 'On Order and Conflict', p. 24 – of course referring to C. Brown, 'Turtles all the Way Down: Anti-Foundationalism, Critical Theory and International Relations', *Millennium*, 23(2), 1994: 213–36.
11. And such dynamics can be observed in many conflict settings in world society, be it with regard to conflicts in South-East Asia or identity-related conflicts in Belgium. Thus, the logic of a creeping antagonization is, of course, not limited to the Middle East or other non-Western regions.
12. This chapter does not aim to apply this theoretical framework to a particular Middle East conflict since this would require a much more specific study on selected aspects of the creeping antagonization of Middle East politics. It should be read as a strong plea for an explicit and systematic application of conflict-theoretical approaches to conflict settings, which should consequently guide the empirical analysis of distinct conflicts, rather than addressing conflicts on the basis of their idiosyncratic features (themes, actors and so on) as is, indeed, often done in academic and policy-oriented studies. See for influential approaches in conflict theories E. E. Azar, *The Management of Protracted Social Conflict*, Aldershot: Dartmouth, 1990; J. Burton, *Violence Explained*, Manchester: Manchester University Press, 1997; R. Dahrendorf, *Class and Class Conflict in Industrialised Societies*, Stanford: Stanford University Press, 1959; J. Galtung, *Peace by Peaceful Means. Peace and Conflict, Development and Civilization*, London: Sage, 1996.
13. See Y. Zerubavel, 'The "Mythological Sabra" and Jewish Past: Trauma, Memory and Contested Identities', *Israel Studies*, 7(2), 2002: 115–44; S. Haugbolle, 'Public and Private Memory of the Lebanese Civil War', *Comparative Studies of South Asia, Africa and the Middle East*, 25(1), 2005: 191–203; L. Khalili, 'Places of Memory and Mourning: Palestinian Commemoration in the Refugee Camps in Lebanon', *Comparative Studies of South Asia, Africa and the Middle East*, 25(1), 2005: 30–45; A. H. Sa'di, 'Catastrophe, Memory and Identity: Al-Nakbah

as a Component of Palestinian Identity', *Israel Studies*, 7(2), 2002: 175–98. See also I. Gur-Ze'ev and I. Pappé, 'Beyond the Destruction of the Other's Collective Memory', *Theory, Culture & Society*, 20(1), 2003: 93–108.

14. See chapter 2, note 5.
15. S. Stetter, 'Regions of Conflict in World Society'.
16. See in detail Chapter 4.
17. This also distinguishes the understanding of world society and world statehood in modern systems theory from the teleological approach of Alexander Wendt, see A. Wendt, 'Why a World State is Inevitable'. See also M. Albert and R. Stichweh, *Weltstaat und Weltstaatlichkeit*.
18. N. Luhmann, *Soziale Systeme*, p. 530.
19. M. Albert et al., 'The Transformative Power of Integration: Conceptualising Border Conflicts', in T. Diez et al. (eds), *The European Union and Border Conflicts: the Power of Integration and Association*, Cambridge: Cambridge University Press, 2008, p. 16.
20. N. Luhmann, *Soziale Systeme*, p. 504. This, of course, closely relates to other (conflict) theories which, in one way or the other, stress the various function of conflicts, for example, by directing attention towards contradictions, unresolved problems or injustices.
21. Ibid., p. 508.
22. N. Luhmann, *Die Politik des Gesellschaft*, p. 94.
23. N. Luhmann, *Die Gesellschaft der Gesellschaft*, p. 466.
24. N. Luhmann, *Soziale Systeme*, p. 509.
25. This is most explicitly communicated in the 'ultimate communication' of suicide attacks or assassinations. Note that the 'the maintenance and stabilisation of a conflict requires more than an empirical move of two or three rejections – a social situation referred to as "conflict episodes". Thus, the stabilisation of a conflict order necessitates the emergence of the expectation on the side of Alter and Ego that communications are repeatedly rejected. It is only in this case that conflicts consolidate their status as a social order which is distinct from its environment. Empirically, one can then distinguish between four stages of conflict communication, depending on the degree to which communications between Alter and Ego are based on the securitisation of the relationship, on the one hand, and the degree to which the societal environment becomes captured by the conflict, on the other', see M. Albert et al., 'On Order and Conflict', pp. 20–1. What matters then is the observation that if a conflict moves from the level of conflict episodes, to issue conflicts, identity conflicts and subordination conflicts (see in detail T. Diez et al., *The European Union and Border Conflicts*; H. Messmer, *Der soziale Konflikt*), the lock-in effects of conflicts are accompanied by an increasing difficulty in crossing the borders I/you as well as here/there, see H. Messmer, 'Contradictions, Conflict and Borders', in S. Stetter, *Territorial Conflicts in World Society*, pp. 101–24.
26. N. Luhmann, *Die Gesellschaft der Gesellschaft*, p. 466.
27. N. Luhmann, *Die Politik der Gesellschaft* p. 133.
28. H. Messmer, 'Contradictions, Conflict and Borders', p. 113.
29. N. Luhmann, *Die Gesellschaft der Gesellschaft*, p. 604.
30. U. Stäheli, *Sinnzusammenbrüche*, p. 279.
31. Ibid., p. 280, quoting N. Luhmann, *Essays on Self-Reference*, New York: Columbia University Press, 1990, p. 14.

32. A. Kieserling, *Kommunikation unter Anwesenden: Studien über Interaktionssysteme*, Frankfurt: Suhrkamp, 1999, p. 282.
33. See, amongst many others, T. Diez, 'Europe's Other and the Return of Geopolitics'; B. Rumelili, 'Constructing Identity and Relating it to Difference: Understanding the EU's Mode of Differentiation', *Review of International Studies*, 30(1), 2004: 27–47; G. Schöpflin, 'The Construction of Identity', paper presented at the Österreichischer Wissenschaftstag 2001; M. Albert et al. (eds), *Identities, Borders, Orders: Rethinking International Relations Theory*, Minneapolis: University of Minnesota Press, 2001.
34. S. N. Eisenstadt and B. Giesen, 'The Construction of Collective Identity', *Archives Européennes de Sociologie*, 36(1), 1995: 75, quoted in M. Albert, *Zur Politik der Weltgesellschaft: Identität und Recht im Kontext internationaler Vergesellschaftung*, Weilerswist: Velbrück, 2002.
35. H. Messmer, 'Contradictions, Conflict and Borders', p. 115.
36. N. Luhmann, *Die Kunst der Gesellschaft*, p. 104.
37. Ibid.
38. S. N. Eisenstadt and B. Giesen, 'The Construction of Collective Identity', 73.
39. Ibid.
40. As implied by Luhmann's remark that 'for all difference-theoretical approaches identity is a rather worrying concept', N. Luhmann, *Die Religion der Gesellschaft*, p. 25 – at least as long as one is impressed by modernity's unity semantics with regard to notions of individuality, subjectivity and collectivism, see N. Luhmann, *Die Gesellschaft der Gesellschaft*, 1016–36 and N. Luhmann, 'Individuum, Individualität, Individualismus'. Only then, it seems, the tension arises of 'how to explain the persistence of identities that are not in line with functional differentiation', U. Stäheli and R. Stichweh, 'Inclusion/Exclusion', p. 4.
41. As Wallerstein has suggested, such a perceived tension between universal features and particularistic identities is, in fact, problematic since it neglects the way in which the dimensions are mutually constituted and, thereby, serve a powerful function for the modern world-system (see also further below in this chapter). Thus, 'the heart of the debate, it seems to me, revolves around the ways in which the presumed antinomies of unity and diversity, universalism and particularism, humanity and race, world and nation, person and man/woman have been manipulated. I have previously argued that the two principal ideological doctrines that have emerged in the history of the capitalist world-system – that is, universalism on the one hand and racism and sexism on the other – are not opposites but a symbiotic pair', I. Wallerstein, 'Culture as the Ideological Battleground of the Modern World-System', in M. Featherstone (ed.), *Global Culture: Nationalism, Globalization and Modernity*, London: Sage, 1990, p. 39. This echoes Luhmann's plea of contrasting 'the universalism of function orientation with the particularism of regional communities', N. Luhmann, *Die Gesellschaft der Gesellschaft*, p. 1051.
42. N. Luhmann, *Die Politik der Gesellschaft*, pp. 218–19.
43. Ibid., p. 218.
44. Ibid., p. 133.
45. On the debate conflict vs. integration see H. Messmer, *Der soziale Konflikt*, pp. 22–8.

46. See for an introductory overview H. Miall, 'Conflict Transformation: a Multi-Dimensional Task', Handbook of the Berghof Research Center for Constructive Conflict Management, http://www.berhof-handbook.net.
47. Of course the same argument can be made for the equally problematic practices of Occidentalism, that is, the portrayal of the 'West' as culturally or morally inferior.
48. P. Bilgin, 'Is the "Orientalist" Past the Future of Middle East Studies?', p. 431.
49. G. M. Steinberg, 'Postcolonialist Theory and the Ideology of Peace Studies'.
50. Of course referring here to B. Anderson, *Imagined Communities: Reflections on the Origin and Spread of Nationalism*, London: Verso, 1991.
51. The problem with civil society is, however, that this term implicitly carries a heavy normative baggage. Who decides who belongs to civil society? This can be well observed in the context of 'civil society' relations between the West and Arab countries and the question of whether those groups which are less open to Habermasian practices of deliberative democracy (on both sides!) belong to civil society, too. Thus, 'the renaissance of this concept … has such enthusiastic-romanticist underpinnings that the answer to the question of what is excluded with this concepts is: reality', N. Luhmann, *Die Politik der Gesellschaft*, p. 12.
52. D. Tuastad, 'Neo-Orientalism and the New Barbarism Thesis'.
53. M. Appleton, 'The Political Attitudes of Muslims Studying at British Universities in the post-9/11 World: Part I', *Journal of Muslim Minority Affairs*, 25(2), 2005: 171–91 as well as Part II in issue 3, 2005: 299–316.
54. G. Piterberg, 'Domestic Orientalism: the Representation of "Oriental" Jews in Zionist/Israeli Historiography', *British Journal of Middle Eastern Studies*, 23(2), 1996: 125–45.
55. D. Tuastad, 'Neo-Orientalism and the New Barbarism Thesis'.
56. Ibid., pp. 591–2.
57. G. Deleuze, 'The Troublemakers', *MIT Electronic Journal of Middle East Studies*, 1, 2001. This underlines the argument that Middle East conflicts do not simply pitch two ethno-religious groups against each other but have a worldwide societal audience.
58. As referred to above this does not exclude the possibility of Occidentalism, thereby celebrating allegedly Middle Eastern cultural and institutional practices as superior to technocratic Western exercises.
59. As already mentioned above, such antagonizations are not specific to any region but are the result of structural world societal communications. The many studies comparing ethnically divided cities are intriguing in that regard, see M. Auga et al., *Divided Cities in Transition*; antagonisms, however, do not only have to relate to ethno-religious division but can also relate to socio-economic inequalities, see R. Scholar, *Divided Cities: the Oxford Amnesty Lectures 2003*, Oxford: Oxford University Press, 2006.
60. F. Azar and E. Mullet, 'Muslims and Christians in Lebanon: Common Views on Political Issues', *Journal of Peace Research*, 39(6), 2002: 735–46.
61. T. Scheffler, 'Religious Communalism and Democratization'.
62. R. Maktabi, 'The Lebanese Census of 1932 Revisited: Who are the Lebanese?', *British Journal of Middle Eastern Studies*, 26(2), 1999: 220.
63. Ibid., p. 239.

64. A. R. Norton, 'Lebanon's Malaise', *Survival*, 42(4), 2000: 35–50.
65. A. N. Hamzeh, 'Clientelism, Lebanon', p. 176.
66. Ibid., pp. 176–7.
67. R. M. Nasser, *Palestinian Identity in Jordan and Israel*.
68. T. Segev, 'The world of Citizen Amal Jamal', Ha-Aretz, http://www.haaretz. com/hasen/spages/770907.html.
69. See for this quote by a politician of the nationalist Yisrael Beitenu party, http://news.bbc.co.uk/2/hi/middle_east/6254691.stm.
70. On the interrelationship between identity, politics and demography see, for the case of Jerusalem, M Auga et al., *Divided Cities in Transition*. It is intriguing in this regard that the official website of the Israeli Foreign Ministry manages in its lengthy descriptions of national minorities in Israel not once to refer to the Arab-speaking minority as 'Palestinians' although arguably the huge majority of them (except for Druze and Circassians) regard themselves, besides being Arab, Israeli or whatever, as Palestinians. See http://www.mfa. gov.il/ MFA/Facts%20About%20Israel/People/SOCIETY-%20Minority%20-Communities. Interesting with regard to this securitization of identity is the emphasis that the Druze in Israel place on the 'concept of *taqiyya*, which calls for complete loyalty by its adherents to the government of the country in which they reside'. This is, of course, not to argue that the problem could merely be solved by referring to Israeli Palestinians as Israeli Palestinians – as long as frozen crossings endure, such semantic nuances might have symbolic importance. Yet they would hardly change the structural setting of an overall antagonization of Middle East politics. They would most likely be smoothly integrated into such antagonistic settings.
71. See in detail D. Sadowski (ed.), *Israel 2025: Szenarien der zukünftigen Entwicklung*, Tel Aviv: Friedrich-Ebert-Foundation, 2001; S. Hasson, 'Haredi and Secular Jews in Jerusalem in the Future: Scenarios and Strategies', Policy Paper, Jerusalem: The Floersheimer Institute for Policy Studies, 1999.
72. C. S. Liebman, 'Reconceptualizing the Culture Conflict among Israeli Jews', *Israel Studies*, 2(2), 2005: 172–89. See also A. Shapira (ed.), *Israeli Identity in Transition*, West Port: Praeger, 2004.
73. In the tradition of J. W. Burton, *Conflict: Human Needs Theory*, Basingstoke: Palgrave, 1990.
74. O. Richmond, *The Transformation of Peace*, p. 208.
75. B. Bliesemann de Guevara, 'Gebrauchshinweise beachten! Die Berichte der International Crisis Group', GIGA Focus, 4, 2007, Hamburg: German Institute of Global and Area Studies.
76. See in detail http://www.crisisgroup.org/home/index.cfm?id=1096&l=1.
77. B. Bliesemann de Guevara, 'Gebrauchshinweise beachten!' p. 6.
78. Ibid., p. 3.
79. And, to respond to an obvious challenge, this of course also relates to this study.
80. See B. Rumelili, 'Constructing Identity and Relating it to Difference'.
81. This is also the experience of many micro-level meetings between conflict parties, for example, at several meetings between Israelis and Palestinians in which the author had the opportunity to participate. It is indeed a stunning experience to observe the differences it makes to encounter the Other as a person compared to the stereotypical confrontation with the Other as a threat as is usually the case within the domestic conflict setting – yet the

problem is the fragility of such learning efforts once participants return to conflict settings 'on the ground'. That might also be the reason why many track III meetings are organized at great physical distances from conflict areas. See, among many others, the activities of dialogue lab, a group of young European, Israeli and Palestinian students on http://www.dialogue-lab.org/homepage.swf.
82. See chapter 2, note 51.
83. I. Wallerstein, *Geopolitics and Geoculture*, p. 180.
84. Ibid., p. 166.
85. See J. W. Meyer and R. L. Jepperson, 'The "Actors" of Modern Society: the Cultural Construction of Social Agency', *Sociological Theory*, 18(1), 2000: 100–20.
86. N. Luhmann, *Die Kunst der Gesellschaft*, p. 104.
87. I. Wallerstein, *Geopolitics and Geoculture*, p. 166.
88. This can actually be studied in social conflicts in which responsibility for the conflict is seldom attributed to the conflict itself but rather to an intransigent and threatening Other. It is, therefore, a central element in conflict resolution to make conflict participants aware of the (often fundamentally) divergent perspectives of the Other. This focus on 'empathy' is seen as crucial for successful conflict resolution, in the sense that the Self distances itself from its 'fatal attraction' with the contradictory logic of conflict communications. Successful conflict resolution is the ability to see the conflict from the 'outside' and to 'move away from individual-centred resolution to the creation of a "third culture" which is not just the result of fusion, but the generation of a new possibility-space for the flourishing of difference', see H. Miall et al., *Contemporary Conflict Resolution: the Prevention, Management and Transformation of Deadly Conflicts*, Cambridge: Polity, 1999, pp. 72–3.
89. N. Luhmann, *Die Gesellschaft der Gesellschaft*, p. 588.
90. N. Luhmann, *Die Religion der Gesellschaft*, p. 311, my emphasis.
91. N. Luhmann, 'Kultur als historischer Begriff', p. 42.
92. H. Messmer, *Der soziale Konflikt*, p. 210.
93. This does not necessarily have to be the other conflict party. It can also be directed towards a (powerful) external third party which is regarded as siding with the Other and, thereby, prolonging the conflict. This is a common topic in Israel-Palestine, with many Israelis accusing the EU of not doing enough to solve the conflict (and indeed to spur conflict dynamics) and many Palestinians being equally critical of the US.
94. H. Messmer, *Der soziale Konflikt*, p. 211.
95. M. Albert et al., 'On Order and Conflict', p. 1.
96. M. Albert et al., 'The Transformative Power of Integration', p. 22.
97. Ibid., the quote in the quote can be found in O. Wæver, 'Securitisation: Taking Stock of a Research Program in Security Studies', draft paper discussed at the PIPES seminar at the University of Chicago, 2003, p. 10.
98. An interesting side note here is Marwan George Rowayheb's emphasis on the political objectives achieved by militias in the Lebanese civil war, thereby arguing that their role cannot adequately be addressed when merely focusing on violence. Thus, 'the militiamen studied may be considered a sample of a population in Lebanon that might be willing to identify itself in terms other than their confessional backgrounds, and challenging the socio-political environments imposed by the Lebanese political system and the civil war

that made confessional identities valuable tools to acquire political power in Lebanon'; see M. G. Rowayheb, 'Lebanese Militias: a New Perspective', *Middle Eastern Studies,* 42(2), 2006: 314. The problem is, of course, that while militias might at times have transcended the (antagonistic) confessional confines of Lebanese politics they have not really been successful in basing their political activities within less antagonistic political structures.

99. A. Wendt, 'Anarchy is What States Make of It: the Social Construction of Power Politics', *International Organization,* 46(2), 1992: 391–425.
100. K. E. Schulze, *The Jews of Lebanon: Between Coexistence and Conflict,* Sussex: Sussex Academic Press, 2001.
101. See T. Docherty (ed.), *Postmodernism: a Reader,* New York: Harvester, 1993, p. 334.
102. B. Milton-Edwards, 'Political Islam in Palestine in an Environment of Peace?', *Third World Quarterly,* 17(2), 1996: 199–225.

6. Beyond Orientalization and civilization: concluding remarks

1. From the opera 'Falstaff' (1893).
2. See Chapter 1, note 9.
3. J. Galtung, *Peace by Peaceful Means: Peace and Conflict, Development and Civilization,* London: Sage, 1996; J. Burton, *Conflict: Human Needs Theory,* Basingstoke: Palgrave, 1990.
4. J. Galtung, *Peace by Peaceful Means.*
5. See M. Fischer, 'Civil Society in Conflict Transformation: Ambivalence, Potentials and Challenges', Handbook of the Berghof Research Center for Constructive Conflict Management, http://www.berghof-handbook.net.
6. D. Senghaas, 'The Civilisation of Conflict: Constructive Pacifism as a Guiding Notion for Conflict Transformation', Handbook of the Berghof Research Center for Constructive Conflict Management, http://www.berghof-handbook.net. Moreover, in a more radical tradition this also comprises a wholesale transformation of the very character of politics, see R. B. J. Walker, 'The Subject of Security', in K. Krause and M. Williams (eds), *Critical Security Studies: Concepts and Cases,* London: UCL Press, 1997.
7. O. P. Richmond, *The Transformation of Peace.*
8. L. Brock, 'Frieden: Überlegungen zur Theoriebildung', in D. Senghaas (ed.), *Den Frieden denken: Si vis pacem, para pacem,* Frankfurt: Suhrkamp, 1995, p. 339.
9. O. P. Richmond, *The Transformation of Peace,* p. 225.
10. Although the use of the plural might also be useful for the many pasts and presents of Middle East politics, that is, the often diametrically opposed understandings of how past and current developments ought to be understood.
11. S. Stetter, 'Regions of Conflict in World Society'.
12. L. Fawcett, *International Relations,* p. 4.
13. F. Braudel, *The Mediterranean and the Mediterranean World.*
14. J. Shamir and K. Shikaki, 'Determinants of Reconciliation among Israelis and Palestinians', *Journal of Peace Research,* 39(2), 2002: 185–202.

15. I. Gur-Ze'ev and I. Pappé, 'Beyond the Destruction of the Other's Collective Memory', p. 94.
16. M. Kayyal, 'A Hesitant Dialogue with "The Other": the Interactions of Arab Intellectuals with the Israeli Culture', *Israel Studies*, 11(2), 2006: 54–74; E. Awwad, 'Broken Lives: Loss and Trauma in Palestinian-Israeli Relations', *International Journal of Politics, Culture and Society*, 17(3), 2004: 405–14; S. Adwan and D. Bar-On, 'Shared History Project: A PRIME Example of Peace-Building under Fire', *International Journal of Politics, Culture and Society*, 17(3), 2004: 513–21.
17. See J. Chaitin, F. Obeidi, S. Adwan and D. Bar-On, 'Palestinian and Israeli Cooperation in Environmental Work During the "Peace Era"', *International Journal of Politics, Culture and Society*, 17(3), 2004: 523–42.
18. J. Slater, 'Lost Opportunities for Peace in the Arab-Israeli Conflict', *International Security*, 27(1), 2002: 79–106; S. Ben-Ami, 'So Close and Yet So Far: Lessons from the Israeli-Palestinian Peace Process', *Israel Studies*, 10(2), 2005: 72–90.
19. And that is why these dynamics are not limited to inter-group relations but relate to 'internal others', too. See J. Massad, 'Zionism's Internal Other: Israel and the Oriental Jews', *Journal of Palestine Studies*, 25(4), 1996: 53–68.
20. Moreover, such perspectives also tend to overemphasize the conflictive dimension of religion in the region. While it is true that many religious groups engage in acts of violence, there is no direct linkage between conflict and religiosity. These dynamics are discussed in the literature from various angles and involving a wide range of (violent or peaceful) religious groups in the Middle East and their actual or potential role in a more peaceful region. See J. Gunning, 'Peace with Hamas? The Transforming Potential of Political Participation', *International Affairs*, 80(2), 2004: 233–55; E. Korn, 'The Man of Faith and Religious Dialogue: Revisiting "Confrontation"', *Modern Judaism*, 25(1), 2005: 290–315; B. Milton-Edwards, 'Political Islam in Palestine in an Environment of Peace?'; M. Abu-Nimer, 'Religion, Dialogue, and Non-Violent Actions in Palestinian-Israeli Conflict', *International Journal of Politics, Culture and Society*, 17(3), 2004: 491–511; J. Reissner, 'Islam in der Weltgesellschaft: Wege in eine eigene Moderne', Berlin: Stiftung Wissenschaft und Politik, 2007; C. Houston, 'Islamism, Castoriadis and Autonomy'.
21. See T. Diez, 'Europe's Other and the Return of Geopolitics'. References to the 'European' experience in overcoming conflict and violence in a war-torn continent are widespread in the Middle East.
22. B. Buzan and O. Wæver, *Regions and Powers*.

Bibliography

Aaronsohn, R., 'Settlement in Eretz Israel: a Colonialist Enterprise? "Critical" Scholarship and Historical Geography', *Israel Studies*, 1(2), 1996.

Abdo, N., 'Gender and Politics under the Palestinian Authority', *Journal of Palestine Studies*, 28(2), 1999.

Abu-Nimer, M., 'Religion, Dialogue, and Non-Violent Actions in Palestinian-Israeli Conflict', *International Journal of Politics, Culture and Society*, 17(3), 2004.

Açikgenç, A., 'An Evaluation of Violence from Islam's Perspective', *Alternatives – Turkish Journal of International Relations*, 1(4), 2002.

Ackerman, W. I., 'Making Jews: an Enduring Challenge in Israeli Education', *Israel Studies*, 2(2), 2005.

Adler, E., 'Seizing the Middle Ground: Constructivism in World Politics', *European Journal of International Relations*, 3(3), 1997.

Adoni, L., 'King Abdallah: in His Father's Footsteps?', *Journal of Palestine Studies*, 29(3), 2000.

Adwan, S. and D. Bar-On, 'Shared History Project: A PRIME Example of Peace-Building under Fire', *International Journal of Politics, Culture and Society*, 17(3), 2004.

Ahmed, A. S., *Islam Under Siege: Living Dangerously in a Post-Honor World*, Cambridge: Polity, 2003.

Al Husban, A. H., 'The Place of Local Councils in the Power Network: a Case Study of the North of Jordan (Halid bin el-Walid Municipality)', *Orient*, 46(4), 2005.

Alagha, J., 'Hizbullah, Terrorism, and September 11', *Orient*, 44(3), 2003.

—— 'Hizbullah and Martydom', *Orient*, 45(1), 2004.

Al-Azm, S. J., 'Islam, Terrorism and the West', *Comparative Studies of South Asia, Africa and the Middle East*, 25(1), 2005.

Albert, M., *Zur Politik der Weltgesellschaft: Identität und Recht im Kontext internationaler Vergesellschaftung*, Weilerswist: Velbrück, 2002.

—— 'On Governance, Democracy and European Systems: on Systems Theory and European Integration', *Review of International Studies*, 28(2), 2002.

—— 'Politik der Weltgesellschaft und Politik der Globalisierung: Überlegungen zur Emergenz von Weltstaatlichkeit', in B. Heintz, R. Münch and H. Tyrell, 2005.

—— 'Einleitung: Weltstaat und Weltstaatlichkeit: Neubestimmungen des Politischen in der Weltgesellschaft', in M. Albert and R. Stichweh, 2007.

Albert, M. and L. Brock, 'Debordering the World of States: New Spaces in International Relations', in M. Albert, L. Brock and K.-D. Wolf, 2000.

Albert, M. and L. Hilkermeier (eds), *Observing International Relations: Niklas Luhmann and World Politics*, London and New York: Routledge, 2004.

Albert, M. and R. Stichweh (eds), *Weltstaat und Weltstaatlichkeit: Beobachtungen globaler politischer Strukturbildung*, Wiesbaden: VS Verlag, 2007.

Albert, M., L. Brock and K.-D. Wolf, *Civilizing World Politics: Society and Community Beyond the State*, Oxford: Rowman & Littlefield, 2000.

Albert, M., T. Diez and S. Stetter, 'The Transformative Power of Integration: Conceptualising Border Conflicts', in T. Diez, M. Albert and S. Stetter, 2008.

Albert, M., D. Jacobsen and Y. Lapid (eds), *Identities, Borders, Orders: Rethinking International Relations Theory*, Minneapolis: University of Minnesota Press, 2001.

Albert, M., O. Kessler and S. Stetter, 'On Order and Conflict: International Relations and the "Communicative Turn"', *Review of International Studies*, Special Issue, 34, forthcoming, 2008.

Albrecht, H.-J., J.-M. Simon, H. Rezaei, H.-C. Rohne and E. Kiza (eds), *Conflicts and Conflict Resolution in Middle Eastern Societies: Between Tradition and Modernity*, Berlin: Duncker & Humblot, 2006.

Ali, A., 'Islamism: Emancipation, Protest and Identity', *Journal of Muslim Minority Affairs*, 20(1), 2000.

Al-Mahadin, S., 'Jordanian Women in Education: Politics, Pedagogy and Gender Discourses', *feminist review*, 78(1), 2004.

Al-Sayyid, M. K., 'The Concept of Civil Society and the Arab World', in B. Korany, R. Brynen and P. Noble, 1995.

Al-Zaydi, M., 'Education and Hope', Asharq Alawsat English, http://www.aawsat.com/english/news.asp?section=2&id=8160.

Andersen, N. A., *Discursive Analytical Strategies: Understanding Foucault, Koselleck, Laclau, Luhmann*, Bristol: Policy Press, 2003.

Anderson, B. S., 'Writing the Nation: Textbooks of the Hashemite Kingdom of Jordan', *Comparative Studies of South Asia, Africa and the Middle East*, 21(1/2), 2001.

Anderson, B., *Imagined Communities: Reflections on the Origin and Spread of Nationalism*, London: Verso, 1991.

Anderson, L., 'Democracy in the Arab World: a Critique of the Political Culture Approach', in R. Brynen, B. Korany and P. Noble, 1995.

—— 'Politics in the Middle East: Opportunities and Limits in the Quest for Theory', in M. Tessler, J. Nachtwey and A. Banda, 1999.

Andoni, L., 'Searching for Answers: Gaza's Suicide Bombers', *Journal of Palestine Studies*, 26(4), 1997.

Antoon, S., 'Mahmud Darwish's Allegorical Critique of Oslo', *Journal of Palestine Studies*, 31(2), 2002.

Appleton, M., 'The Political Attitudes of Muslims Studying at British Universities in the Post-9/11 World: Part I', *Journal of Muslim Minority Affairs*, 25(2), 2005.

—— 'The Political Attitudes of Muslims Studying at British Universities in the Post-9/11 World: Part II', *Journal of Muslim Minority Affairs*, 25(3), 2005.

Arad, R., S. Hirsch and A. Tovias, *The Economics of Peacemaking: Focus on the Egyptian-Israeli Situation*, London: Macmillan, 1983.

Archbigu, D. and D. Held (eds), *Cosmopolitan Democracy: an Agenda for a New World Order*, Cambridge: Polity Press, 1995.

Arjomand, S. A., 'Islam, Political Change and Globalization', *Thesis Eleven*, 76(1), 2004.

Armstrong, D. (ed.), Governance and Resistance in World Politics, *Review of International Studies*, Special Issue, 29, 2003.

Armstrong, K., 'The Holiness of Jerusalem: Asset or Burden?', *Journal of Palestine Studies*, 27(3), 1998.

Arnason, J. and G. Stauth, 'Civilization and State Formation in the Islamic Context: Re-Reading Ibn-Khaldun', *Thesis Eleven*, 76(1), 2004.

Aronson, S., 'The Post-Zionist Discourse and Critique of Israel: a Traditional Zionist Perspective', *Israel Studies*, 8(1), 2003.

Auga, M., S. Hasson, R. Nasrallah and S. Stetter (eds), *Divided Cities in Transition: Challenges Facing Jerusalem and Berlin*, Jerusalem: Al-Manar Press, 2005.

Awwad, E., 'Broken Lives: Loss and Trauma in Palestinian-Israeli Relations', *International Journal of Politics, Culture and Society*, 17(3), 2004.

Ayish, M. E., 'Arab World Television in Transition: Current Trends and Future Prospects', *Orient*, 41(3), 2000.

Ayubi, N. N., *Over-Stating the Arab State: Politics and Society in the Middle East*, London: Tauris, 1995.

Azar, E. E., *The Management of Protracted Social Conflict*, Aldershot: Dartmouth, 1990.

Azar, F. and E. Mullet, 'Muslims and Christians in Lebanon: Common Views on Political Issues', *Journal of Peace Research*, 39(6), 2002.

Azaryahu, M., 'Mount Herzl: the Creation of Israel's National Cemetery', *Israel Studies*, 1(2), 2005.

Badawi, A., 'Policy Failure, Power Relations and the Dynamics of Elite Change in Palestine', *Orient*, 44(4), 2003.

Baecker, D., 'Gewalt im System', *Soziale Welt*, 47(1), 1996.

—— 'Lenin's Twist, or the R-Factor of Communication', *Soziale Systeme*, 8(1), 2002.

—— 'Die Gewalt des Terrorismus', unpublished paper, 2006.

Bahlul, R., 'Toward an Islamic Conception of Democracy: Islam and the Notion of Public Reason', *Critique: Critical Middle Eastern Studies*, 12(1), 2003.

Balchin, C., 'With Her Feet on the Ground: Women, Religion and Development in Muslim Communities', *development*, 46(4), 2003.

Bank, A., 'Re-ORIENTing IR: Innerstaatliche Gewaltkonflikte als Treffpunkt Internationaler Beziehungen und Vergleichender Orientforschung', paper presented at the Offene Sektionstagung der Sektion Internationale Politik der Deutschen Vereinigung für Politische Wissenschaft, Mannheim, September 2006.

Bank, A. and M. Valbjørn, 'Signs of a New Arab Cold War: the 2006 Lebanon War and the Sunni-Shi'i Divide', *Middle East Report*, Spring, 2007.

Bar-Joseph, U., 'The Paradox of Israeli Power', *Survival*, 46(4), 2004.

Barnett, M., *Dialogues in Arab Politics: Negotiations in Regional Order*, New York, Columbia University Press, 1998.

—— (ed.), *Israel in Comparative Perspective: Challenging the Conventional Wisdom*, Albany: State University of New York Press, 1998.

—— 'On the Uniqueness of Israel: Multiple Readings', in M. Barnett, *Israel in Comparative Perspective*, 1998.

Barnett, M. and R. Duvall, 'Power in International Relations', *International Organization*, 59(1), 2005.

Bar-On, T. and H. Goldstein, 'Fighting Violence: a Critique of the War on Terrorism', *International Politics*, 42(2), 2005.

Baumgarten, H., 'Die Hamas: Wahlsieg in Palästina: Islamistische Transformation zur Demokratie in einem neopatrimonialen Rentier-System', *Orient*, 47(1), 2006.

Beck, M., 'Von theoretischen Wüsten, Oasen und Karawanen: Der Vordere Orient in den Internationalen Beziehungen', *Zeitschrift für Internationale Beziehungen*, 9(2), 2002.

Beck, M., C. Harders, A. Jünemann and S. Stetter (eds.), *Der Nahe Osten im Umbruch: Theoretische Perspektiven auf eine Region zwischen Transformation und Autoritarismus*, Wiesbaden: VS-Verlag, forthcoming, 2008.

Beck, U., *Der kosmopolitische Blick oder: Krieg ist Frieden*, Frankfurt: Suhrkamp, 2004.

Beckermann, Z., 'Israeli Traditionalists and Liberals: a Social-Constructivist Perspective', *Israel Studies*, 4(2), 1999.

Ben-Ami, S., 'So Close and Yet So Far: Lessons from the Israeli-Palestinian Peace Process', *Israel Studies*, 10(2), 2005.

Ben-Porat, G., 'A State of Holiness: Rethinking Israeli Secularism', *Alternatives*, 25(2), 2000.

——— 'A New Middle East? Globalization, Peace and the "Double Movement"', *International Relations*, 19(1), 2005.

Ben Rafael, E., 'Critical Versus Non-Critical Sociology: an Evaluation', *Israel Studies*, 2(1), 2005.

Benvenisti, M., 'The Stale Myth of Battlefield Bravado', *Ha-Aretz*, 13 April 2007.

Ben-Yehuda, N., 'The Masada Mythical Narrative and the Israeli Army', in E. Lomsky-Feder and E. Ben-Ari, 2000.

Bilgin, P., 'Is the "Orientalist" Past the Future of Middle East Studies?', *Third World Quarterly*, 25(2), 2004.

——— 'Whose Middle East? Geopolitical Interventions and Practices of Security', *International Relations*, 18(1), 2004.

——— *Regional Security in the Middle East: a Critical Perspective*, London and New York: Routledge, 2005.

Binder, L. (ed.), *Ethnic Conflict and International Politics in the Middle East*, Gainesville: University of Florida Press, 1999.

Bliesemann de Guevara, B., 'Gebrauchshinweise beachten! Die Berichte der International Crisis Group', GIGA Focus, 4, 2007, Hamburg: German Institute of Global and Area Studies, 2007.

Bohn, C. and A. Hahn, 'Patterns of Inclusion and Exclusion: Property, Nation and Religion', *Soziale Systeme*, 8(1), 2002.

Bonacker, T., 'Debordering by Human Rights: the Challenge of Postterritorial Conflicts in World Society', in S. Stetter, *Territorial Conflicts*, 2007.

Bonacker, T and C. Weller (eds), *Konflikte in der Weltgesellschaft: Akteure, Strukturen, Dynamiken*, Frankfurt and New York: Campus, 2006.

Bora, A., '"Wer gehört dazu?" Überlegungen zur Theorie der Inklusion', in K. U. Hellman and R. Schmalz-Bruns, 2002.

Boulding, E., *Building Peace in the Middle East: Challenges for States and Civil Society*, Boulder: Lynne Rienner, 1994.

Bowker, R., *Palestinian Refugees: Mythology, Identity, and the Search for Peace*, Boulder: Lynne Rienner, 2003.

Brand, L. A., *Jordan's Inter-Arab Relations: the Political Economy of Alliance Making*, New York: Columbia University Press, 1994.

——— 'The Effects of the Peace Process on Political Liberalization in Jordan', *Journal of Palestine Studies*, 28(2), 1999.

——— 'Academic Freedom: the "Danger" of Critical Thinking', *International Studies Perspective*, 8(4), 2007.

Braudel, F., *The Mediterranean and the Mediterranean World in the Age of Phillip II*, 2 vols, Berkeley: University of California Press, 1996.

Brock, L., 'Frieden: Überlegungen zur Theoriebildung', in D. Senghaas (ed.), *Den Frieden denken: Si vis pacem, para pacem*, Frankfurt: Suhrkamp, 1995.

——— 'World Society from the Bottom Up', in M. Albert and L. Hilkermeier, 2004.

Brodocz, A., M. Llanque and G. Schaal (eds), *Bedrohungen der Demokratie*, Wiesbaden: VS Verlag, forthcoming, 2008.

Brown, C., 'Turtles all the Way Down: Anti-Foundationalism, Critical Theory and International Relations', *Millennium*, 23(2), 1994.

Brown, N. J., 'Democracy, History, and the Contest over the Palestinian Curriculum', Washington, DC: Adam Institute, 2001.

Brubaker, W. R., 'Immigration, Citizenship, and the Nationstate in France and Germany: a Comparative Historical Perspective', *Ethnic and Racial Studies*, 18(5), 1990.

Brücher, G., 'The Irony of Terror: the Morality-Sensitive Nerve in the Criticism of Violence', in S. Stetter, *Territorial Conflicts*, 2007.

Bull, H., *The Anarchical Society: a Study of Order in World Politics*, London and New York: Columbia University Press, 1977.

Burton, J. W., *World Society*, Cambridge: Cambridge University Press, 1972.

——— *Violence Explained*, Manchester: Manchester University Press, 1997.

——— *Conflict: Human Needs Theory*, London: Palgrave, 1990.

Butterworth, C. E. and I. W. Zartman (eds), *Between the State and Islam*, Cambridge: Cambridge University Press, 2001.

Buzan, B., *From International to World Society: English School Theory and the Social Structure of Globalisation*, Cambridge: Cambridge University Press, 2004.

Buzan, B. and O. Wæver, *Regions and Powers: the Structure of International Security*, Cambridge: Cambridge University Press, 2005.

Chaitin, J., F. Obeidi, S. Adwan and D. Bar-On, 'Palestinian and Israeli Cooperation in Environmental World During the "Peace Era"', *International Journal of Politics, Culture and Society*, 17(3), 2004.

Charles, T., 'Syria: a State and its Narratives', *Middle Eastern Studies*, 37(2), 2001.

Chase-Dunn, C., 'Globalizations: a World-Systems Perspective', *Journal of World-Systems Research*, 5(2), 1999.

Clark, J., 'Social Movement Theory and Patron Clientelism: Islamic Social Institutions and the Middle Class in Egypt, Jordan and Yemen', *Comparative Political Studies*, 37(8), 2004.

Cohen, E. A., M. J. Eisenstadt and A. J. Bacevich, 'Israel's Revolution in Security Affairs', *Survival*, 40(1), 1998.

Cohen-Almagor, R., 'Cultural Pluralism and the Israeli Nation-Building Ideology', *International Journal of Middle East Studies*, 27(4), 1995.

Collins, J., 'Global Palestine: a Collision for Our Time', *Critique: Critical Middle Eastern Studies*, 16(1), 2007.

Dahrendorf, R., *Class and Class Conflict in Industrialised Societies*, Stanford: Stanford University Press, 1959.

Dalacoura, K., 'Islamist Terrorism and the Middle East Democratic Deficit: Political Exclusion, Repression and the Causes of Terrorism', *Democratization*, 13(3), 2006.

Damir-Geilsdorf, S., 'Das Ende – eine politische Wende? Gegenwärtige muslimische Erinnerungen an die Zukunft', *Orient*, 44(2), 2003.

Darwish, M., *Wir haben ein Land aus Worten*, Zurich: Ammann, 2002.

Del Sarto, R. A., *Contested State Identities and Regional Security in the Euro-Mediterranean Area*, Basingstoke: Palgrave Macmillan, 2006.

Deleuze, G., 'The Troublemakers', *MIT Electronic Journal of Middle East Studies*, 1, 2001.

Diez, T., 'Europe's Other and the Return of Geopolitics', *Cambridge Review of International Affairs*, 17(2), 2004.

Diez, T., M. Albert and S. Stetter (eds), *The European Union and Border Conflicts: the Power of Integration and Association*, Cambridge: Cambridge University Press, 2008.

Diez, T., S. Stetter and M. Albert, 'The European Union and Border Conflicts: the Transformative Power of Integration', *International Organization*, 60(3), 2006.

Diner, D., *Versiegelte Zeit: Über den Stillstand in der islamischen Welt*, Berlin: Propyläen, 2005.

Divine, D. R., 'Zionism and the Transformation of Jewish Society', *Modern Judaism*, 20(3), 2000.

Docherty, T. (ed.), *Postmodernism: a Reader*, New York: Harvester, 1993.

Dowding, K., 'Three-Dimensional Power: a Discussion of Steven Lukes' *Power: a Radical View*', *Political Studies Review*, 4(2), 2006.

Dumper, M., 'The Christian Churches in Jerusalem in the Post-Oslo Period', *Journal of Palestine Studies*, 31(2), 2002.

Duncker, A., 'Ungleiches Recht für alle? Zur Rechtsgleichheit in islamischen Menschenrechtserklärungen', *Orient*, 45(4), 2004.

Ehteshami, A., 'Is the Middle East Democratizing', *British Journal of Middle Eastern Studies*, 26(2), 1999.

—— 'Islam, Muslim Polities, and Democracy', *Democratization*, 11(4), 2004.

Ehteshami, A. and E. C. Murphy, 'Transformation of the Corporatist State in the Middle East', *Third World Quarterly*, 17(4), 1996.

Eisenstadt, S. N., 'The Continual Reconstruction of Multiple Modern Civilizations and Collective Identities', in G. Preyer and M. Bös, 2002.

—— *Comparative Civilizations and Multiple Modernities*, Leiden and Boston: Brill, 2003.

Eisenstadt, S. N. and B. Giesen, 'The Construction of Collective Identity', *Archives Européennes de Sociologie*, 36(1), 1995.

Elie, S. D., 'The Harem Syndrome: Moving beyond Anthropology's Discursive Colonialization of Gender in the Middle East', *Alternatives*, 29(2), 2004.

El-Khatib, A., 'Jerusalem in the Qur'an', *British Journal of Middle Eastern Studies*, 28(1), 2001.

El-Shagi, E., 'Islam und wirtschaftliche Entwicklung', *Orient*, 44(3), 2003.

Esposito, J. L., *Unholy War: Terror in the Name of Islam*, Oxford: Oxford University Press, 2002.

Euro-Mediterranean Human Rights Network, '2006 Change is Possible and Necessary: Achieving Gender Equality in the Euro-Mediterranean Region', Copenhagen: EMHRN, 2006.

Faist, T., J. Gerdes and B Rieple, 'Dual Citizenship as a Path-Dependent Process', *International Migration Review*, 37(4), 2004.

Fandy, M., 'Enriched Islam: the Muslim Crisis of Education', *Survival*, 49(2), 2007.

Faqir, F., 'Intrafamily Famicide in Defence of Honour: the Case of Jordan', *Third World Quarterly*, 22(1), 2001.

Farah, R., ' "To Veil or Not to Veil is Not the Question: Palestinian Refugee Women Voices on Other Matters', *development*, 45(1), 2002.

Fathi, S., 'Jordanian Survival Strategy: the Election Law as a "Safety Valve" ', *Middle Eastern Studies*, 41(6), 2005.

Fawcett, L. (ed.), *International Relations of the Middle East*, Oxford: Oxford University Press, 2005.

Fawcett, L. and Y. Sayigh (eds), *The Third World Beyond the Cold War: Continuity and Change*, Oxford: Oxford University Press, 1999.

Featherstone, M. (ed.), *Global Culture: Nationalism, Globalization and Modernity*, London: Sage, 1990.

Ferrero, M., 'Martyrdom Contracts', *Journal of Conflict Resolution*, 50(6), 2006.

Fischer, M., 'Civil Society in Conflict Transformation: Ambivalence, Potentials and Challenges', Handbook of the Berghof Research Center for Constructive Conflict Management, http://www.berghof-handbook.net.

Forte, T., 'Sifting People, Sorting Papers: Academic Practice and the Notion of State Security in Israel', *Comparative Studies of South Asia, Africa and the Middle East*, 23(1/2), 2003.

Foucault, M., *Discipline and Punish*, New York: Vintage Books, 1979.

Frisch, H., 'Nationalising a Universal Text: the Quran in Arafat's Rhetoric', *Middle Eastern Studies*, 41(3), 2005.

Fuchs, P., 'Kein Anschluß unter dieser Nummer oder Terror ist wirklich blindwütig', http://www.fen.ch/texte/gast_fuchs_terrorismus.htm.

Gabriel, S., 'Is the Jewish Diaspora Unique? Reflections on the Diaspora's Current Situation', *Israel Affairs*, 10(1), 2005.

Galchinsky, M., 'The Jewish Settlements in the West Bank: International Law and Israeli Jurisprudence', *Israel Studies* 9(3), 2005.

Galtung, J., *Peace by Peaceful Means: Peace and Conflict, Development and Civilization*, London: Sage, 1996.

Gambill, G. C., 'The Balance of Terror: War by Other Means in the Contemporary Middle East', *Journal of Palestine Studies*, 28(1), 1998.

Gause III, F. G., 'Systemic Approaches to Middle East International Relations', *International Studies Review*, 1(1), 1999.

Gershoni, I., 'Rethinking the Formation of Arab Nationalism in the Middle East, 1920–1945: Old and New Narratives', in J. Jankowski and I. Gershoni, 1997.

Ghadbian, N., *Democratization and the Islamist Challenge in the Arab World*, Boulder: Westview Press, 1997.

Ghanem, A., N. Rouhana and O. Yiftachel, 'Questioning "Ethnic Democracy": a Response to Sammy Smooha', *Israel Studies*, 3(2), 1997.

Gholamasad, D., 'Zur Sozio-und Psychogenese der Selbstmordattentate der Islamisten', *Orient*, 43(3), 2002.

Ghrawi, Y. and P. Sass, 'The Political Reform Debate in the Middle East and North Africa: Arabic Newspapers and Journals June 2004–Feburary 2005', Working Paper FG 6, 2005/01, Berlin: Stiftung Wissenschaft und Politik, 2005.

Goldberg, E., R. Kasaba, and J. S. Migdal (eds), *Rules and Rights in the Middle East: Democracy, Law, and Society*, Seattle: University of Washington Press, 1993.

Gongora, T., 'War Making and State Power in the Contemporary Middle East', *International Journal of Middle East Studies*, 29(3), 1997.

Gottheil, F., 'UNRWA and Moral Hazard', *Middle Eastern Studies*, 42(3), 2006.

Guazzone, L., (ed.), *The Islamist Dilemma: the Political Role of Islamist Movements in the Contemporary Arab World*, Reading: Ithaca, 1995.

—— (ed.), *The Middle East in Global Change: the Politics and Economics of Interdependence and Fragmentation*, Basingstoke: Macmillan, 1997.

Gunning, J., 'Peace with Hamas? The Transforming Potential of Political Participation', *International Affairs*, 80(2), 2004.

Gur-Ze'ev, I. and I. Pappé, 'Beyond the Destruction of the Other's Collective Memory', *Theory, Culture & Society*, 20(1), 2003.

Guzzini, S., 'Structural Power: the Limits of Neorealist Analysis', *International Organization*, 47(3), 1993.

——— 'Constructivism and International Relations: an Analysis of Luhmann's Conceptualization of Power', in M. Albert and L. Hilkermeier, 2004.

Habermas, J., *Faktizität und Geltung: Beiträge zur Diskurstheorie des Rechts und des demokratischen Rechtsstaats*, Frankfurt: Suhrkamp, 1992.

Hafez, M., *Why Muslims Rebel: Repression and Resistance in the Islamic World*, Boulder: Lynne Rienner, 2003.

Hakimian, H. and Z. Moshaver (eds), *The State and Global Change: the Political Economy of Transition in the Middle East and North Africa*, 2001, Richmond: Curzon.

Halliday, F., *Islam and the Myth of Confrontation: Religion and Politics in the Middle East*, London: Tauris, 1996.

——— *Nation and Religion in the Middle East*, Boulder: Lynne Rienner, 2000.

——— *The Middle East in International Relations: Power, Politics and Ideology*, Cambridge: Cambridge University Press, 2005.

Hallote, R. S. and A. H. Joffe, 'The Politics of Israeli Archaeology: Between "Nationalism" and "Science" in the Age of the Second Republic', *Israel Studies*, 7(3), 2002.

Hamzawy, A., 'Vom Primat der Verschwörung: Zeitgenössische arabische Debatten', *Orient*, 43(3), 2002.

Hamzeh, A. N., 'Lebanon's Hizbullah: from Islamic Revolution to Parliamentary Accommodation', *Third World Quarterly*, 14(2), 1993.

——— 'Lebanon's Islamists and Local Politics: a New Reality', *Third World Quarterly*, 21(5), 2000.

——— 'Clientelism, Lebanon: Roots and Trends', *Middle Eastern Studies*, 37(3), 2001.

Hanieh, A., 'The Camp David Papers', *Journal of Palestine Studies*, 30(2), 2001.

Harb, M. and R. Leenders, 'Know the Enemy: Hizbullah, "Terrorism", and the Politics of Perception', *Third World Quarterly*, 26(1), 2005.

Hart, J., 'Three Approaches to the Measurement of Power in International Relations', *International Organization*, 30(2), 1976.

Hashai, N., 'Forecasting Trade Potential between Former Non-Trading Neighbors: the Israeli-Arab Case', *Journal of World Trade*, 38(2), 2004.

Hass, S., *Natiney Ha-Shemesh*, Tel Aviv: Ha-Kibbutz Ha-Meuchad, 2005.

Hasso, F. S., 'Discursive and Political Developments by/of the 2002 Palestinian Women Suicide Bombers/Martyrs', *feminist review*, 81(1), 2005.

Hasson, S., 'Haredi and Secular Jews in Jerusalem in the Future: Scenarios and Strategies', Policy Paper, Jerusalem: The Floersheimer Institute for Policy Studies, 1999.

Hatem, M. V., 'In the Eye of the Storm: Islamic Societies and Muslim Women in Globalization Discourses', *Comparative Studies of South Asia, Africa and the Middle East*, 26(1), 2006.

Haugbolle, S., 'Public and Private Memory of the Lebanese Civil War', *Comparative Studies of South Asia, Africa and the Middle East*, 25(1), 2005.

Hefner, R. W. (ed.), *Remaking Muslim Politics: Pluralism, Contestation, Democratization*, Princeton: Princeton University Press, 2005.

—— 'Introduction: Modernity and the Remaking of Muslim Politics', in R. W. Hefner, 2005.

Heintz, B., R. Münch and H. Tyrell (eds), *Weltgesellschaft: Theoretische Zugänge und empirische Problemlagen*, Sonderheft der Zeitschrift für Soziologie, Stuttgart: Lucius & Lucius, 2005.

Held, D., *Democracy and the Global Order*, Cambridge: Polity, 1995.

Heller, J., 'Alternative Narratives and Collective Memories: Israel's New Historians and the Use of Historical Context', *Middle Eastern Studies,* 42(4), 2006.

Hellmann, K.-U., 'Einleitung', in K.-U. Hellmann and R. Schmalz-Bruns, 2002.

Hellmann, K.-U. and R. Schmalz-Bruns (eds), *Theorie der Politik: Niklas Luhmanns politische Soziologie*, Frankfurt: Suhrkamp, 2002.

Henry, C. M. and R. Springborg, *Globalisation and the Politics of Development in the Middle East*, Cambridge: Cambridge University Press, 2001.

Henry, C. M., 'The Clash of Globalisations in the Middle East', in L. Fawcett, 2005.

Herzog, H., 'Homefront and Battlefront: the Status of Jewish and Palestinian Women in Israel', *Israel Studies,* 3(1), 2005.

Hilal, J., 'Problematizing Democracy in Palestine', *Comparative Studies of South Asia, Africa and the Middle East,* 23 (1/2), 2003.

Hinnebusch, R., 'Syria: the Politics of Economic Liberalisation', *Third World Quarterly*, 18(2), 1997.

—— *The International Politics of the Middle East*, Manchester: Manchester University Press, 2003.

—— 'The Politics of Identity in Middle East International Relations' in L. Fawcett, 2005.

—— 'Authoritarian Persistence, Democratization Theory and the Middle East: an Overview and Critique', *Democratization,* 13(3), 2006.

Hinnebusch, R. and A. Ehteshami (eds), *The Foreign Policies of Middle East States*, Boulder: Lynne Rienner, 2002.

Houston, C., 'Islamism, Castoriadis and Autonomy', *Thesis Eleven,* 76(1), 2004.

Hoyt, P. D., 'Legitimacy, Identity and Political Development in the Arab World: Book Review', *International Studies Review*, 42(1), 1998.

Hudson, M. C., *Arab Politics: the Search for Legitimacy*, New Haven: Yale University Press, 1979.

Hunter, S. T., 'The Rise of Islamist Movements and the Western Response: Clash of Civilizations or Clash of Interest?', in L. Guazzone, 1995.

Hurd, E. S., 'Appropriating Islam: the Islamic Other in the Consolidation of Western Modernity', *Critique: Critical Middle Eastern Studies*, 12(1), 2003.

Innis, H. A., *Empire and Communications*, Toronto: University of Toronto Press, 1972.

Jacobson, D. C., 'The Ma'ale School: Catalyst for the Entrance of Religious Zionists into the World of Media Production', *Israel Studies,* 9(1), 2004.

Jacoby, T. A. and B. E. Sasley (eds), *Redefining Security in the Middle East*, Manchester: Manchester University Press, 2002.

Jamal, A., 'The Palestinian Media: an Obedient Servant or a Vanguard of Democracy?', *Journal of Palestine Studies*, 29(3), 2000.

—— 'State-Building, Institutionalization and Democracy: the Palestinian Experience', *Mediterranean Politics,* 6(3), 2001.

Jankowski, J. and I. Gershoni (eds), *Rethinking Nationalism in the Arab Middle East*, New York: Columbia University Press, 1997.

Japp, K. P., 'Zur Soziologie des fundamentalistischen Terrorismus', *Soziale Systeme*, 9(1), 2003.

Japp, K. P. and I. Kusche, 'Die Kommunikation des politischen Systems: Zur Differenz von Herstellung und Darstellung im politischen System', *Zeitschrift für Soziologie*, 33(6), 2004.

Jung, D. (ed.), *The Middle East and Palestine: Global Politics and Regional Conflict*, Basingstoke: Palgrave Macmillan, 2004.

Kalin, I., 'Islam and the West: Deconstructing Monolithic Perceptions – a Conversation with Professor Esposito', *Journal of Muslim Minority Affairs*, 21(1), 2001.

Kamil, O., 'The Synagogue as Civil Society, or How Can We Understand the Shas Party', *Mediterranean Quarterly*, 12(3), 2001.

Kampmark, B., 'Hanan Ashrawi and the Prize Protest: the Value and Limits of Debating Peace in the Australian Diaspora', *Journal of Muslim Minority Affairs*, 25(3), 2005.

Kamrava, M., 'Non-Democratic States and Political Liberalisation in the Middle East: a Structural Analysis', *Third World Quarterly*, 19(1), 1998.

—— 'The Politics of Weak Control: State Capacity and Economic Semi-Formality in the Middle East', *Comparative Studies of South Asia, Africa and the Middle East*, 22(1/2), 2002.

Karawan, I. A., 'Political Parties between State Power and Islamist Opposition', in C. E. Butterworth and I. W. Zartman, 2001.

Kaufman, A., ' "Tell Us Our History": Charles Corm, Mount Lebanon and Lebanese Nationalism', *Middle Eastern Studies*, 40(3), 2004.

Kayyal, M., 'A Hesitant Dialogue with "The Other": the Interactions of Arab Intellectuals with the Israeli Culture', *Israel Studies*, 11(2), 2006.

Kedar, M., 'In Search of Legitimacy: Assad's Islamic Image in the Syrian Official Press', in M. Ma'oz, J. Ginat and O. Winckler, 1999.

Keohane, R. O. and J. S. Nye, Jr (eds), *Governance in a Globalizing World*, Washington, DC: Brookings Institution Press, 2000.

Kermani, N., *Gott ist schön: Das ästhetische Erleben des Koran*, Munich: Beck, 2000.

Kerr, M. H., *The Arab Cold War: Gamal 'Abd Al-Nasir and His Rivals, 1958–1970*, Oxford: Oxford University Press, 1971.

Khalidi, R., *Palestinian Identity: the Construction of Modern National Consciousness*, New York: Columbia University Press, 1997.

—— 'The Centrality of Jerusalem to an End of Conflict Agreement', *Journal of Palestine Studies*, 30(3), 2001.

—— 'The Middle East as an Area in an Era of Globalization', in A. Mirsepassi, A. Basu and F. Weaver, 2003.

Khalili, L. 'Places of Memory and Mourning: Palestinian Commemoration in the Refugee Camps in Lebanon', *Comparative Studies of South Asia, Africa and the Middle East*, 25(1), 2005.

Khashan, H., 'Collective Palestinian Frustration and Suicide Bombings', *Third World Quarterly*, 24(6), 2003.

Khoury, P. S. and J. Kostiner (eds), *Tribes and State Formation in the Middle East*, London and New York: Tauris, 1991.

Kieserling, A., *Kommunikation unter Anwesenden: Studien über Interaktionssysteme*, Frankfurt: Suhrkamp, 1999.

Kimmerling, B., 'Jurisdiction in an Immigrant-Settler Society: the "Jewish and Democratic" State', *Comparative Political Studies*, 35(10), 2002.

Kliot, N. and D. Newman, *Geopolitics at the End of the Twentieth Century: the Changing World Political Map*, Frank Cass: London, 2000.
Koenig, M., 'Weltgesellschaft, Menschenrechte und der Formwandel des Nationalstaats', in B. Heintz, R. Münch and H. Tyrell, 2005.
Kook, R., 'Between Uniqueness and Exclusion: the Politics of Identity in Israel', in M. Barnett, 1998.
Korany, B., R. Brynen and P. Noble (eds), *Political Liberalization and Democratization in the Arab World*, 2 vols, Boulder: Lynne Rienner, 1995 and 1998.
Korn, E., 'The Man of Faith and Religious Dialogue: Revisiting "Confrontation"', *Modern Judaism*, 25(1), 2005.
Krause, D., *Luhmann-Lexikon: Eine Einführung in das Gesamtwerk von Niklas Luhmann*, 3rd edn, Stuttgart: Lucius & Lucius, 2001.
Kuhm, K., 'Raum als Medium gesellschaftlicher Kommunikation', *Soziale Systeme*, 6(2), 2000.
Kuperman, R. D., 'Strategies of Asymmetric Warfare and their Implementation in the South Lebanon Conflict', *Foreign Policy Analysis*, 2(1), 2006.
Laclau, E., *New Reflections on the Revolution of Our Time*, London: Verso, 1990.
Lahoud, N., 'Tradition in Contemporary Arabic Political Discourse', *Critique: Critical Middle Eastern Studies*, 13(3), 2004.
Layne, L. L., *Home and Homeland: the Dialogics of Tribal and National Identity in Jordan*, Princeton: Princeton University Press, 1994.
Le More, A., 'Killing with Kindness: Funding the Demise of a Palestinian State', *International Affairs*, 81(5), 2005.
Levy, G., 'From Subjects to Citizens: on Educational Reforms and the Demarcation of the "Israeli Arabs"', *Citizenship Studies*, 9(3), 2005.
Lewis, B., *The Middle East: 2000 Years of History from the Rise of Christianity to the Present Day*, London: Weidenfeld & Nicolson, 1995.
Liebman, C. S., 'Reconceptualizing the Culture Conflict among Israeli Jews', *Israel Studies*, 2(2), 2005.
Lissak, M., '"Critical" Sociology and "Establishment" Sociology in the Israeli Academic Community: Ideological Struggles or Academic Discourse?', *Israel Studies*, 1(1), 2005.
Lochery, N., 'Scholarship or Propaganda: Works on Israel and the Arab-Israeli Conflict, 2001', *Middle Eastern Studies*, 37(4), 2002.
Lodo, S., 'Palestinian Transnational Actors and the Construction of the Homeland', unpublished manuscript.
Lohlker, R., 'Cyberjihad: Das Internet als Feld der Agitation', *Orient*, 43(3), 2002.
Lomsky-Feder, E. and E. Ben-Ari (eds), *The Military and Militarism in Israeli Society*, Albany: State University of New York Press, 1999.
Lowrance, S., 'Deconstructing Democracy: the Arab-Jewish Divide in the Jewish State', *Critique: Critical Middle Eastern Studies*, 13(2), 2004.
—— 'Identity, Grievances, and Political Action: Recent Evidence from the Palestinian Community in Israel', *International Political Science Review*, 27(2), 2006.
Lucas, R. E., 'Press Laws as a Survival Strategy in Jordan, 1989–99', *Middle Eastern Studies*, 39(4), 2003.
Luciani, G., 'Resources, Revenues, and Authoritarianism in the Arab World: Beyond the Rentier State', in B. Korany, R. Brynen and P. Noble, 1995.
—— 'Oil and Political Economy in the International Relations of the Middle East', in L. Fawcett, 2005.

Luhmann, N., 'Symbiotische Mechanismen', in *Soziologische Aufklärung 3: Soziales System, Gesellschaft, Organisation*, Opladen: Westdeutscher Verlag, 1981.

—— *Soziale Systeme: Grundriß einer allgemeinen Theorie*, Frankfurt: Suhrkamp, 1987.

—— 'Frauen, Männer und George Spencer Brown', *Zeitschrift für Soziologie*, 17(1), 1988.

—— *Essays on Self-Reference*, New York: Columbia University Press, 1990.

—— *Die Wissenschaft der Gesellschaft*, Frankfurt: Suhrkamp, 1992.

—— 'Individuum, Individualität, Individualismus', in *Gesellschaftsstruktur und Semantik: Studien zur Wissenssoziologie der modernen Gesellschaft, Band 3*, Frankfurt: Suhrkamp, 1993.

—— *Das Recht der Gesellschaft*, Frankfurt: Suhrkamp, 1995.

—— *Soziologische Aufklärung 6: Die Soziologie und der Mensch*, Opladen: Westdeutscher Verlag, 1995.

—— 'Inklusion und Exklusion', in *Soziologische Aufklärung 6: Die Soziologie und der Mensch*, 1995.

—— 'Kausalität im Süden', *Soziale Systeme*, 1(1), 1995.

—— 'Kultur als historischer Begriff', in *Gesellschaftsstruktur und Semantik: Studien zur Wissenssoziologie der modernen Gesellschaft, Band 4*, 1999.

—— *Die Kunst der Gesellschaft*, Frankfurt: Suhrkamp, 1997.

—— *Die Gesellschaft der Gesellschaft*, Frankfurt: Suhrkamp, 1998.

—— 'Jenseits von Barbarei', in *Gesellschaftsstruktur und Semantik: Studien zur Wissenssoziologie der modernen Gesellschaft, Band 4*, Frankfurt: Suhrkamp, 1999.

—— *Die Politik der Gesellschaft*, Frankfurt: Suhrkamp, 2000.

—— 'Die Rückgabe des zwölften Kamels: Zum Sinn einer soziologischen Analyse des Rechts', *Zeitschrift für Rechtssoziologie*, 21(1), 2000.

—— *Aufsätze und Reden*, ed. O. Jahraus, Stuttgart: Philipp Reclam, 2001.

—— 'Die Paradoxie als Form', in *Aufsätze und Reden*, 2001.

—— 'Vorbemerkungen zu einer Theorie sozialer Systeme', in *Aufsätze und Reden*, 2001.

—— *Macht*, 3rd edn, Stuttgart: Lucius & Lucius, 2003.

Lukes, S., *Power: a Radical View*, London: Macmillan, 1974.

Lustick, I. S., 'The Oslo Agreements as an Obstacle to Peace', *Journal of Palestine Studies*, 27(1), 1997.

—— 'Hegemony and the Riddle of Nationalism', in L. Binder, 1999.

—— 'Yerushalayim and al-Quds: Political Catechism and Political Realities', *Journal of Palestine Studies*, 30(1), 2000.

Lust-Okar, E., *Structuring Conflict in the Arab World: Incumbents, Opponents, and Institutions*, Cambridge: Cambridge University Press, 2005.

—— 'Elections under Authoritarianism: Preliminary Lessons from Jordan', *Democratization*, 13(3), 2006.

Lynch, M., *State Interests and Public Spheres: the International Politics of Jordan's Identity*, New York: Columbia University Press, 1999.

Ma'oz, M., J. Ginat and O. Winckler (eds), *Modern Syria: from Ottoman Rule to Pivotal Role in the Middle East*, Brighton: Sussex University Press, 1999.

Maiguashca, B., 'Governance and Resistance in World Politics', *Review of International Studies*, Special Issue, 29, 2003.

Maktabi, R., 'The Lebanese Census of 1932 Revisited: Who are the Lebanese?', *British Journal of Middle Eastern Studies*, 26(2), 1999.

——— 'Turn in Religion, Turn on Pluralism, Drop out Citizenship? Membership and Political Participation in Jordan, Kuwait and Lebanon', in B. O. Utvik and T. S. Vikor, 2000.

Mandaville, P., 'Sufis and Salafis: the Political Discourse of Transnational Islam', in R. W. Hefner, 2005.

March, A. F., 'The Demands of Citizenship: Translating Political Liberalism into the Language of Islam', *Journal of Muslim Minority Affairs*, 25(3), 2005.

Marchart, O., 'On Drawing a Line: Politics and the Significatory Logics of Inclusion/Exclusion', *Soziale Systeme*, 8(1), 2002.

Marshall, T.H., *Class, Citizenship, and Social Development, Essays*, Garden City: Doubleday, 1964.

Massad, J. A., 'Zionism's Internal Other: Israel and the Oriental Jews', *Journal of Palestine Studies*, 25(4), 1996.

——— *Colonial Effects: the Making of Jordanian National Identity*, New York: Columbia University Press, 2001.

Messmer, H., *Der soziale Konflikt: Kommunikative Emergenz und systemische Reproduktion*, Stuttgart: Lucius & Lucius, 2003.

——— 'Contradictions, Conflict and Borders', in S. Stetter, *Territorial Conflicts*, 2007.

Meyer, J. W. and R. L. Jepperson, 'The "Actors" of Modern Society: the Cultural Construction of Social Agency', *Sociological Theory*, 18(1), 2000.

Meyer, J. W., J. Boli and G. M. Thomas (eds), *Institutional Structure: Constituting State, Society, and the Individual*, Newbury Park: Sage, 1987.

Meyer, J. W., J. Boli, G. M. Thomas and F. O. Ramirez, 'World Society and the Nation-State', *American Journal of Sociology*, 103(1), 1997.

Miall, H., 'Conflict Transformation: a Multi-Dimensional Task', Handbook of the Berghof Research Center for Constructive Conflict Management, http://www.berhof-handbook.net.

Miall, H., O. Ramsbotham and T. Woodhouse, *Contemporary Conflict Resolution: the Prevention, Management and Transformation of Deadly Conflicts*, Cambridge: Polity, 1999.

Migdal, J. S., 'State Building and the Nation State', *Journal of International Affairs*, 58(1), 1994.

Milton-Edwards, B., 'Political Islam in Palestine in an Environment of Peace?', *Third World Quarterly*, 17(2), 1996.

Mirsepassi, A., A. Basu and F. Weaver (eds), *Localizing Knowledge in a Globalizing World: Recasting the Area Studies Debate*, Syracuse: Syracuse University Press, 2003.

Morris, B., *The Birth of the Palestinian Refugee Problem, 1947–1949*, Cambridge: Cambridge University Press, 1987.

Morrison, S., ' "Os Turcos": the Syrian-Lebanese Community of Sao Paolo, Brazil', *Journal of Muslim Minority Affairs*, 25(3), 2005.

Mufti, M., 'Elite Bargains and the Onset of Political Liberalization in Jordan', *Comparative Political Studies*, 32(1), 1999.

Muhibbu-Din, M. A., 'Ahl al-Kitab and Religious Minorities in the Islamic State: Historical Context and Contemporary Challenges', *Journal of Muslim Minority Affairs*, 20(1), 2000.

Murphy, R., *Social Closure: the Theory of Monopolization and Exclusion*, Oxford: Clarendon Press, 1988.

Muscati, S. A., 'Reconstructing "Evil": a Critical Assessment of Post-11 September Political Discourses', *Journal of Muslim Minority Affairs*, 23(2), 2003.

Mushlih, M., 'Hamas: Strategy and Tactics', in L. Binder, 1999.

Nasrallah, R. et al., *The Wall: Fragmenting the Palestinian Fabric to Jerusalem*, Jerusalem: International Peace and Cooperation Centre, 2006.

Nassehi, A., 'Exclusion Individuality or Individualization by Inclusion', *Soziale Systeme*, 8(1), 2002.

—— 'Politik des Staates oder Politik der Gesellschaft: Kollektivität als Problemformel des Politischen', in K.-U. Hellmann and R. Schmalz-Bruns, 2002.

—— 'Die Theorie funktionaler Differenzierung im Horizont ihrer Kritik', *Zeitschrift für Soziologie*, 33(2), 2004.

Nasser, R. M., *Palestinian Identity in Jordan and Israel: the Necessary 'Other' in the Making of a Nation*, London: Routledge, 2005.

Nathanson, R. and S. Stetter (eds), *The Middle East under Fire? EU-Israel Relations in a Region between War and Conflict Resolution*, Berlin and Tel Aviv: Friedrich-Ebert Stiftung, 2007.

Nevo, J. and I. Pappé (eds), *Jordan in the Middle East: the Making of a Pivotal State, 1948–1988*, London: Frank Cass, 1994.

Newman, D., 'The Threat to Academic Freedom in Israel-Palestine', *Tikkun*, 19(4), 2003.

Newman, S., 'The Place of Power in Political Discourse', *International Political Science Review*, 25(2), 2004.

Neyestani, M. R., 'Cultural and Religious Identities in an Era of Information and Communication Globalization', *Alternatives: Turkish Journal of International Relations*, 4(4), 2005.

Nocke, A., 'Israel and the Emergence of Mediterranean Identity: Expressions of Locality in Music and Literature', *Israel Studies*, 11(1), 2006.

Nonnemann, G., 'Rentiers and Autocrats, Monarchs and Democrats, State and Society: the Middle East between Globalization, Human "Agency", and Europe', *International Affairs*, 77(1), 2001.

Norton, A. R., 'Associational Life: Civil Society in Authoritarian Political Systems', in M. Tessler, J. Nachtwey and A. Banda, 1999.

—— 'Lebanon's Malaise', *Survival*, 42(4), 2000.

Palmer Harik, J., 'Democracy (Again) Derailed: Lebanon's Ta'if Paradox', in B. Korany, R. Brynen and P. Noble, 1995.

Pappé, I., 'Post-Zionist Critique on Israel and Palestinians: Part I: the Academic Debate', *Journal of Palestine Studies*, 26(2), 1997.

—— 'Post-Zionist Critique on Israel and the Palestinians Part II: the Media', *Journal of Palestine Studies*, 26(3), 1997.

—— 'The Tantura Case in Israel: the Katz Research and Trial', *Journal of Palestine Studies*, 30(3), 2001.

Parkin, F., *Marxism and Class Theory: a Bourgeois Critique*, London: Tavistock, 1979.

Patomäki, H., 'Problems of Democratizing Global Governance: Time, Space and the Emancipatory Process', *European Journal of International Relations*, 9(3), 2003.

Pawelka, P., 'Der Vordere Orient in der Weltpolitik: Sozialwissenschaftliche Modelle und Forschungsperspektiven', *Orient*, 41(1), 2000.

Peled, Y., 'Ethnic Identity and the Legal Construction of Citizenship: Arab Citizens of the Jewish State', *American Political Science Review*, 86(2), 1992.

230 *Bibliography*

———— 'Restoring Ethnic Democracy: the Or Commission and Palestinian Citizenship in Israel', *Citizenship Studies*, 9(1), 2005.

Perko, F. M. S. J., 'Towards a "Sound and Lasting Basis": Relations between the Holy See, the Zionist Movement, and Israel, 1986–1996', *Israel Studies*, 2(1), 1997.

Perthes, V., 'The Political Economy of the Syrian Succession', *Survival*, 43(1), 2001.

———— (ed.), *Germany and the Middle East: Interest and Options*, Berlin: Heinrich-Böll-Stiftung / Stiftung Wissenschaft und Politik, 2002.

———— 'Editorial: Elites in the Orient, or: Why Focus on Middle Eastern Elites?', *Orient*, 44(4), 2003.

Peteet, J., 'Words as Interventions: Naming in the Israeli-Palestinian Conflict', *Third World Quarterly*, 26(1), 2005.

Pinker, S., *The Blank Slate: the Modern Denial of Human Nature*, London: Allen Lane, 2002.

Piterberg, G., 'Domestic Orientalism: the Representation of "Oriental" Jews in Zionist/Israeli Historiography', *British Journal of Middle Eastern Studies*, 23(2), 1996.

Powell, W. W. and P. J. DiMaggio, *The New Institutionalism in Organizational Analysis*, Chicago: University of Chicago Press, 1991.

Preyer, G. and M. Bös (eds), *Borderlines in a Globalized World*, Dordrecht: Springer, 2002.

Rasler, K., 'Shocks, Expectancy, and the De-Escalation of Protracted Conflicts: the Israeli-Palestinian Case', *Journal of Peace Research*, 37(6), 2000.

Reich, B., 'Israel's Quest for Peace', *Mediterranean Quarterly*, 13(2), 2002.

Reissner, J., 'Islam in der Weltgesellschaft: Wege in eine eigene Moderne', Berlin: Stiftung Wissenschaft und Politik, 2007.

Reiter, Y., 'Higher Education and Sociopolitical Transformation in Jordan', *British Journal of Middle Eastern Studies*, 29(2), 2002.

Rejwan, N., *Israel's Place in the Middle East: a Pluralist Perspective*, Gainesville: University of Florida Press, 1998.

Richmond, O., *The Transformation of Peace*, Basingstoke: Palgrave Macmillan, 2005.

Risse, T., ' "Let's Argue!": Communicative Action in World Politics', *International Organization*, 54(1), 2000.

Ritzer, G., *The McDonaldization of Society*, London: Sage, 1995.

Robertson, R., *Globalization: Social Theory and Global Culture*, London: Sage, 1992.

Robinson, G. E., 'Defensive Democratization in Jordan', *International Journal of Middle East Studies*, 30(3), 1998.

Rogan, E. L., 'The Emergence of the Middle East into the Modern State System', in L. Fawcett, 2005.

Rougier, B., 'Religious Mobilizations in Palestinian Refugee Camps in Lebanon: the Case of Ain el-Helweh', in D. Jung, 2004.

Rowayheb, M. G., 'Lebanese Militias: a New Perspective', *Middle Eastern Studies*, 42(2), 2006.

Rumelili, B., 'Constructing Identity and Relating it to Difference: Understanding the EU's Mode of Differentiation', *Review of International Studies*, 30(1), 2004.

Rynhold, J., 'Israel's Fence: Can Separation Make Better Neighbours?', *Survival*, 46(1), 2004.

Sa'di, A. H., 'Modernization as an Explanatory Discourse of Zionist-Palestinian Relations', *British Journal of Middle Eastern Studies*, 24(1), 1997.

—— 'Catastrophe, Memory and Identity: Al-Nakbah as a Component of Palestinian Identity', *Israel Studies*, 7(2), 2002.

Sadowski, D. (ed.), *Israel 2025: Szenarien der zukünftigen Entwicklung*, Tel Aviv: Friedrich-Ebert-Foundation, 2001.

Sagi, A. and Y. Stern, 'Wanted, a Leader of Vision', *Ha-Aretz*, 12 January 2007.

Said, E. W., *Orientalism*, Harmondsworth: Penguin, 1995.

—— 'Projecting Jerusalem', *Journal of Palestine Studies*, 25(1), 1995.

—— *Das Ende des Friedensprozeß*, Berlin: Berlin Verlag, 2000.

—— *Reflections on Exile, and Other Literary and Cultural Essays*, London, Granta: 2001.

Salibi, K., *The Modern History of Jordan*, London: I.B. Tauris, 1993.

Sarsar, S., 'Jerusalem: Between the Local and the Global', *Alternatives – Turkish Journal of International Relations*, 1(4), 2001.

Sasley, B. E., 'The Effects of Political Liberalization on Security', in T. A. Jacoby and B. E. Sasley, 2002.

Sayigh, Y., 'Armed Struggle and State Formation', *Journal of Palestine Studies*, 26(4), 1997.

—— 'Globalization Manqué: Regional Fragmentation and Authoritarian-Liberalism in the Middle East', in L. Fawcett and Y. Sayigh, 1999.

Sayigh, Y. and A. Shlaim, *The Cold War and the Middle East*, Oxford: Clarendon, 1997.

Schechla, J., 'The Invisible People Come to the Light: Israel's "Internally Displaced" and the "Unrecognized Villages"', *Journal of Palestine Studies*, 31(1), 2001.

Scheffler, T., 'Religious Communalism and Democratization: the Development of Electoral Law in Lebanon', *Orient*, 44(1), 2003.

Schirmer, W., 'Addresses in World Societal Conflicts: a Systems Theoretical Contribution to the Theory of the State in International Relations', in S. Stetter, *Territorial Conflicts*, 2007.

Schlichte, K., *Der Staat in der Weltgesellschaft: Politische Herrschaft in Asien, Afrika und Lateinamerika*, Frankfurt and New York: Campus, 2005.

Scholar, R., *Divided Cities: the Oxford Amnesty Lectures 2003*, Oxford: Oxford University Press, 2006.

Schöpflin, G., 'The Construction of Identity', paper presented at the Österreichischer Wissenschaftstag 2001.

Schulze, K. E., *The Jews of Lebanon: Between Coexistence and Conflict*, Sussex: Sussex Academic Press, 2001.

Seale, P., *Asad of Syria: the Struggle for the Middle East*, Berkeley: University of California Press, 1988.

Sedgwick, M., 'Marginal Muslims in Cyberspace: Traditionalists, New Communities and the Blurring of Distinctions', in B. O. Utvik and K. S. Vikor, 2000.

Senghaas, D., 'The Civilisation of Conflict: Constructive Pacifism as a Guiding Notion for Conflict Transformation', Handbook of the Berghof Research Center for Constructive Conflict Management, http://www.berghof-handbook.net.

Shafir, G., 'Israeli Decolonization and Critical Sociology', *Journal of Palestine Studies*, 25(3), 1996.

Shamir, J. and K. Shikaki, 'Determinants of Reconciliation among Israelis and Palestinians', *Journal of Peace Research*, 39(2), 2002.

Shapira, A. (ed.), *Israeli Identity in Transition*, Westport: Praeger, 2004.

Shaykhk Muhammad Husayn Fadlallah and J. Massad, '11 September, Terrorism, Islam, and the Intifada', *Journal of Palestine Studies*, 31(2), 2002.

Shehaded, L. R., 'The Legal Status of Married Women in Lebanon', *International Journal of Middle East Studies*, 30(4), 1998.

—— 'Coverture in Lebanon', *feminist review*, 76(1), 2004.

Shlaim, A., 'The Rise and Fall of the Oslo Peace Process', in L. Fawcett, 2005.

Slater, J., 'Lost Opportunities for Peace in the Arab-Israeli Conflict', *International Security*, 27(1), 2002.

Sluglett, P., 'The Cold War and the Middle East', in L. Fawcett, 2005.

Smooha, S., 'Ethnic Democracy: Israel as an Archetype', *Israel Studies*, 2(2), 1995.

Sørli, M. E., N. P. Gleditsch and H. Strand, 'Why is there so much Conflict in the Middle East?', *Journal of Conflict Resolution*, 49(1), 2005.

Stäheli, U., *Sinnzusammenbrüche: Eine dekonstruktive Lektüre von Niklas Luhmanns Systemtheorie*, Weilerswist: Velbrück, 2000.

—— 'Fatal Attraction? Popular Modes of Inclusion in the Economic System', *Soziale Systeme*, 8(1), 2002.

Stäheli, U. and R. Stichweh, 'Inclusion/Exclusion: Systems Theoretical and Poststructuralist Perspectives', *Soziale Systeme*, 8(1), 2002.

Stasiulis, D. and D. Ross, 'Security, Flexible Sovereignty, and the Perils of Multiple Citizenship', *Citizenship Studies*, 10(3), 2006.

Steinberg, G., 'Boycotting the Jews (*Wall Street Journal* European Edition)', available on http://faculty.biu.ac.il/~steing/conflict/oped/boycott.html.

—— 'Postcolonial Theory and the Ideology of Peace Studies', *Israel Studies*, 13(4), 2007.

Steinberg, S., 'Discourse Categories in Encounters between Palestinians and Israelis', *International Journal of Politics, Culture and Society*, 17(3), 2004.

Stetter, S., 'Democratisation without Democracy: the Implementation of EU Assistance for Democratisation Processes in Palestine', *Mediterranean Politics*, 8(3), 2003.

—— 'The Politics of De-Paradoxification in Euro-Mediterranean Relations: Semantics and Structures of "Cultural Dialogue"', *Mediterranean Politics*, 10(3), 2005.

—— 'Theorising the European Neighbourhood Policy: Debordering and Rebordering in the Mediterranean', EUI Working Papers, RSCAS No. 2005/34, European University Institute, Robert Schuman Centre for Advanced Studies, Mediterranean Programme Series: Florence, 2005.

—— 'Of Separate and Joint Universes: National Parliamentary Elections in Israel and Palestine', *Mediterranean Politics*, 11(3), 2006.

—— *EU Foreign and Interior Policies: Cross-Pillar Politics and the Social Constructions of Sovereignty*, London and New York: Routledge, 2007.

—— (ed.), *Territorial Conflicts in World Society: Modern Systems Theory, International Relations and Conflict Studies*, London and New York: Routledge, 2007.

—— 'Regions of Conflict in World Society: the Place of the Middle East and Sub-Saharan Africa', in S. Stetter, *Territorial Conflicts*, 2007.

—— 'Entgrenzung von Politikfeldern in der Weltgesellschaft? Eine Bedrohung für die Demokratie?' in A. Brodocz, M. Llanque and G. Schaal, forthcoming, 2008.

Stichweh, R., *Die Weltgesellschaft: Soziologische Analysen*, Frankfurt: Suhrkamp, 2000.

—— 'Strangers, Inclusion, and Identities', *Soziale Systeme*, 8(1), 2002.

——— 'Zur Theorie der politischen Inklusion', in *Inklusion und Exklusion*, 2005.

——— *Inklusion und Exklusion: Studien zur Gesellschaftstheorie*, Bielefeld: transcript, 2005.

——— 'Der 11. September und seine Folgen für die Entwicklung der Weltgesellschaft: Zur Genese des terroristischen Weltereignisses', in T. Bonacker and C. Weller, 2006.

Stolow, J., 'Transnationalism and the New Religio-Politics: Reflections on a Jewish Orthodox Case', *Theory, Culture & Society*, 21(2), 2004.

Suleiman, Y., *A War of Words: Language and Conflicts in the Middle East*, Cambridge: Cambridge University Press, 2004.

Telhami, S., 'Power, Legitimacy, and Peace-Making in Arab Coalitions: the New Arabism', in L. Binder, 1999.

Telhami, S. and M. Barnett (eds), *Identity and Foreign Policy in the Middle East*, Ithaca: Cornell University Press, 2002.

Tessler, M, J. Nachtwey and A. Banda (eds), *Area Studies and Social Science: Strategies for Understanding Middle East Politics*, Bloomington and Indianapolis: Indiana University Press, 1999.

Tibi, B., *Islamischer Fundamentalismus, moderne Wissenschaft und Technologie*, Frankfurt: Suhrkamp, 1992.

——— *Arab Nationalism: Between Islam and the Nation-State*, Basingstoke: Macmillan, 1997.

——— *The Challenge of Fundamentalism*, Berkeley: University of California Press, 1998.

Treacher, A. and H. Shukrallah, 'Editorial: the Realm of the Possible: Middle Eastern Women in Political and Social Spaces', *feminist review*, 80(1), 2005.

Tschirgi, D., 'Resolving the Palestinian Refugee Problem: Edward A. Norman's Unintended Contribution to Relevant Lessons in Perspectives, Values, and Consequences', in D. Jung, 2004.

Tuastad, D., 'Neo-Orientalism and the New Barbarism Thesis: Aspects of Symbolic Violence in the Middle East Conflict(s)', *Third World Quarterly*, 24(4), 2003.

Tuathail, G. Ó, *Critical Geopolitics: the Politics of Writing Global Space*, Minneapolis: University of Minnesota Press, 1996.

Tuathail, G. Ó, S. Dalby and P. Routledge, *The Geopolitics Reader*, London and New York: Routledge, 2006.

Turner, M., 'The Shared Cultural Significance of Jerusalem', in M. Auga, S. Hasson, R. Nasrallah and S. Stetter, 2005.

Tyrell, H., 'Singular oder Plural: Einleitende Bemerkungen zu Globalisierung und Weltgesellschaft', in B. Heintz, R. Münch and H. Tyrell, 2005.

UNESCO, 'Report of the Technical Mission to the Old City of Jerusalem (27 February–2 March 2007)', New York: UNESCO, 2007.

United Nations Development Programme and Arab Fund for Economic and Social Development (eds), *The Arab Human Development Report 2005: Building a Knowledge Society*, New York: UNDP, 2005.

United Nations Development Programme, Arab Fund for Economic and Social Development and Arab Gulf Programme for United Nations Development Organizations (eds), *Arab Human Development Report 2004: Towards Freedom in the Arab World*, New York: UNDP, 2004.

Utvik, B. O. and K. S. Vikor (eds), *The Middle East in a Globalized World*, Bergen: Nordic Society for Middle Eastern Studies, 2000.

Valbjørn, M., 'The Meeting of the Twain: Bridging the Gap between International Relations and Middle East Studies', *Cooperation and Conflict*, 38(2), 2003.

——— 'Toward a "Mesopotamian Turn": Disciplinary and the Study of the International Relations of the Middle East', *Journal of Mediterranean Studies*, 14(1/2), 2004.

Vathakou, E., 'The Autopoiesis of Conflict Transformation: an Example of a "Butterfly Effect" in Greek-Turkish Relations', in S. Stetter, *Territorial Conflicts*, 2007.

Volpi, F. and F. Cavatorta, 'Forgetting Democratization? Recasting Power and Authority in a Pluralist Muslim World', *Democratization*, 13(3), 2006.

Wæver, O., 'Securitisation: Taking Stock of a Research Program in Security Studies', draft paper discussed at the PIPES seminar at the University of Chicago, 2003.

Walker, R. B. J., 'The Subject of Security', in K. Krause and M. Williams (eds), *Critical Security Studies: Concepts and Cases*, London: UCL Press, 1997.

Wallerstein, I., *The Modern World-System: Capitalist Agriculture and the Origins of the European World-System*, New York: Academic Press, 1974.

——— *The Capitalist World-Economy: Essays*, Cambridge: Cambridge University Press, 1980.

——— 'Culture as the Ideological Battleground of the Modern World-System', in M. Featherstone, 1990.

——— *Geopolitics and Geoculture: Essays on the Changing World-System*, Cambridge: Cambridge University Press, 1994.

Walter, J., 'Politik als System? Systembegriffe und Systemmetaphern in der Politikwissenschaft und in den Internationalen Beziehungen', *Zeitschrift für Internationale Beziehungen*, 12(2), 2005.

Wasserstein, B., *Israel and Palestine: Why They Fight and Can They Stop?*, London: Profile, 2003.

Waxman, C. I., 'Critical Sociology and the End of Ideology in Israel', *Israel Studies*, 2(1), 2005.

Weingrod, A. and A. Manna, 'Living along the Seam: Israeli Palestinians in Jerusalem', *International Journal of Middle East Studies*, 30(3), 1998.

Weiss, D., 'Wege zu einer arabischen Wissensgesellschaft', *Orient*, 45(1), 2004.

Wendt, A., 'Anarchy is What States Make of It: the Social Construction of Power Politics', *International Organization*, 46(2), 1992.

——— 'Why a World State is Inevitable', *European Journal of International Relations*, 9(4), 2005.

Wiktorowicz, Q., 'The Salafi Movement in Jordan', *International Journal of Middle East Studies*, 32(2), 2000.

——— *The Management of Islamic Activism: Salafis, the Muslim Brotherhood, and State Power in Jordan*, New York: State University of New York Press, 2001.

Wiktorowicz, Q. and S. T. Farouki, 'Islamic NGOs and Muslim Politics: a Case from Jordan', *Third World Quarterly*, 21(4), 2000.

Wildangel, R., *Zwischen Achse und Mittelmacht: Palästina und der National-sozialismus*, Berlin: Klaus Schwarz, 2007.

Wimmer, A., 'Globalization *Avant la Lettre*: a Comparative View of Isomorphization and Heteromorphization in an Inter-Connecting World', *Comparative Studies in Society and History*, 43(3), 2001.

——— *Nationalist Exclusion and Ethnic Conflict: Shadows of Modernity*, Cambridge: Cambridge University Press, 2002.

Zahhar, M. and H. Hijazi, 'Hamas: Waiting for Secular Nationalism to Self-Destruct: an Interview with Mahmud Zahhar', *Journal of Palestine Studies*, 24(3), 1995.

Zerubavel, Y., 'The "Mythological Sabra" and Jewish Past: Trauma, Memory and Contested Identities', *Israel Studies*, 7(2), 2002.

Zisser, E., 'A False Spring in Damascus', *Orient,* 44(1), 2003.

—— 'Bashar Al-Asad and his Regime: Continuity and Change', *Orient,* 45(2), 2004.

—— 'Who's Afraid of Syrian Nationalism? National and State Identity in Syria', *Middle Eastern Studies*, 42(2), 2006.

Žižek, S., *For They Know Not What They Do: Enjoyment as Political Factor*, London: Verso, 1991.

Zohar, Z., 'Oriental Jewry Confronts Modernity: the Case of Rabbi Ovadiah Yosef', *Modern Judaism*, 24(2), 2004.

Zubaida, S., *Law and Power in the Islamic World*, London: Tauris, 2005.

Zureik, E., 'Constructing Palestine through Surveillance Practices', *British Journal of Middle Eastern Studies*, 28(2), 2001.

Index

11 September 2001, 96, 98

Abbas, Mahmoud, 47
Abdallah, King of Jordan, 3
action/reaction scheme, 96, 98
Aflaq, Michel, 22
Agudat Israel, 137–8
Al-Aqsa brigades, 71,75
Al-Arabiyya, 19
Al-Assad, Bashir, 3
Al-Assad, Hafiz, 3, 89
Alawites, 89
Al-Azm, Sadiq, 98
Al-Jazeera, 19, 37
Al-Nakba, 50
Al-Qaradawi, Sheik Yusuf, 98
Amman, 50
anti-Semitism, 16, 129, 166
Arab Human Development Reports,
    33, 63, 81, 109, 123–32, 173
Arabism, 5, 22, 35, 109
Arafat, Yassir, 3, 50, 60, 89
area studies controversy, 10, 15–16
Ashkenazim, 129, 160
authoritarianism, 3, 64, 81–6, 158–9

Beirut, 50
borders
    border conflicts, 69
    functional borders, 29, 38, 42–50,
        62–5, 80, 109, 117–18
    symbolic borders, 29, 54, 159
    territorial borders, 37, 41, 45

Camp David Summit, 59–60, 174
censorship, 123
census, Lebanon, 158
Christians, 59, 95
citizenship, 21, 49, 90, 105–6, 111, 121
civil society, 23, 55, 82, 105–6, 137, 173
civil war, Lebanon, 74, 82
civilization, 5, 8, 11, 23–4, 64, 142,
    172–3
Clinton, Bill, 60–1
cobwebs, 18–19, 25, 64

colonialism, 16, 22, 69, 96–7, 126–8,
    156
communication, 6–7, 18, 26–9, 36–9,
    42, 94–7, 120–2, 146, 168
    political communication, 31–2, 40,
        46, 50, 54–5, 62–4, 73–81
confessional groups, Lebanon, 157–9
conflict
    conflict resolution, 144, 153, 160–2,
        168, 173
    conflict system, 144–54, 167
    function of conflict, 33, 144–6,
        149–52, 168–9
    Israel/Palestine conflict, 14, 32,
        157, 165
consociational democracy, 157
constitutions, 50, 82, 106, 133, 158
contingency, 7–8, 33, 38, 52, 74–9,
    99, 108, 115–18, 124, 135, 145,
    167–8
    double contingency, 94
cooperation, 4, 14, 82–3, 154, 169–75
Corm, Charles, 69
creeping antagonization, 6, 33–4, 94–5,
    103, 108, 118–19, 136, 143–4,
    151–7, 162–7
culture
    cultural dialogue, 71, 156, 168
    cultural frame, 163–4, 175
    cultural heritage, 40, 43, 55–61

Damascus, 50, 96
debordering, 36, 38–9, 41–3
deep perturbation, 34, 143, 145, 152–3,
    167, 174–6
democracy
    democratization, 3, 14, 71, 171
    ethnic democracy, 82, 85, 90–1
    global democracy, 55
deparadoxification, 77, 80, 88–9,
    103, 121
de-politicization, 73, 80, 86, 95, 103
de-securitization, 33, 173